America Adopts the Automobile,
1895–1910

America Adopts the Automobile, 1895–1910

James J. Flink

The MIT Press Cambridge, Massachusetts, and London, England

Set in Linofilm Janson by Allservice
Phototypesetting Co.
Printed and
bound in the United States of
America by The Maple Press Co.

ISBN 0 262 06036 1 (hardcover)

Library of Congress catalog card
number: 74-107989

For my
most influential teachers,
Thomas C. Cochran and
Gerald T. White

Illustrations

Tables

Acknowledgments

Some of the personal and intellectual debts that I have incurred while seeing this book into print never can be acknowledged adequately. My wife, Iona Rogers Flink, truly has been "more precious than rubies." Beyond transcribing most of the notes and typing several drafts of the manuscript, Iona managed to be a severe and effective critic while remaining a compassionate wife. She joins me in dedicating this book to Thomas C. Cochran, my major professor in graduate school, and to Gerald T. White, whose undergraduate courses first awakened my interest in social and economic history. Professors Cochran and White best exemplify the scholarly and gentlemanly standards of conduct that we value. We appreciate more than we can say their encouragement and help during the researching and writing of this book.

I am extremely grateful to the many other people who gave me help and extended courtesies. Jay Martin, Murray G. Murphey, Peter Nickels, John B. Rae, Charles E. Rosenberg, and John L. Shover read the manuscript. Their comments were invaluable. Robert A. Jones did the statistical correlations and researched state motor vehicle laws for me. I am indebted to Dolores B. Axam, Mary M. Cattie, and Florence M. Jenkins of the Automobile Reference Collection of the Free Library of Philadelphia for many favors and for their constant cooperation over the past five years. Permission to use illustrations was given by the Free Library of Philadelphia, the Smithsonian Institution, and the Ford Archives of the Henry Ford Museum. Donald H. Berkebile of the Smithsonian Institution helped in the selection of illustrations, and William Fredericks did the photographic work on the illustrations from the Free Library of Philadelphia.

James J. Flink
Irvine, California
December 7, 1969

America Adopts the Automobile,
1895–1910

Introduction

Impact in America

An anonymous resident of "Middletown" chided the Lynds, in their classic 1929 study of a typical American community: "Why on earth do you need to study what's changing this country? . . . I can tell you what's happening in just four letters: A-U-T-O!"[1] Most Americans felt similarly at the time, and historians will undoubtedly someday refer to the first half of the twentieth century as the age of the automobile. For, since its introduction in the United States in 1895, the motor vehicle has been the most significant force shaping the development of modern American civilization.

In addition to the overwhelming impact of the motorcar itself, innovations in the automobile industry transformed American social and economic institutions. With the introduction of the moving-belt assembly line and the $5-day in 1913–1914, Henry Ford created a new class of semiskilled industrial worker and set a new standard of remuneration for manual labor. At General Motors under Alfred P. Sloan, the decentralized, multidivisional structure of the modern industrial corporation, modern management techniques, and consumer installment credit as we know it were pioneered in the 1920s. Applied to the manufacture of many other items, these innovations have called the tune and set the tempo of modern American life, and they underlie our unparalleled standard of living and our emergence as the foremost commercial and military power in the world.

The automobile industry has been the mainstay and prime mover of the American economy in the twentieth century. Automobile sales became the backbone of a new consumer-goods-oriented economy that emerged during the 1920s. About 9.6 million new cars were sold in the United States in 1968, and one out of every six jobs was directly related to the automobile industry. Since the 1920s the automobile industry

[1] Robert S. Lynd and Helen M. Lynd, *Middletown* (New York: Harcourt, Brace & World, 1929), p. 251.

has also been the lifeblood of the oil industry, one of the chief customers of the steel industry, and the biggest consumer of many other industrial products, including plate glass, rubber, and lacquers. Construction of streets and highways remains one of the largest items of governmental expenditure in the United States. The motorcar has also been responsible both for a continuing suburban real estate boom and for the rise of many new types of small businesses, such as service stations and tourist accommodations. The eminent economic historian Thomas C. Cochran noted this central role of the automobile industry in recent American economic development and concluded: "No one has or perhaps can reliably estimate the vast size of capital invested in reshaping society to fit the automobile. Such a figure would have to include expenditures for consolidated schools, suburban and country homes, and changes in business location, as well as the more direct investments mentioned above."[2]

Widespread adoption of the automobile did indeed reshape American lifeways. Patterns of courtship, residence, socialization of children, education, work habits, and use of leisure time were all radically altered by the adoption of the automobile. The rise of a standardized, middle-class national culture in the United States was greatly encouraged by the contributions of the motor vehicle to the decline of localism, ethnicity, and class differences. The modern industrial city with its residential suburbs is a product of automobility, as are most of the formidable problems for municipal and national government associated with the uncontrolled growth of megalopolis. The motor vehicle has also played a major role in the systematic destruction of the scenic beauty of America and in the shameful depletion of its land and water resources. Automobile accidents have killed or maimed more American citizens during the last several decades than either foreign wars or domestic violence.

[2] Thomas C. Cochran, *The American Business System* (Cambridge, Mass.: Harvard University Press, 1957), p. 44.

Moreover, while the precise effects remain incalculable, medical authorities feel assured that exhaust fumes from the ever-present motorcar constitute a major cause of notable increases in heart and respiratory diseases. Responsible ecologists have recently in fact become alarmed that atmospheric pollution due largely to the continued, widespread use of the gasoline automobile poses a grave threat not only to the future of American man but to the future of life itself in any form on earth.

Sources and Scope of Study

The hows and whys of the spectacular rise of the automobile and the automobile industry from obscurity to predominance in American civilization within the very short time span of one generation, and the social revolution this rise incurred, form the subject matter of the present book and of another upon which I am currently engaged in research. Developments from the introduction of the motor vehicle in the United States to the end of the formative stage of the American automobile industry, so well symbolized by the opening of the Ford Motor Company's Highland Park plant on January 1, 1910, are dealt with in this volume. The succeeding one will trace the course of events from that point to the coming of age of the American automobile industry with the establishment of mature market conditions in the late 1920s.

  Because the opening of the Ford Highland Park plant represented a critical turning point in the development of the American automobile movement, 1910 is an ideal point at which to terminate the present book. Until that time, the story of the automobile in the United States is mainly one of the impact of the American social and cultural milieu on the acceptance of a European technological innovation and the formation of a new industry. This subject will constitute the focus of attention in the following chapters. The emphasis must shift after 1910 to the theme of how the effective implementation of Henry Ford's business strategy of volume production of a static-model, reliable car for the masses began to transform American life and precipitated the end of an era in American historical development.

In view of the centrality of the automobile to the historical development of the American people in the twentieth century, the energy expended by professional historians on the automobile and the automobile industry has indeed been meager. Since the publication of two revised doctoral dissertations in 1928,[3] a number of other scholarly books and articles have substantially advanced our factual knowledge and interpretation of the development of the American automobile industry and the careers of significant automotive entrepreneurs. Thanks mainly to the automobile buff turned amateur historian, we also know a good deal about automobile racing and the mechanical evolution of the modern motorcar. But many important facets of the American automotive revolution still remain unexplored, and no comprehensive history of the American automobile industry has yet been written. The monumental study of the Ford Motor Company undertaken by Allan Nevins in collaboration with Frank E. Hill[4] has been the only multivolume history to appear on any aspect of the general topic. The publisher of John B. Rae's recent (1965) and excellent but very brief volume, *The American Automobile*, could claim on its dust jacket that the book was "the first complete, authoritative treatment of the whole span of the automobile industry, which has given modern American society its pace and direction and stimulated an amazing number of related industrial and social changes."[5]

The most crucial void in our knowledge has been that attention has remained far

[3] Ralph C. Epstein, *The Automobile Industry* (Chicago and New York: A. W. Shaw Co., 1928), and Lawrence H. Seltzer, *A Financial History of the American Automobile Industry* (Boston and New York: Houghton Mifflin, 1928).
[4] Allan Nevins, with the collaboration of Frank E. Hill, *Ford: The Times, The Man, The Company, 1865–1915; Ford: Expansion and Challenge, 1915–1933;* and *Ford: Decline and Rebirth, 1933–1962* (New York: Charles Scribner's Sons, 1954, 1957, 1963).
[5] John B. Rae, *The American Automobile* (Chicago: University of Chicago Press, 1965).

too narrowly focused upon the internal dynamics of the automobile industry and its more prominent individual manufacturers, which has led to the rather complete neglect of many significant relationships between the development of the industry as a whole and the changing social and cultural milieu within which this development occurred. And this is the void that I hope at least partially to fill in the present book and its successor.

Concentration upon the internal dynamics of the automobile industry, its prominent companies, and outstanding individuals has undoubtedly been encouraged by several considerations. The industrial biographer has been understandably attracted to the career of the atypical individual whose unique accomplishments have already been widely acclaimed. Henry Ford, of course, is the prime example among automobile manufacturers.[6] One must also acknowledge that business historians, with notable exceptions, have not been inclined to deal with "soft" social and cultural variables.[7] Probably the most important consideration, however, has been the relative unavailability of many types of data to the historian who would venture beyond conventional limitations to write a broad social history of the American automobile industry during its formative years. Business records have not survived for the lion's share of the approximately 1,500 firms that have been active at some time in the American automobile industry. The stock of memoirs and personal documents is scanty for even the

[6] Henry Ford is in fact the only important figure in the early automobile industry to have received extensive biographical treatment. While Glenn A. Niemeyer's definitive volume, *The Automotive Career of Ransom E. Olds* (East Lansing: Michigan State University Press, 1963), fills a major gap in our knowledge about Ford's closest rival for fame, we still lack full-length, scholarly biographies of Benjamin Briscoe, William C. Durant, Albert A. Pope, and Alexander Winton, to name only a few of the more prominent early automotive entrepreneurs who deserve attention.

[7] The outstanding exception has been the work produced by the scholars who were associated with the Research Center in Entrepreneurial History at Harvard University from 1948 through 1958. The conceptual approach and substantive contributions of this group of scholars have been summarized well in Arthur C. Cole, *Business Enterprise in Its Social Setting* (Cambridge, Mass.: Harvard University Press, 1959).

more important entrepreneurs in the early industry and virtually nonexistent for the pioneer automobile dealers, mechanics, club officials, and owners. Relevant public documents and governmental records are also sparse and scattered before at least 1910. Except for the framing of rudimentary motor vehicle legislation and a long legal battle in the federal courts over the monopoly threat to the industry supposedly posed by the Selden patent on the gasoline automobile,[8] the federal government and state governments gave little formal recognition to the automobile. The American automobile revolution did not become a topic for serious scholarly study until almost a generation after the introduction of the motor vehicle in the United States, and then no one had the foresight to survey systematically the man in the street about what he thought had happened.

The periodical literature of the day thus constitutes the major source, in some cases the sole source, of information on many aspects of the early social history of the automobile industry in the United States. While this body of data has the limitations that the evidence is secondhand and that one cannot facilely generalize the views expressed in a periodical as necessarily representative of the views of its readers, all types of historical data have drawbacks. The wealth of information available in the automobile trade journals and articles on the automobile in popular magazines during the formative years of the automobile industry in the United States has been neglected far too long.

The appearance of *Motocycle* in October and *Horseless Age* in November 1895 antedated the first sales of motor vehicles in the United States and the formation of the first American automobile manufacturing firm. Several more automobile journals, written by and for devotees of the new "sport," soon joined these periodicals to cru-

[8] For the history of the Selden patent, see William Greenleaf, *Monopoly on Wheels: Henry Ford and the Selden Patent Suit* (Detroit: Wayne State University Press, 1961).

sade for the universal adoption of the motor vehicle, and they chronicle even the more minute details of progress toward this goal. As self-acknowledged champions of an innovation they expected would soon revolutionize American life, these journals were interested in reporting and commenting on a much broader range of phenomena than just the mechanical evolution of the motorcar and the development of the American automobile industry. Anything related to the automobile was grist for their mill. Their topics ranged from panegyrics about the utopian virtues of an imminent horseless society to the mundane reporting of the proceedings of the automobile clubs and the first purchases of motor vehicles in remote hamlets, from pronouncements by public officials and captains of industry about the potential of the horseless carriage to fashions for would-be lady motorists and complaints that mechanics were incompetent and dishonest. Although the automobile journals were biased partisans of the motor vehicle, they rarely misread public opinion by confusing it with their own. Rather, the motorist was consistently cast in the role of a victimized underdog, and evidence of public apathy about the automobile or legitimate criticism of automobilists was all too characteristically overreacted to as "rabid motorphobia." Except for this lapse, however, the reporting seems on the whole to have been fairly objective and has the decided merit of having been done by participant observers who had a high degree of technical competence in their subject matter.

From the outset of its diffusion in the United States, the motor vehicle was given extensive and overwhelmingly favorable coverage in popular periodicals — coverage well beyond what an objective appraisal of the innovation's importance and potential at the time could have justified. Sensationalistic newspapers discovered early that automobile news printed on the sports page or in the Sunday supplement fascinated readers from all walks of life. Even the more staid mass-circulation magazines quickly became aware that articles about the automobile had an especially great appeal for the middle-class reader, who could envision becoming an automobile owner himself in the foreseeable future. Often lacking the technological knowledge that could have served as a realistic restraint, writers in popular periodicals were on the whole even more optimistic about the imminent appearance of a cheap car for the masses and the beginning of a new horseless age than were the automobile journals. The latter at times chided the popular press for its naive statements that might bring discredit upon the reputable manufacturer who was still struggling to produce a reliable car for a limited market at a moderate price. The reasons for popular enthusiasm about the motor vehicle that emerge from an analysis of articles on the automobile in the popular periodicals of the day have an internal logical consistency, and they accord well with what we already know about the temper of the period. Therefore, in the absence of conflicting evidence, they deserve credence as widely held sentiments.

  Faced with the alternatives of either basing the first volume of my study largely upon these less than ideal but nonetheless very valuable and underexploited sources or not writing the book at all, I have not hesitated to choose the former course of action. Furthermore, in the interest of economy of research effort and in the belief that the writing of history must be a cumulative process based upon considerable trust in one's predecessors, I have not hesitated to deal synthetically, in the main, with those aspects of the history of the automobile industry that have already been examined in detail by others and to eschew firsthand reexamination of the various industry sources upon which previous studies have been primarily based. My effort has been invested instead, wisely I believe, in an exhaustive page by page, cover to cover examination of the leading automobile journals and a liberal sample of popular magazines of the period.* The reader must, of course, be the ultimate judge of whether this task

*In quotations from these periodicals, I have taken the liberty of correcting the typographical errors and changing some capitalization and spelling to conform with present-day practice.

has been worthwhile. At the very least, I hope he finds in the following chapters an empathic account of what a generation of Americans thought the automobile revolution was all about.

1
Gaining Acceptance

European Development

The gasoline automobile originated and was initially developed in Germany and France in the late nineteenth century. Etienne Lenoir, a Belgian mechanic, first patented an internal-combustion engine in France in 1860, and demand from small industrial plants needing a cheap and simple source of power soon stimulated the invention of more advanced internal-combustion engines. The most important of these from the standpoint of automotive technology was a four-cycle engine introduced by Nicholas Otto, a German manufacturer, in 1878. Conceived as a stationary source of power, the original Otto engine was too cumbersome and slow to be efficient in a self-propelled vehicle. However, by 1885 Gottlieb Daimler, who had been one of Otto's engineers, and his assistant William Maybach had developed a 1.5 horsepower, 110-pound, 600-rpm, vertical, "high-speed" engine that proved to be the prototype of the modern motorcar's power plant. To demonstrate the capability of their engine, Daimler and Maybach built four experimental motor vehicles between 1885 and 1889.

Carl Benz, another German manufacturer of stationary gasoline engines, pioneered the automobile to the stage of commercial feasibility. The first Benz car, built in 1885, was a tricycle powered by a one-cylinder, 0.8-horsepower engine. His third vehicle was exhibited at the Paris Exposition in 1887 and was sold shortly afterward to a Frenchman named Emile Roger, who became Benz's agent in France. Motor vehicles were now for the first time offered for sale to the public. In 1891 Benz came out with a vastly improved four-wheel automobile that featured Ackermann steering and a redesigned engine capable of 700 rpm. This automobile was fairly reliable and sold well, given the limited performance expectations and market of the day. It was widely imitated. Aside from minor changes, however, Benz retained the same design for ten years, so he was soon surpassed technically by other manufacturers.

Emile Constant Levassor innovated the basic mechanical arrangement of the modern motorcar. The newly founded engineering firm of Panhard and Levassor acquired the French manufacturing rights for the Daimler motor in 1890 and decided to produce complete motor vehicles rather than just internal-combustion engines. In his 1891 car, Levassor placed the engine vertically in front of the chassis instead of under the seats or in the back, which put the crankshaft parallel with the longitudinal line of the car instead of parallel with the axles. The great importance of this new mechanical arrangement, called the *système* Panhard, was that it was now possible for motor vehicles to accommodate larger and more powerful engines. A secondary consideration was that for the first time the carriage silhouette was broken away from in an automotive design. Then in 1895 Panhard and Levassor began to use the new Daimler "Phoenix" engine, which had two cylinders arranged in tandem and developed (by French rating) 4 horsepower at 750 rpm. Levassor drove one of these cars over the 727-mile course of the 1895 Paris-Bordeaux-Paris race at the then incredible average speed of 15 mph, with the longest stop for servicing being only twenty-two minutes.

In 1894 *Le Petit Journal* sponsored a 78-mile reliability run from Paris to Rouen, in which all thirteen entries powered by internal-combustion engines and four of the eight steam-driven entries managed to finish. The Automobile Club of France was founded soon afterward, in early 1895, to encourage the development of the motor vehicle and to regulate future automotive sporting events. The Paris-Bordeaux-Paris race that began on July 11, 1895, was the new club's initial endeavor. Nine of the twenty-two vehicles that started ultimately completed the formidable distance, and the best driving time was Levassor's impressive forty-eight hours. Although he was ostensibly the winner, Levassor was disqualified on a technicality, and first place was given to a Peugeot that finished eleven hours behind him. Eight of the nine successful entries were powered by internal-combustion engines.

The Paris-Bordeaux-Paris race underlined French superiority in automotive technology. Encouraged by a favorable press and the lack of any repressive governmental restrictions, experimentation with self-propelled road vehicles flourished in France. Next to Emile Constant Levassor's modernization of the gasoline automobile, the most significant single technological achievement was probably Léon Serpollet's invention of the "flash boiler," an instantaneous steam generator that allowed the modern steam-powered car to be developed and enjoy a brief period of popularity. Perhaps the best indication of French leadership is that motor vehicles by 1895 were already beginning to be produced in quantity for sale by several French firms — Panhard-Levassor, Roger-Benz, Peugeot, De Dion-Bouton, and Bollée. As a consequence, the automobile was already a common sight on the streets of Paris. Nowhere else was this true at the time.

Before 1895, few Americans had seen a motor vehicle, much less thought about its potential use as a practical means of transportation. Six motor vehicles were exhibited at the Columbian Exposition in Chicago in 1893, but they attracted little attention. Several American inventors had also managed to build experimental cars by 1895. However, these machines were exceptionally primitive in comparison with the best contemporary French designs and were not produced in quantity for sale. No one could have foreseen that the United States would soon develop into the world's foremost automobile culture.

Early Interest in America

One of the first Americans to recognize the future importance of the motor vehicle was George B. Selden, a Rochester, New York, patent attorney and neophyte inventor, who had seen a crude two-cycle engine invented in 1872 by George B. Brayton, an American engineer, at the 1876 Philadelphia Centennial Exposition. Selden was

Plate 2. Illustration from the Selden patent papers, showing plan views of vehicle. Courtesy Smithsonian Institution.

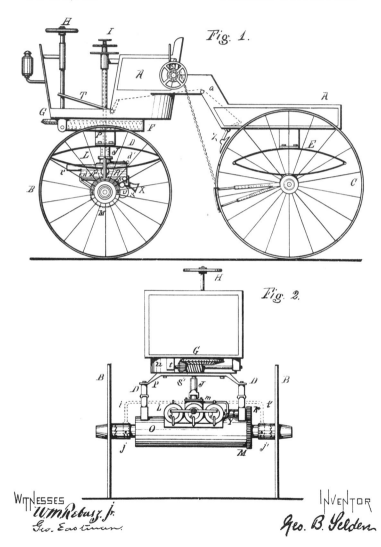

G. B. SELDEN.
ROAD ENGINE.

No. 549,160.

Patented Nov. 5, 1895.

granted United States patent no. 549,160 on November 5, 1895, for an "improved road engine." He claimed to have solved the basic problems involved in the design of a self-propelled road vehicle through a unique combination of components that had been separately developed in the prior technological art with "a liquid-hydro-carbon engine of the compression type." Thus the Selden patent covered the basic elements necessary for the construction of a motor vehicle propelled by a petroleum product, despite the important considerations that Selden had not yet constructed an operational model of his design at the time the patent was issued and that the actual state of the prior technological art in no sense supported his allegation of priority.

Selden filed his original patent application in 1879 and then used evasive legal tactics to delay the patent's acceptance until conditions seemed favorable for the commercial exploitation of his patent rights. In this manner he was able to maintain adequate security for his claims while he deferred the outset of the seventeen-year period of exclusive rights to his invention provided by law. Having assiduously kept track of the course of developments in the automotive field, Selden was forced to act in 1895 — in part due to a tightening of Patent Office rules on delayed applications, and in part because recent developments indicated that the time was now ripe and delay might be disastrous.

Other American inventors had progressed beyond George Selden's paper accomplishments during the early 1890s by designing motor vehicles that performed well enough in actual road tests to be considered successful. Ransom E. Olds, a Lansing, Michigan, machinist, completed steam-powered vehicles in his family-owned shop in 1887 and 1891 and made the first sale of an American automobile in 1893, when he sold the latter vehicle for $400 to a London patent-medicine firm, the Francis Times Company, for use at its branch house in Bombay, India. An electric car de-

signed by William Morrison of Des Moines, Iowa, was driven on the streets of Chicago in 1892. In 1894 another electric automobile, the "Electrobat," was built by Henry G. Morris and Pedro G. Salom in Philadelphia. More directly relevant to the claims of the Selden patent was the first successful American gasoline automobile turned out by J. Frank and Charles E. Duryea in 1893. The Duryea brothers were Springfield, Massachusetts, bicycle mechanics who were motivated to design their own automobile after reading a description of the Benz car in the 1889 *Scientific American*. Their feat was duplicated in 1894 by Elwood P. Haynes, superintendent of the Indiana Natural Gas and Oil Company, who built his vehicle with the help of two Kokomo, Indiana, machinists, Edgar and Elmer Apperson, and their assistant, Jonathan D. Maxwell. A number of other Americans also began to build experimental gasoline automobiles about this time. Significant among those who had succeeded by 1896 were Hiram Percy Maxim, Charles B. King, Ransom E. Olds, Alexander Winton, and Henry Ford.

The accomplishments of these American inventors were undoubtedly less important in influencing George Selden to act on his patent than the greatly increased interest in motor vehicles evident in the United States during the summer and fall of 1895. This interest was engendered by newspaper and magazine coverage of the Paris-Bordeaux-Paris race. Widespread dissemination of information about the French contest by American periodicals had immediate impact. Over 500 applications for patents relating to the automobile were on file in the United States Patent Office by September 1895. Most of these applications had been received that summer, and government officials attributed the influx to interest stimulated by the French long-distance race. The race had other important effects. Two American periodicals, the *Chicago Times-Herald* and *Cosmopolitan Magazine*, were encouraged to sponsor the first American automobile races, and incentive was provided for the inauguration

Plate 4.   Elwood P. Haynes in his
1894 gasoline automobile. Courtesy
Free Library of Philadelphia.

of the first two specialized American automobile periodicals, *Motocycle* in October
and *Horseless Age* in November 1895. Gimbel Brothers, Hilton Hughes & Company,
and the R. H. Macy Company were also prompted to offer the first European automobiles for sale in the United States.

The Paris-Bordeaux-Paris race demonstrated to many Americans the feasibility
of using motor vehicles for long-distance, high-speed transportation, and an aura of
optimism about the automobile prevailed among technical experts in the United
States throughout 1895. Opinions ventured late in that year by prominent inventors
and leading figures in the transportation industry were overwhelmingly favorable.
P. H. Studebaker, whose family firm was then the world's leading producer of carriages and wagons, addressed an open congratulatory letter to Herman H. Kohlsaat,
the sponsor of the 1895 *Chicago Times-Herald* race. Thomas A. Edison, when inter-
viewed by a reporter from the *New York World*, stated that "the horseless vehicle
is the coming wonder. . . . It is only a question of time when the carriages and trucks
in every large city will be run with motors."[1]

Similarly, the predominant opinion expressed in popular periodicals was that motor
vehicles would eventually be improved, sold in quantity, and become an important
part of the American transportation system. As early as January, *Scientific American*
voiced the general assumption that "with the stimulus of such races as the present
[Paris-Bordeaux-Paris race] for substantial monetary prizes, the development cannot
fail to be rapid. When the machinery shall be still more simplified we may expect to
see the automobile carriage come into extensive use."[2] Even the most skeptical article
conceded "that this class of vehicle is destined to become a prominent factor none
can doubt, and it is well to be prepared. . . . the prospects are more than ever favorable,

[1] Cited in Rudolph E. Anderson, *The Story of the American Automobile* (Washington, D.C.: Public Affairs Press,
1950), p. 67.
[2] "Another Race of Carriages Without Horses," *Scientific American*, 72:387 (January 22, 1895).

Plate 5.   The first page of the
first issue of *Horseless Age*. Courtesy Free Library of Philadelphia.

THE HORSELESS AGE.

A MONTHLY JOURNAL

DEVOTED TO THE INTERESTS OF THE MOTOR VEHICLE INDUSTRY.

VOL. I.   NEW YORK, NOVEMBER, 1895.   NO. 1.

THE HORSELESS AGE.

E. P. INGERSOLL, Editor and Proprietor.

PUBLICATION OFFICE:

157-159 WILLIAM STREET, NEW YORK.

SUBSCRIPTION, FOR THE UNITED STATES AND CANADA,
$2.00 a year, payable in advance.   For all foreign
countries included in the Postal Union, $2.50.

ADVERTISEMENTS.—Rates will be made known on application.   When change of copy is desired it should be sent
in not later than the fifteenth of the month.

COMMUNICATIONS.—The Editor will be pleased to receive
communications on trade topics from any authentic
source.   The correspondent's name should in all cases
be given as an evidence of good faith, but will not be
published if specially requested.

Address all correspondence, and make all checks, drafts, and
money orders payable to
THE HORSELESS AGE, 157-159 William Street, New York.

Salutatory.

WE PRESENT to the trade and the public the first
number of the HORSELESS AGE, a journal which
will be published monthly hereafter in the interest of
the motor vehicle.   The appearance of a journal devoted to a branch of industry yet in an embryonic
state, may strike some as premature, and the somewhat desultory character of this number may provoke
criticism in some quarters.   But those who have taken
the pains to search below the surface for the great
tendencies of the age, know what a giant industry is
struggling into being there.   All signs point to the
motor vehicle as the necessary sequence of methods of
locomotion already established and approved.   The
growing needs of our civilization demand it; the public
believe in it, and await with lively interest its practical
application to the daily business of the world.

In such a condition of expectancy the chief want is
news.   Not only those directly concerned in the perfection of the new vehicle, but the reading public as
well, wish to be informed of the progress of this great
mechanical movement; to know the forms or styles in
which the new vehicle is to appear, and to examine the
claims that are offered, no less than the facts that
are accomplished.   To satisfy this demand is the work
to which the journalist should bend his energies.
Criticism, at such a time, may properly be left to the
mechanical expert or the intending purchaser.   His
chosen task is to collect the materials upon which an
intelligent judgment may be based.

At this formative period of the motor vehicle
industry, exact data are difficult to obtain.   All over
the country mechanics and inventors are wrestling with
the problems of trackless traction.   Much of their work
is in an unfinished state; many of their theories lack
demonstration; but enough has already been achieved
to prove absolutely the practicability of the motor
vehicle.   What is here presented, however, is merely
an earnest of what is to come.

The second number of the HORSELESS AGE will
contain a detailed account of the *Times-Herald* contest,
which is to be held at Chicago on November 2nd, and
many new illustrations.   In succeeding numbers, topics
of importance to the trade will be taken up for discussion.   Several projects bearing broadly on the future
development of the industry are now under editorial
consideration, and will be announced in due time.

The Horseless Age.

It has a fascinating sound, and ere the close of 1895, the
idea will have been proved as practical as the sound is
fascinating.

It is often said that a civilization may be measured by its
facilities of locomotion.   If this is true, as seems abundantly
proved by present facts and the testimony of history, the new
civilization that is rolling in with the horseless carriage will be
a higher civilization than the one we now enjoy.

and we do not doubt their use in many places where the conditions are favorable."
Its author merely wished to enter a caveat against "an endless amount of nonsense
[that] is being published in the public press. . . . The horse will not be dethroned;
neither will the time ever come when the horseless vehicle will hold other than a
secondary place."[3]

Faith in the future of the motor vehicle and national pride were strong enough to
allow a most favorable interpretation of the equivocal results of the first two American
automobile races. Just five of the eleven entrants started in the *Chicago Times-Herald*
race held on Thanksgiving Day, November 28, 1895. The Duryea car that won and
a Benz driven by Charles B. King were the only two vehicles able to complete the
55-mile distance. J. Frank Duryea's winning average speed was less than 8 miles
per hour. However, the *Times-Herald* report the following day pointed out that the
race had been run in thirty-degree temperatures "through deep snow, and along
ruts that would have tried horses to their utmost." Thus the race was generally in-
terpreted as a convincing demonstration that the Duryea and Benz automobiles could
perform tolerably under the worst possible conditions and gave substantial impetus
to automotive activity in the United States.

The *Cosmopolitan Magazine* race run the following spring from New York City Hall
to Irvington, New York, merely seemed to confirm the superiority of the Duryea
car. Four Duryeas and a lone Benz were the only vehicles entered, and three of the
Duryeas managed to finish the race. The press generally overlooked the fact that a
$3,000 first prize had been able to attract so few entries.

The optimism concerning the Duryea car proved to be well founded. Two redesigned Duryea cars participated in a race from London to Brighton, England, on
November 14, 1896. Despite the regressive surrey style of these cars, the one driven

[3] "The Horseless Vehicle," ibid., 73:107 (August 17, 1895).

Plate 6.   Charles E. Duryea in
the car that J. Frank Duryea drove
to victory in the *Chicago Times-
Herald* race. Courtesy Smithsonian
Institution.

by J. Frank Duryea managed to defeat the Panhard and Levassor automobile that had won the most recent European long-distance race.

Formation of the Industry

An American automobile industry formed during the closing years of the nineteenth century. Paying no heed to the Selden patent, J. Frank and Charles E. Duryea capitalized on their success in the *Times-Herald* race and initiated manufacture for a commercial market in the United States by organizing the Duryea Motor Company in the fall of 1895. The Duryeas subsequently made the first sale of an American gasoline automobile in February 1896 and produced twelve more vehicles that year. This was the first time that more than one car of the same design was made in the United States. Their firm became the Duryea Manufacturing Company of Peoria, Illinois, in 1897. Elwood P. Haynes and the Apperson brothers similarly took advantage of their early start in building an operational gasoline automobile by forming the Haynes-Apperson Company at Kokomo, Indiana. Haynes-Apperson began to produce vehicles for a commercial market in 1898. Alexander Winton, a Cleveland, Ohio, bicycle manufacturer, entered the competition when the Winton Motor Carriage Company was organized in 1897. Winton started in the automobile business by building six small omnibuses for municipal service in Cleveland, but, meeting with public protests and damage suits on the trial runs, he turned to the production of private passenger cars. The quality of Winton automobiles gained national recognition when Winton drove one of his cars 800 miles from Cleveland to New York City in less than seventy-nine hours' driving time in the summer of 1897. Winton sold his first automobile in March 1898 and by December had delivered twenty-two vehicles.

Other American companies were manufacturing electric cars for a commercial market by 1898. One of these was the Electric Carriage and Wagon Company formed

Plate 7.   Scene at the Duryea factory, Springfield, Massachusetts, in 1896 during the assembling of the first American cars made from the same pattern. Courtesy Smithsonian Institution.

Plate 8.   1898 Winton, the first
Winton car sold. Courtesy Smithsonian Institution.

Plate 9.   1895–1897 Morris and
Salom "Electrobat" cab, one of
the first American electric cars.
Courtesy Free Library of Philadelphia.

by Henry G. Morris and Pedro G. Salom, which began to operate twelve of its electric vehicles as a fleet of public cabs on the streets of New York City in January 1897. The company then moved to Hartford, Connecticut, and was absorbed by the Electric Vehicle Company, a New Jersey holding company. The most important early manufacturer of not only electric but all motor vehicles in the United States was the Pope Manufacturing Company of Hartford, Connecticut. Pope was the nation's leading bicycle manufacturer. Its motor vehicle department, started by Hiram Percy Maxim in 1895, began to produce electric automobiles in 1897. By the end of 1898 Pope had made some 500 electric and 40 gasoline automobiles. The Pope motor vehicle division became the Columbia Automobile Company and was consolidated with the aforementioned Electric Vehicle Company in 1899.

Quantity production of steam cars was initiated in the Boston area by George E. Whitney and by Francis E. and Freelan O. Stanley. Whitney built several successful steam cars in 1896 and went on to form the Whitney Motor Wagon Company in 1898. In the fall of 1898 the Stanley twins sold one of two steamers they had built and also organized a company to produce steam vehicles. This company was purchased by John Brisbane Walker, the owner of *Cosmopolitan Magazine*, and Amzi Lorenzo Barber, an asphalt magnate. Walker and Barber split up in 1899 to form rival companies that made identical cars—the Mobile Company of America at Tarrytown, New York, and the Locomobile Company of America at Bridgeport, Connecticut. The Stanleys then reentered the automobile business by acquiring the Whitney Motor Wagon Company in 1899 and changing its name to the Stanley Manufacturing Company of Boston, Massachusetts.

With these companies in the lead, and allowing for changes of name and early failures, thirty American automobile manufacturers produced an estimated 2,500 motor vehicles in 1899, the first year for which separate figures for the automobile

Plate 10.   The Stanley twins in
their first steamer, built in 1897.
Courtesy Smithsonian Institution.

industry were compiled in the *United States Census of Manufactures*. Eight companies were located in Massachusetts and two in Connecticut. These ten New England firms concentrated on the production of steam and electric cars and were responsible for the most significant proportion of the total 1899 output. The Middle West was the center for the manufacture of gasoline automobiles and was also represented by ten firms. The remaining ten automobile manufacturers active in 1899 were located in the Middle Atlantic states.

The output of these thirty active manufacturers is only a partial indication of the extent of automotive activity in the United States at the close of the nineteenth century. *Motor Age* estimated in 1899 that, in addition, experimental automobile work was "being carried on on such a scale that if the conditions in New England were approached in other parts of the country. . . . it may perhaps be estimated that one thousand such shops exist in the United States today, and probably one hundred of them have been in operation for two years or longer without yet having advanced to the stage of manufacture, except in a very few instances." The periodical pointed out that "the majority of these workers in the east have small hopes of ever conducting factories under their own control." Rather, the goal of most was to produce patentable features of design that could be tested in experimental vehicles, then sold for a high price to an established company or an individual who had the capital to develop them.[4]

Early Expectations

The future of the American automobile industry seemed assured at the beginning of the twentieth century. Phenomenal progress was made by the manufacturer from 1900 to 1910 both in improvement of product and in the capacity to produce moder-

[4] "Manufacture in New England," *Motor Age*, 1:4 (September 12, 1899).

Plate 11.   Reproduction of the
Detroit shop in which Henry Ford
built his first car in 1896. Courtesy
of the Ford Archives, Henry Ford
Museum, Dearborn, Michigan.

Plate 12.   Illustration of the Packard plant in Detroit, 1904. Courtesy
Free Library of Philadelphia.

ately priced vehicles in quantity. However, the growth of the industry never surpassed popular expectations. Aware of the many problems that had to be solved, persons who could claim some technical expertise were apt to be more cautious than the man in the street about predicting the imminent arrival of an automobile for the masses that would rapidly displace the horse. The principal examiner at the United States Patent Office stated in 1901: "The self-propelled vehicle is with us; it is obvious to the least observant of laymen that it has come to stay, while the expert has a justifiable belief in its future. . . . To say that the future of the automobile is assured is merely to voice an impression which is as common as it is usually vague." He went on to say that most assessments of how fast the automobile would replace the horse were too optimistic and lacked appreciation of the specific technological problems that had to be solved: "To judge from frequent printed references to the horseless age, the speedy extinction of the horse is popularly anticipated. I do not take this view. . . . He may be relegated to comparative obscurity, and possibly, in course of time to the zoo; but it is not we who shall live to see his extinction."[5]

Little popular prejudice toward the motor vehicle was evident either in absolute terms or compared with earlier responses to innovation in transportation, particularly the bicycle and the self-propelled trolley car. An official of the Locomobile Company gave a typical assessment of this in 1902: "The introduction of the mechanical carriage has been relatively quiet. To be sure, there have been some accidents, and these happenings in or near metropolitan districts have attracted more or less attention and possibly have been given undue publicity by publications of a sensational nature. Yet, if we look back to the early days of the trolley car and the bicycle, it will be fairly evident that the introduction of the automobile has been very free from unpleasant incidents."[6]

[5] W. W. Townsend, "Future of the Industry Assessed," ibid., 3:999–1001 (February 6, 1901).
[6] J. A. Kingman, "The Automobile in the Country," *Country Life in America*, 2:139 (August 1902).

High popular expectations were encouraged by influential figures in finance and in the transportation industry, who publicly expressed reckless confidence in the immediate future of the automobile industry. One of these outspoken individuals was Colonel Albert A. Pope, then head of the American Bicycle Company — a short-lived "bicycle trust" capitalized at $40 million that had grown out of the 1899 dissolution of the Pope Manufacturing Company. Pope, in a statement released in late 1900 through the Boston News Bureau, a financial information agency, said: "The automobile will in time be the universal means of transportation, and the future of the American Bicycle Co. rests on the adoption and development of the automobile. . . . I predict that inside of ten years there will be more automobiles in use in the large cities of the United States than there are now horses in these cities." The sale of some $4.2 million worth of new stock was expected to provide additional working capital for expansion of the firm's automobile business, carried on by the Waverley Company of Indianapolis, a manufacturer of electric vehicles, and the H. A. Lozier plant at Toledo, Ohio, which first made steam and later gasoline cars. The two companies became organized as the International Motor Car Company. Pope declared that 15,000 of his bicycle agents throughout the country were "fairly howling" for automobiles to meet an "enormous demand." Pope knew the need was for a reliable automobile that would sell for less than $1,000. Although he recognized that the current automobiles fell far short of this standard, he confidently hoped that "next year we will certainly have a machine near perfection."[7]

After 1902, predictions began to be made quite freely that an automobile for the masses would inevitably be produced in the foreseeable future. The fact that the innovation was no longer a novelty and the appearance of the curved-dash Oldsmobile the preceding year at the moderate retail price of $650 appeared to offer substantial

[7] "Fairly Howling," *Motor World*, 1:17 (October 11, 1900).

ground for this expectation. *World's Work* typically commented in early 1903: "The excitement of the innovation is gone, and the machine is so common they go by unnoticed. . . . Looking into the future, prophets are seeing individual machines possible to the rich and poor alike."[8] Henry Norman, the English editor of *World's Work*, stated: "For my part, I am convinced that ten years hence there will not be a horse left in the streets of London or New York except for the few kept purely for pleasure and pride in their beauty and strength for police and military use." The response to Norman's article from readers demonstrated that his opinion was widely shared. In a follow-up article a few months later, he reported that "the extraordinary fact is that almost every commentator seems prepared to accept my rather audacious prophecies as probably well founded."[9]

By the time the Ford Motor Company was organized in 1903, the belief was common that the automobile would soon replace the horse, and mass ownership of reliable motor vehicles seemed probable in the near future. Henry Ford's conception of a universal car for the masses might indeed have been derived from any of a significant number of articles that expressed this belief in the periodical literature of the day.

Demonstrating the Capabilities of the Horseless Vehicle

Predictions that the automobile would soon displace the horse in the United States seemed credible by 1903 because it had already been demonstrated a number of times that American-made motor vehicles could, without excessive mechanical trouble, negotiate primitive roads over distances that would have been impossible for horses.

Alexander Winton's 1897 drive from Cleveland to New York City resulted in so much favorable publicity that he repeated the trip two years later with Charles B.

[8] "The Advancing Automobile," *World's Work*, 5:3253 (March 1903).
[9] Henry Norman, "The Coming of the Automobile," ibid., 5:3308 (April 1903), and "Can I Afford an Automobile?" ibid., 6:3502 (June 1903).

Shanks, a newspaper reporter. The articles written by Shanks to publicize the journey attracted much attention and drew interested crowds all along their route. James R. Doolittle, writing the first comprehensive history of the industry in 1916, called Shanks's articles "the first real effort at intelligent publicity with which the new industry had been favored." He estimated that "when Winton reached New York a million people saw his car and part of the credit for that crowd must be given to Shanks." The fact that Winton's 1899 Cleveland–New York run had taken less than forty-eight hours' driving time, combined with Shanks's effective publicity, appear to have marked a turning point in popular demand for automobiles. Other manufacturers gave Winton credit for a general increase in sales. Winton's own records showed that before the trip his "sales were made almost exclusively to engineers who desired to buy and experiment with an automobile that would really run, but after the trip, the sales were made to the public at large."[10]

Ransom E. Olds decided in the fall of 1901 to emulate Winton's practical demonstration of the motor vehicle. The Olds Motor Works was by then committed to volume production of the curved-dash Oldsmobile, having been the first company to mass-produce gasoline automobiles by manufacturing some 425 vehicles in 1901. A New York City to Buffalo endurance run sponsored by the Automobile Club of America had indicated the possibility of long-distance automobile touring by private owners, and Olds hoped to capture the market in the heavily populated eastern cities by providing convincing evidence that his moderately priced, light car was as reliable for touring as more expensive, heavy vehicles.

Roy D. Chapin, then a tester at the Olds factory, was picked to drive a new curved-dash from Detroit to the New York automobile show. Chapin left Detroit on October 27. Despite one stop for major repairs and the handicap of extremely muddy roads,

[10] James R. Doolittle et al., *The Romance of the Automobile Industry* (New York: Klebold Press, 1916), pp. 322–323.

he arrived in New York City on November 5. His average speed for the total distance of 820 miles was 14 mph, and he used 30 gallons of gasoline, 80 gallons of water, and all of the numerous spare parts he had carried along. The favorable publicity given his feat was in large part responsible for Olds's sale of 750 cars in New York City alone the following year, something never before approximated by any automobile manufacturer.

That American automobiles could withstand hard use under the most adverse driving conditions was conclusively demonstrated by three transcontinental crossings during the summer of 1903. The first was made by Dr. H. Nelson Jackson, a Burlington, Vermont, physician, and his chauffeur, Sewall K. Crocker. They traveled from San Francisco to New York City in a new Winton in sixty-three days. Then a Packard sent out by the factory for advertising purposes was driven from San Francisco to New York by Tom Fetch in just fifty-three days. Not to be outdone, the Olds Motor Works shipped a curved-dash to California; the car was driven back to Detroit by Eugene Hammond and L. L. Whitman between July 6 and September 7. All three events received substantial publicity, and the reputations of Winton, Packard, and Oldsmobile cars were deservedly enhanced. For Ransom E. Olds this was an important achievement that helped him to lead the industry with a record 4,000 sales in 1903. The comparative reliability of the moderately priced, light car now had been established for the American public. Winton, probably Olds's closest competitor, sold about 700 cars that year.

The mechanical breakdowns suffered by all three transcontinental cars were not viewed with much concern at the time. Dr. Jackson reported, for example, that despite primitive roads and very bad weather he had used only two sets of tires and added: "Nor did the car give me much trouble. A broken bolt coming over the mountains, two connecting rod breakages and an axle nut dropping off and letting the balls out—

Plate 13.   Dr. H. Nelson Jackson and Sewall K. Crocker, his chauffeur, in their 1903 Winton at a typical stop during the first transcontinental trip across the United States. Courtesy Smithsonian Institution.

Plate 14.   Restored 1903 curved-dash Oldsmobile, the first mass-produced car in the world. The curved-dash sold for only $650 and was the most popular American car from its introduction in 1901 to about 1904. Courtesy Smithsonian Institution.

this was the sum total. I telegraphed for new connecting rods and put them in with as little delay as possible; while as to the balls, an old mower yielded some to take their place and a machinist made a new cup and cone while we waited."[11]

These successful crossings of the American continent encouraged an estimated several thousand Americans to take cross-country automobile vacations in 1904 and stimulated interest in organized reliability runs. Under the auspices of the American Automobile Association, a major tour from New York to the St. Louis Exposition was organized in 1904. No prize was offered. Although some advance arrangements were made to ensure adequate service facilities along the general route of travel, it was strictly a "go-as-you-please" affair for the automobile club members who participated in the event between July 25 and August 10. Fifty-nine of the seventy-one cars that started managed to complete the trip. Then in 1905 two Oldsmobiles ran a transcontinental race from New York to Portland, Oregon, in only forty-four days. These events indicated to Americans that the reliable automobile had arrived and that lower-priced American-made cars could perform over rough terrain as well as or better than the finest European machines.

The reliability run reached its zenith in the famous Glidden reliability tours, run annually for handsome trophies between 1905 and 1913. The motivating force behind the tours was Charles J. Glidden, a Boston millionaire and automobile enthusiast. The Glidden tours were open to members of the American Automobile Association and any club it recognized. Since Glidden's aim was to promote touring by private owners rather than to give publicity to manufacturers, he stipulated that each car entered must be driven by its owner. This turned out to be of little practical consequence, however, because any executive of the automobile industry could comply

[11] "Dr. Jackson Arrives," *Motor World*, 6:659, 668 (July 30, 1903).

with the rule by driving one of his firm's most recent models himself. Thus most contestants in the Glidden tours were representatives of the automobile industry.

The first Glidden tour was held from July 11 to July 22, 1905, and covered 870 miles from New York through New England and return. Twenty-seven of the thirty-four entries finished, and the cup was won by Percy P. Pierce, who had driven a heavy Pierce touring car that carried five passengers. One of the participants summed up the results: "The tour has proved that the automobile is now almost foolproof. It has proved that American cars are durable and efficient. It has shown the few who took part how delightful their short vacation may be, and it has strengthened our belief in the permanence of the motorcar."[12]

Track and road races that placed primary emphasis upon speed were more important for their contribution to automotive technology as tests for weaknesses in design than as publicity for the motor vehicle. The first American track races were held at Narragansett, Rhode Island, on September 7, 1896, between five Duryeas and two electric cars—a Ricker and a Morris and Salom "Electrobat." The Ricker won all five heats—something that would have been impossible for an electric over any reasonably long distance. Spectators considered the performance dull and in protest originated the cry, "Get a horse!" Progress in achieving extremely high speeds on the track was very rapid. The 1896 Ricker ran a mile at an average of 26.8 mph; only ten years later, a Stanley Steamer driven by Fred Marriott averaged 127.66 mph in a mile run at Ormond Beach, Florida. Long-distance road races emphasizing speed were also held on the public highways over closed courses. The most important American road races were the international events sponsored by the American Automobile Association for a trophy donated by William K. Vanderbilt, Jr. The first

---

[12] George O. Draper, "A View of the Tour from One Participating," *Horseless Age*, 16:153 (July 26, 1905).

Plate 16.   Alexander Winton in
his 1903 "Bullet No. 2" racing car,
one of the first cars to use an eight-
cylinder, in-line engine. This car
was driven one mile in 43 seconds
by Barney Oldfield at Daytona
Beach on January 28, 1904. Courtesy Smithsonian Institution.

race for the Vanderbilt Challenge Cup was run over a 284-mile Long Island course on October 8, 1904, and won by a Panhard averaging 52.2 mph.

The 1904 Vanderbilt Cup and other road races met with wide public disapproval. They were considered dangerous exhibitions, unwarranted because their importance for the development of a reliable family car seemed remote. Track racing did not excite as much condemnation, but the vehicles designed to achieve maximum speed over short distances on the track were specialized monstrosities rather than practical road vehicles. Consequently, track races were viewed by the public as little more than exciting spectacles. Public opinion notwithstanding, contests stressing speed undoubtedly did contribute much to automotive technology. To counterbalance this gain, some hostility to the motor vehicle was perhaps aroused; the publicity given to the automobile by speed contests, in contrast with that accorded by long-distance reliability runs, was mainly unfavorable. By about 1905 the trade journals generally questioned even the advertising benefits to be gained from racing by individual manufacturers. As *Motor Age* commented, "The amount of direct benefit to all but a few concerns has proved so small that it is doubtful if even the winners can see any great profit in the outcome, whereas it is certain the losers . . . have lost more by failing to make the showing they expected to make."[13]

The 1906 San Francisco earthquake proved a much more severe and impressive test of the motor vehicle than either speed contests or reliability runs. Walter C. White organized a caravan of motortrucks to bring needed supplies to the disaster area. Even more important, some 200 privately owned automobiles in the stricken city were immediately impressed for public service by the military and civic officials for a multiplicity of emergency uses. An indication of the extensive use to which these vehicles were put is that the gasoline automobiles among them consumed an

[13] "What Does Racing Prove?" *Motor Age*, 8:6 (July 13, 1905).

estimated 15,000 gallons of fuel donated by the Standard Oil Company. After tires exploded from the heat of the pavement, cars were run for days on their wheel rims at as fast a speed as they were capable of over obstacle-laden streets. Passenger cars were called upon to tow several moving vans after the horses pulling them had expired from the heat and strain. Mechanical failures under these extremely severe conditions turned out to be surprisingly infrequent.

  Reports of the automobile's role in saving lives and property during the San Francisco disaster were ecstatic in their praise. Both the War Department and municipal governments were encouraged to adopt motor vehicles more extensively, and the average citizen was given convincing proof that the automobile was a practical and beneficial machine. John Dougherty, acting chief of the San Francisco Fire Department, telegraphed the Electric Vehicle Company on April 24: "Three of your 45-horsepower Columbias have been used by myself and assistants, Shaugnessy and Wills, continuously night and day since the earthquake April 18, and are still in service. . . . Their work has been perfect at all times and I marvel that my automobile can stand up to such an unusual and severe test. I was skeptical about the automobile previous to the disaster, but now give it my hearty endorsement." One of Dougherty's firemen told a reporter that "hereafter it would be nothing but automobiles in the fire department."[14] According to the *San Francisco Chronicle,* "that the automobile played an all but indispensable part in saving the western part of San Francisco, and at the same time has proved invaluable in the serious business of governing the city through its greatest stress, is conceded by every man who has had his eyes open during the ten days or so that have elapsed since the earthquake. Old men in the bread lines who had previously occupied much of their time in supper-table denunciation of the whizz-wagons now have nothing but praise for them. Men high in

[14] "Motor Car Triumphs in Crisis," ibid., 9:3 (May 3, 1906).

official service . . . go even further and say that but for the auto it would not have been possible to save even a portion of the city or to take care of the sick or to preserve a semblance of law and order."[15]

The San Francisco earthquake of 1906 thus capped the need for demonstration of the reliability of the motor vehicle. Following the disaster, L. L. Whitman drove a Franklin automobile to San Francisco from New York in the then incredible time of just fifteen days and a few hours. By 1907, gasoline economy runs had replaced tours to demonstrate reliability as the focus of public interest.

The Automobile Show

The rapid rise of the motor vehicle from an obscure curiosity item in the late nineteenth century to a secure position of acceptance in American life is illustrated well by the institutionalization of the automobile show in the United States by about 1905. Following the stimulus engendered by the initial developments in diffusion, *Referee*, a bicycle periodical, suggested in 1896 that there was a need to display motor vehicles; a Daimler car was shown at the 1896 Sportsmen's Exhibition in Madison Square Garden; Montgomery Ward, the Chicago mail-order house, sent a motor vehicle about the country in a special railroad coach for advertising purposes; and both Barnum and Bailey and the Franklin Brothers circuses displayed Duryea automobiles as attractions in 1896. Electric cars were exhibited at an indoor bicycle race in Chicago in 1897 and again at the Electrical Exposition in Madison Square Garden the following year. The automobile was beginning to be used as a drawing card at country fairs as well by about 1900.

Public interest on such occasions was so great that it soon became feasible to devote exhibits solely to motor vehicles. Thus in 1900 the automobile show was initi-

[15] Reprinted in "Credit to Auto for Its Frisco Work," *Automobile*, 14:807 (May 17, 1906).

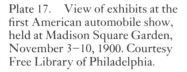

Plate 17.   View of exhibits at the
first American automobile show,
held at Madison Square Garden,
November 3–10, 1900. Courtesy
Free Library of Philadelphia.

ated; five automobile shows, all advertised as "firsts," were held that year. However, credit as the first successful such event of importance should go to the November 3 – 10, 1900, show held at Madison Square Garden under the joint auspices of two newly formed organizations – the National Association of Automobile Manufacturers (NAAM) and the Automobile Club of America (ACA). Joint sponsorship of the important automobile shows in the United States by the NAAM and a local auto- mobile club was continued as common practice until 1905. After that date, separate annual shows were held in New York City under the respective auspices of the Association of Licensed Automobile Manufacturers (ALAM), a trade association of those companies given the right to manufacture gasoline cars under the Selden patent, and the American Motor Car Manufacturers' Association (AMCMA), a rival group of so-called independents who had organized to fight the Selden claims. The annual New York shows were by far the most important; they were approached in prestige only by the exhibitions held in Chicago.

The essential nature of the automobile show had changed by 1905, and its phe- nomenal success by then surpassed even the most optimistic early expectations. Originally, the automobile show primarily had served manufacturers as a retail outlet for their products. Beginning about 1905, however, dealerships were well enough established that the shows lost this function and became mainly a place to preview new models and, as Colonel Albert A. Pope put it, act as "a sort of festival for society and the automobiling class."[16] Public interest in the automobile show had grown to such proportions in just a few years that by 1905 the New York show at Madison Square Garden was probably the nation's leading industrial exposition.

[16] Arthur N. Jervis, "How the Auto Show Idea Developed," ibid., 16:37–38 (January 10, 1907). For the history of the automobile show see also Harry W. Perry, "From the Earliest Show to the Latest," *Motor*, 13:52, 232, 234 (January 10, 1910), and Anderson, *Story of the American Automobile*, pp. 123–131.

From Novelty to Necessity

The period of trial was definitely over for the motor vehicle in the United States by 1906. Reliability demonstrations were hardly necessary after this date, and writers in popular periodicals had begun to refer to the automobile as a necessity and to anticipate the imminent appearance of a universal car for the masses. Almost all contemporary observers now agreed with Frank A. Munsey that "the uncertain period of the automobile is past. It is no longer a theme for jokers, and rarely do we hear the derisive expression, 'Get a horse!'"[17] Despite the 1907 financial panic, a writer in *Harper's Weekly* predicted that "there is no question but that [the automobile] business is going to get steadily better. There is one reason for this which must not be overlooked — that is, the fact that the automobile is essential to comfort and happiness."[18]

Spokesmen for the automobile industry reflected this new-found confidence. The secretary for the Mitchell Motor Car Company stated in January 1907 that "the possibilities of the automobile have developed more, and have been more generally understood and appreciated, within the past twelve months than during its entire previous life. . . . There is no doubt but that there is a shortage today and that the country could absorb twice the number of cars that will be made during the year of 1907." Colonel Albert A. Pope expressed the common experience of manufacturers when he said, "In the present state of the industry it is more difficult to produce good cars than to sell them."[19]

Sales of motor vehicles had increased substantially during 1907 despite the general business recession and an apparent saturation of the upper-class market. Conditions

[17] Frank A. Munsey, "The Automobile in America," *Munsey's Magazine*, 34:403 (January 1906).
[18] Charles L. Palms, "The Automobile Outlook," *Harper's Weekly*, 51:1499 (October 12, 1907).
[19] See the brief articles by these and other manufacturers in "Present and Future of a Great Industry," *Automobile*, 16:151–157 (January 17, 1907).

ir own. The whole family
·rs generally prefer to
·nditions of past years
·as been gained by 1910,
·ates awaited only the
·iable motor vehicles at

· vehicle began to pose a
·0, 1899, the National
·verse effect of the auto-
· potential threat severe
· to horses. It responded as
· examination and licensing
·the crippling of horses

·ng a period of exceptionally
·several important makers
·s a hedge against antici-
·Manufacturing Company
·sh, its general counsel,
·er sold its first motor
·· was formed in 1904 to
·arly, James H. Whiting,
·ne 3, 1909).

·okesman for the Elmore
·ne nature of an evolution
·along without the auto-
·ubted that a broad
·become a reality.
·fter 1906 was that manu-
·neir products in cross-
·nnual Glidden tours
·he 1909 Glidden offi-
·nanufacturers "were
·er this contest when we
·· us no good.'"21
·ur from Cincinnati
·he culminating event.
·rn roads and was con-
·l to ensure the stock-
·onsored by Frank A.
·D.C., via New En-
·importance that could
·of the automobile

·integral part of Ameri-
·ortant pioneers in-
·of owning an auto-

·ne, 24:49 (July 14, 1909).

mobile has largely worn off. The neighbors have one of th
has become so accustomed to auto riding that some memb
ride alone or remain behind while others go. In short, the
are not with us so strongly today."[22] Acceptance having th
the development of an automobile culture in the United S
ability of the industry to provide a sufficient quantity of re
prices the average man could afford.

Decline of the Horse, Carriage, and Wagon
During the first decade of the twentieth century, the moto
threat to horse-drawn transportation. As early as October
Master Horseshoers' Association discussed the possible ac
mobile upon the use of horses. The association thought th
enough to warrant action to remove some of the objection
strongly as it could by initiating a movement to compel th
of horseshoers in the hope that this would at least prevent
by incompetent workmen.[23]

   Although carriage and wagon manufacturers were enjoy
high demand for their products at the turn of the century,
of horse-drawn vehicles entered the automobile business a
pated future market conditions. The Studebaker Brothers
of South Bend, Indiana, was stimulated by Frederick S. F
to begin to experiment with electric cars in 1898. Studeba
vehicle in 1902, and the Studebaker Automobile Compan
manufacture both electric and gasoline automobiles. Simi

[22] Charles E. Duryea, "How to Select an Automobile," *Independent*, 66:1213 (
[23] "Horseshoers' Sensible Action," *Motor Age*, 1:113 (October 17, 1899).

president of the Flint Wagon Works of Flint, Michigan, became convinced that the motor vehicle would soon replace the horse and, consequently, bought the Buick Motor Company from Benjamin and Frank Briscoe in 1904. William C. Durant, whose Durant-Dort Carriage Company was one of the leaders in the carriage and wagon industry, was persuaded to join Whiting in the Buick venture. Among the other important carriage and wagon manufacturers that turned to the production of motor vehicles before 1905 were the Standard Wheel Company of Terre Haute, Indiana, which became the Overland Automobile Company, and the Mitchell Wagon Company of Racine, Wisconsin.

Owners of livery stables too began to feel the effects of the automobile on their business, and a few of the more enterprising started automobile rental services or opened garages. The vice-president and manager of the Antler Stables Company, located in the heart of Cleveland, Ohio, justified his firm's switch from horses to motor vehicles in 1905 by pointing out that "a year ago we were keeping 130 horses and doing a big boarding business. Today we have but sixty horses, less than half, and only about fifteen belong to the boarding class. So you see what the automobile is doing to the livery trade."[24] One of three New Haven, Connecticut, livery stable owners who began to rent automobiles the following year expected that, due to the popularity of the motor vehicle, "there would be little or no renting of livery outfits in the near future."[25]

Each year the prospects of the city livery stable grew dimmer. By 1907 it was apparent that the automobile industry's inability to produce reliable, low-cost vehicles in sufficient quantity was all that prevented the rapid disappearance of the horse from American cities. *Automobile* observed: "The horse reigns only in the fields in

[24] "Puts Livery in Background," ibid., 8:12 (August 31, 1905).
[25] "Liverymen Putting in Automobiles," *Automobile*, 14:798 (May 17, 1906).

which his supremacy has not been disputed. . . . He is no longer used by the ultra-fashionable and the pleasure loving to the extent that he once was. The riding and driving clubs all over the country are losing membership, and even closing their clubhouse doors, and livery stables are losing money or being transformed into garages. The remaining stronghold of the horse is guarded solely by low prices." The horse would disappear as soon as the automobile industry was able to produce "something like a million a year of two-passenger, $250 conveyances!" and it appeared evident that "the day of the low-priced car is dawning."[26]

The demand for horses still remained high, however, and the number of farm horses alone in use in 1908 was 19,992,000 versus only 198,000 motor vehicles registered that year. An investigation made by the chief of the Division of Foreign Markets of the United States Department of Agriculture further indicated that the motor vehicle had thus far displaced only about 60,000 horses, compared with an estimated 500,000 horses displaced by electricity in urban streetcar service.[27]

Nevertheless, the trend was unmistakable. By 1912 the number of horses on farms had remained relatively stable at 20,509,000, while motor vehicle registrations had increased substantially to 944,000. The automobile industry (including the manufacture of bodies and parts) had, moreover, clearly become more important to the American economy by 1909 than the carriage and wagon industry. That year, 735 establishments in the American automobile industry were capitalized at $173,837,000, employed 85,359 persons, paid salaries and wages of $58,173,000, and turned out a product valued at $249,202,000, with $117,556,000 being the value added by manufacture. In comparison, 5,492 carriage and wagon firms (including material manufacturers also) in the United States in 1909 were capitalized at $175,474,000, employed 82,944 persons, paid salaries and wages of $45,555,000, and turned out a product

[26] Victor Lougheed, "The Horse and the Automobile," ibid., 16:315–316 (February 14, 1907).
[27] "Farm Horse Giving Way to Its Rival, the Auto," ibid., 18:246 (February 20, 1908).

valued at $159,893,000, with $77,942,000 being the value added by manufacture. The carriage and wagon industry from 1904 to 1909 increased only 2.6 percent in value of product and declined by 10.2 percent in number of wage earners employed. On the other hand, between 1904 and 1909 the automobile industry increased 729.7 percent in value of product and 529.4 percent in number of wage earners employed.[28] Traffic counts also demonstrated that the motor vehicle had come to constitute an appreciable part of some urban transportation systems by the time Henry Ford opened his Highland Park plant on January 1, 1910.[29]

Registration and Production Statistics

Contemporary commentators found it very difficult to estimate accurately either the number of motor vehicles in use in the United States or the growth of the American automobile industry from available registration and production statistics. A 1901 article in the *Review of Reviews* complained: "It is quite difficult to get exact figures of the number of machines being used in this country, as there are no definite methods of registration and the vehicles are pretty widely distributed all over the United States."[30] Five years later, Frank A. Munsey experienced equal difficulty. He informed his readers that "facts and figures about the beginning and progress of the automobile industry here at home are so conflicting, and there is such a dearth of accurate knowledge on the subject, that I cannot show, year by year, our growth in the manufacture of automobiles." Munsey admitted that "just how many there

[28]Various editions of U.S., Bureau of Foreign and Domestic Commerce, *Statistical Abstract of the United States* (Washington, D.C.: Government Printing Office).
[29]See, for example, "Automobile Traffic Growth in New York," *Scientific American*, 97:343 (November 9, 1907); "Chicago Counts Its Boulevard Traffic," *Motor Age*, 16:9 (September 30, 1909); and "Motor Traffic in New England," *Motor World*, 20:1105 (September 30, 1909).
[30]J. A. Kingman, "Automobile Making in America," *American Monthly Review of Reviews* (hereafter cited as *Review of Reviews*), 24:300 (September 1901).

are in the whole United States I have been unable to learn."[31] Estimates of the number of motor vehicles in use that appeared in the periodicals of the day consequently show considerable variation.

Several considerations place clear limitations on the acceptance of any registration figures as an accurate index of the number of motor vehicles in use in these early years.[32] A major problem is that one can expect registration figures to be reasonably accurate only from those states that had compulsory registration laws. For the other states, the figures given must be considered mere guesses. Compulsory registration laws were virtually nonexistent before 1903, and until 1915 they were not universal. New York in 1901 was the first state to require registration; by 1904 it was required in thirteen states; and thirty-six states had compulsory registration laws as of 1910. Even in those states where it was compulsory, the nature of registration raises other problems. For most of the 1901–1910 period, perennial registration was practiced — that is, registration was not subject to annual renewal. All state registration laws were of this type until 1905, and as late as 1910 perennial registration was practiced in fifteen of the thirty-six states that required registration. Thus many motor vehicles that had been scrapped remained in existence in inflated state registration figures. Another factor contributing to overestimation was that, until reciprocal registration laws gained general acceptance, a motor vehicle had to be registered separately in each state through which it was driven that required registration. This condition had been remedied in most states well before 1910, but while it lasted many vehicles were counted several times in each year's registration figures. For example, reregistration by nonresidents evidently accounted for about 11 percent of the motor vehicles

[31]Munsey, "Automobile in America," p. 403.
[32]For details on motor vehicle registration see U.S., Department of Commerce, *Highway Statistics, Summary to 1955* (Washington, D.C.: Government Printing Office, 1957).

registered in Massachusetts and 10 percent of the Connecticut registrations for 1904.[33] Finally, in several states — notably Missouri, Pennsylvania, South Carolina, and Texas — motor vehicles were for some time registered only at the county or municipal level. One wonders how many times each car was counted in the registration figures for these states while this practice was in effect.

Beyond these considerations, one must also be aware that registration figures, especially in these early years, could not be used as an index of the number of automobile owners in the population, even if they were accurate. Multiple ownership was extensively practiced. In addition to the fleets of motor vehicles owned by businesses and municipalities, *Harper's Weekly* estimated in 1906, for example, that "there are more than 200 persons in New York who have from five to ten cars apiece. John Jacob Astor alone is credited with thirty-two. The string of vehicles owned by an enthusiast of this class will include two or three touring cars, a pair of racers, a couple of broughams, a runabout, a station-car, and a work car."[34]

Statistics on motor vehicle production and sales are, of course, no reliable index of either the number of automobile owners in the population or the number of motor vehicles in use. There is reason to believe, furthermore, that production and sales figures given for the early years of the American automobile industry's existence are extremely crude estimates that may understate actual production. Many companies did not keep adequate business records, and many other firms considered production and sales data confidential information. Over 600 companies engaged in automobile manufacturing in the United States prior to 1910. Most were extremely small and ephemeral and never produced more than a few cars. Although the aggregate output of these insignificant firms must have been considerable, precisely how

[33] "Some Automobile Statistics," *Horseless Age*, 14:303–304 (September 28, 1904).
[34] Henry Jay Case, "The Rise of the Motor Car," *Harper's Weekly*, 50:49 (January 13, 1906).

great it was must remain a moot question. Even for a firm as important as REO, adequate data on output are lacking for the period with which we are concerned.

Although registration and production statistics do have the shortcomings just noted, these data nevertheless constitute the best of several possible measures of the diffusion of the motor vehicle in the United States. Therefore, the most reliable data available for 1900–1912 deserve presentation, explication, and analysis.

Table 1.1 shows the phenomenal growth in state motor vehicle registrations from an estimated 8,000 in 1900, before any state in fact required registration, to 944,000 in 1912. Gains over the previous year range from a high of 85 percent in 1901 to a low of 32 percent in 1907. Since percent gains become more significant as the base figure increases, the respective gains of 57, 50, 36, and 48 percent for the years 1909

Table 1.1 Summary of State Motor Vehicle Registrations, by Year, 1900–1912

Year	Automobiles	Percent Gain over Previous Year	Trucks	Percent Gain over Previous Year	Total Motor Vehicles	Percent Gain over Previous Year
1900	8,000				8,000	
1901	14,800	85			14,800	85
1902	23,000	55			23,000	55
1903	32,950	43			32,950	43
1904	54,590	67	700		55,290	68
1905	77,400	42	1,400	100	78,800	43
1906	105,900	37	2,200	57	108,100	37
1907	140,300	33	2,900	32	143,200	32
1908	194,400	38	4,000	38	198,400	38
1909	305,950	57	6,050	51	312,000	57
1910	458,377	49	10,123	67	468,500	50
1911	618,727	35	20,773	105	639,500	36
1912	901,596	46	42,404	104	944,000	48

Source: U.S., Department of Commerce, *Highway Statistics, Summary to 1955* (Washington, D.C.: Government Printing Office, 1957), p. 28. This source contains a note that the data were "compiled principally from State authorities, but it was necessary to draw on other sources and to make numerous estimates in order to present a reasonably complete series."

through 1912 are particularly impressive. Since declining percent gains in adoption after an innovation has diffused among the majority of its potential adopters must necessarily occur, these continuing high annual gains indicate that the potential number of new adopters of the automobile remained high through 1912. (Annual percent gains do not begin to taper off until after 1917 and only become regularly less than 10 percent after 1927, which is also the first year in which replacement demand accounted for a larger percentage of new car sales than initial and multiple car sales combined. The outset of the Great Depression in 1930 marked the first years in which registrations show percent losses over previous years.)

Table 1.2 shows the similarly impressive increase in number and wholesale value of motor vehicle factory sales between 1900 and 1912. From 4,192 factory sales at a wholesale value of slightly less than $5 million in 1900, the automobile industry grew

Table 1.2 Number and Wholesale Value of United States Motor Vehicle Factory Sales, by Year, 1900–1912

Year	Automobiles		Trucks		Total Motor Vehicles	
	Number	Value (Thousands)	Number	Value (Thousands)	Number	Value (Thousands)
1900	4,192	$ 4,899		$	4,192	$ 4,899
1901	7,000	8,183			7,000	8,183
1902	9,000	10,395			9,000	10,395
1903	11,235	13,000			11,235	13,000
1904	22,130	23,358	700	1,273	22,830	24,630
1905	24,250	38,670	750	1,330	25,000	40,000
1906	33,200	61,460	800	1,440	34,000	62,900
1907	43,000	91,620	1,000	1,708	44,000	93,400
1908	63,500	135,250	1,500	2,550	65,000	137,800
1909	123,990	159,766	3,297	5,334	127,287	165,099
1910	181,000	215,340	6,000	9,660	187,000	225,000
1911	199,319	225,000	10,681	21,000	210,000	246,000
1912	356,000	335,000	22,000	43,000	378,000	378,000

Source: Automobile Manufacturers Association, Inc., *Automobiles of America* (Detroit: Wayne State University Press, 1962), p. 104.

to 378,000 factory sales valued wholesale at $378 million in 1912.

Both Table 1.1 and Table 1.2 further illustrate the minimal importance of the commercial motor vehicle in the United States during this period. Almost exclusive emphasis was at first placed upon the development and production of private passenger cars. Until at least 1909, the factory sales of trucks were insignificant, the 1908 figures showing registration of only 4,000 trucks compared with 194,400 passenger cars. After 1910, however, increased attention to the manufacture of commercial vehicles resulted in percent gains in registrations for trucks that were significantly higher than the corresponding percent gains for passenger cars: trucks gained, respectively, 67, 105, and 104 percent in the years 1910 through 1912, for example, while passenger cars gained 49, 35, and 46 percent in these years. In 1912, 22,000 trucks with a wholesale value of $43 million were sold, and 42,404 trucks were registered. Thus, although starting several years later than the passenger car, the commercial vehicle was beginning to be adopted in significant quantity by the end of the period with which we are concerned.

Americanization of the Automobile

Table 1.3 indicates that imports of foreign automobiles were an insignificant source of supply in the United States both in absolute numbers and in comparison with

Table 1.3 United States Imports and Exports of Motor Vehicles, by Year, 1901–1912

Year	1901	1902	1903	1904	1905	1906	1907	1908	1909	1910	1911	1912
Imports	26	265	267	605	1,054	1,106	1,176	1,045	1,625	1,473	972	868
Exports						1,850	2,862	2,477	3,184	6,926	15,807	23,720

Source: U.S., Bureau of Foreign and Domestic Commerce, *Statistical Abstract of the United States* (annual editions, 1901–1912). No reliable figures on numbers of exports of motor vehicles before 1906 are available.

domestic production and that exports of American-made motor vehicles were much greater than imports from Europe during the 1901–1912 period. Imports reached their highest point for these years with 1,625 cars in 1909, then declined to only 868 in 1912. For any given year from 1901 to 1912, imported cars accounted for less than 2 percent of the total registrations in the United States. Most European-made automobiles were found in the New England and Middle Atlantic states, but an analysis of the 1905 registrations in these nine states plus the District of Columbia shows that even here imported cars accounted for only about 5 percent of the total registrations.[35]

A 45 percent ad valorem duty retained in the Payne-Aldrich tariff probably had something to do with the poor showing the foreign car made in the early American market. In any event, each year exports of motor vehicles gained over imports. Between 1906 and 1912, a total of 56,826 American-made motor vehicles were exported while only 8,265 foreign cars were imported into the United States; in 1912 alone exports overshadowed imports 23,720 to 868, accounting for about 6 percent of United States factory sales. European automobiles never sold well in the United States, and in January 1908 *Motor Age* predicted: "Whatever may have been the success of the foreign car in America it is apparent that its days as a material factor in competition here are numbered, as indicated by the lack of interest in the importers' show now in progress in Madison Square Garden. . . . Foreign cars will always be sold in America, but the number will grow so small that in a year or so the profits that may be derived from their sales will barely keep alive a couple of agencies."[36]

Thus the automobile was Americanized during the first decade of the twentieth century. Automobile ownership became much more widespread in the United States

[35] "Uncle Sam and John Bull," *Motor Age*, 8:8 (August 3, 1905).
[36] "Served Its Purpose," ibid., 13:16 (January 2, 1908).

than in Europe. Moreover, despite the considerable technological lead the foreign manufacturer had enjoyed at the turn of the century, the diffusion of the motor vehicle in the United States depended almost entirely upon the rapid development of a native American automobile industry that produced a type of car specifically designed to suit the needs and tastes of a broad middle-class market. By 1910 the American automobile industry had approached the critical turning point at which traditional American emphasis upon a democratic production ethic and the peculiar American genius for production engineering could begin to transform the uniquely American motorcar that had evolved from a pleasure vehicle for the upper and upper-middle classes into a necessity of life for the masses as well. John B. Rae has aptly stated, "By the end of the first decade of the twentieth century the automobile in the United States could no longer be regarded either as a novelty or as a rich man's plaything; it was already potentially what it would become in fact — an item of incredible mass consumption."[37]

[37] John B. Rae, *American Automobile Manufacturers* (Philadelphia: Chilton, 1959), p. 103.

2
Developing
a Mass Market

A mass market for automobiles was foreshadowed in popular sentiment long before it was realized in fact. From its introduction in the United States, the automobile had great appeal for the average man. At the turn of the century, *Motor Age* found that "interest in automobilism seems to be universally permeating. Every line and every lecture delivered on the subject is received with eager attention."[1] Within a few years, the most characteristic attitude of the man in the street was unconcealed enthusiasm for the motorcar. To a writer in the *Independent*, it seemed obvious by 1906 that "the automobile is the idol of the modern age. . . . The man who owns a motorcar gets for himself, besides the joys of touring, the adulation of the walking crowd, and the daring driver of a racing machine that bounds and rushes and disappears in the perspective in a thunder of explosions is a god to the women."[2]

Opposition to the Horseless Vehicle

Horse breeders, livery stable owners, and horse-drawn vehicle drivers' associations are the only groups for which a clear case of vehement opposition to the motor vehicle can be clearly established. Unlike carriage manufacturers and blacksmiths, who were able to profit from the demands for their services arising from the new mode of transportation, these other horse-drawn interests, with few exceptions, viewed the motor vehicle as a threat to their established economic interests and chose to fight the innovation rather than accommodate to it. Frequently, these groups presented petitions to ban the automobile from public roads on the grounds that it constituted a menace to public safety and was merely a "fad of the very rich."

Motorists often attacked antispeed organizations for being motivated primarily by prejudice against the automobile, but spokesmen for the antispeed organizations

[1] "New Yorkers Enthusiastic," *Motor Age*, 1:487 (February 15, 1900).
[2] George Dupuy, "The Conquering Automobile," *Independent*, 60:848 (April 12, 1906).

unequivocally maintained that they were pro-automobile and against only its abuse. For example, Townsend Scudder, the legal counsel for the Long Island Protective Society, said upon the society's incorporation in September 1902: "Our purpose is to enforce the speed law against the reckless drivers of automobiles and also those of fast horses. . . . It is not a society antagonistic to automobiles. We recognize that the automobile is the twentieth-century vehicle, and that it is with us to stay. Many of our members own and operate automobiles, but we are for a free highway and a safe highway and intend to harmonize the interests of the automobilists, the horse drivers, and the pedestrians."[3]

   The little opposition to the automobile that was evident among the urban lower class could be attributed to class-conscious envy and was apparently easily overcome. *Horseless Age* blamed what lower-class prejudice did exist up to 1902 on "many of the newspapers circulating chiefly among the working class [which] try to make capital out of class hatred and lose no opportunity to hold up the automobile as a means of oppression of the poor by the wealthy." But the appearance of labor leaders in automobiles in the 1902 New York City Labor Day parade was taken as an indirect acknowledgment on the part of labor that about 10,000 skilled workmen were already being employed in some phase of automobiling, and that the masses too would be "benefited by the advent of the automobile, as they have been benefited by all other mechanical developments that have preceded it."[4] Sporadic outbursts of stone throwing by "hoodlums and mischievous boys" constituted the only serious expression of urban lower-class hostility to the motor vehicle. During the summer of 1904, stone throwing attacks on motorists in a few lower-class New York City neighborhoods became serious enough to require special police protection along several thorough-

[3] "Object to the Abuse of Automobiling," *Motor World*, 4:662 (September 4, 1902).
[4] "To Conciliate the Masses," *Horseless Age*, 10:266 (September 10, 1902).

fares. These attacks were attributed to the disruption of street games by motor vehicles because "at this season of the year the city's streets become the playgrounds for children and the interruption of their sports by passing vehicles, especially automobiles, is often resented in as forcible an expression as they are capable of."[5] The following year, the Chicago Automobile Club and several other automobile clubs successfully began to combat stone throwing by giving automobile outings to potential culprits. The automobile clubs also began about this time to make attempts to gain popular sympathy through well-publicized automobile outings for underprivileged groups. The most typical event of this kind was an annual automobile outing for orphans.

Hostility to the motor vehicle was generally acknowledged to have been most pervasive in rural areas among farmers. Even as late as 1909, *Overland Monthly* commented that "it is no secret that the average farmer has more or less antipathy for the motorist, and he is not inclined to rush with open arms to greet one when he might happen to cross his path."[6] However, the farmers' opposition to the automobile was fairly well confined to just a few years. Before 1904 little rural prejudice had been apparent, and after 1906 the farmer became the mainstay of the market for automobiles. Overwhelmingly rural and agricultural states such as the Dakotas, Nebraska, and Kansas emerged as some of the more innovative states in the adoption of the motor vehicle by 1910.

Early assessments of farmers' opinions of the motor vehicle by the automobile trade journals found little prejudice against the innovation. At the turn of the century, *Horseless Age* found it "gratifying to learn that the farmers in many sections of the

---

[5] "To Prevent Ruffian Attacks on Automobiles in New York City" and "Specially Protected New York Thoroughfares," ibid., 13:585 (June 1, 1904).
[6] Will Barry, "The Automobile as the Agent of Civilization: California and Good Roads," *Overland Monthly*, n.s. 53:246 (March 1909).

country are taking a very sensible attitude toward the automobile. Recognizing it as the inevitable, soon to be as common on our roads as the horse vehicle, they are improving every opportunity to accustom their horses to it. . . . this is a very hopeful sign, and proves that more than half the battle for the automobile in rural districts is already won."[7] Two years later *Horseless Age* was even more optimistic. The periodical felt that the press falsely assumed that antispeed crusades in rural areas indicated prejudice, when "as a matter of fact, the average farmer is not, and never has been, a decided opponent of the automobile movement. . . . The broad class of the agricultural population regard automobiles with curiosity and the movement itself with more or less indifference." The more progressive farmers were already thinking of adopting the automobile "for their own domestic uses," and some had "traveled far and wide to the automobile factories to find a machine suitable for their requirements."[8]

The ire of farmers was unexpectedly aroused against the automobile, however, with the advent of widespread informal automobile touring during the summer of 1904. Speeding automobile tourists constituted a danger both to stock and to horsedrawn traffic and raised clouds of dust that damaged crops and settled on farmhouses, barns, and washes hung out to dry. These problems were much more severe in rural than in urban areas because of the absence of the traffic congestion that reduced speed in cities and because of the general lack of any paving whatever on country roads. Moreover, in 1904 the farmer could not easily anticipate owning an automobile himself soon, for most reputable manufacturers made no serious attempt to design cars suited to the farmers' needs and purses until forced to by the apparent saturation of the urban luxury market about 1906.

Reaction in some localities was extreme. To cite a few examples: farmers in the vi-

[7] "Prejudice on the Wane in the Rural Districts," *Horseless Age*, 6:10–11 (September 5, 1900).
[8] "The Farmers' Attitude," ibid., 10:184 (August 20, 1902).

cinity of Rochester, Minnesota, plowed up roads, making them unsuited to automobile travel but still passable by horse and carriage; local businessmen in Fayette County, Ohio, were warned by the local farmers to expect a boycott should they dare to purchase automobiles, and the farmers there took to carrying guns and stretching barbed wire across country roads to halt speeding motorists; a session of the Farmers' Institute in Marion, Indiana, passed a resolution asking that all automobiles be banned from using the public roads in the state; and the Farmers' Club of Harlington, New Jersey, dissatisfied with that state's liberal speed limits, unanimously adopted a resolution not to support any candidate for political office who owned an automobile. By 1905 there seemed to be good sense in a Kansas editor's comment that "if we were running for Congress we would not accept an automobile as a gift." *Horseless Age* commented that it longed for a return of the "friendly regard for automobilists [that] prevailed among farmers, as was the rule until several years ago."[9]

  The increase in farmers' hostility to the motor vehicle from 1904 through 1906 notwithstanding, the important point is that reactionary opposition to the motor vehicle among farmers did remain localized. Both the *American Agriculturalist* (circulation ca 85,000) and the *Farm Journal* (circulation ca 500,000) expressed concern about speed and reckless driving on rural roads and asked for more severe motor vehicle legislation and better enforcement of existing laws. Neither periodical, however, proposed reactionary legislation or came out against the motor vehicle. At the thirty-ninth annual session of the National Grange, Patrons of Husbandry, held in Atlantic City, New Jersey, in November 1905, Worthy Master Aaron Jones also spoke moderately about the automobile in his opening speech to the delegates: "Accidents of the most shocking nature have been of common occurrence. In some sections of the country travel upon the country roads [with horses] has been reduced to the driving

[9] "Antagonism of Farmers," ibid., 16:242 (August 25, 1905).

absolutely necessary, cutting out all pleasure driving. There is no doubt of the right
of automobilists to legitimately use the highways, but that use should be regulated
by wise laws vigorously enforced and the penalties for their violation should be sufficiently severe to serve as an effectual warning against violations by others. Automobilists should unite with the people in the work." After some heated debates among
the delegates, the grange on the last day of the convention adopted as its official
position on the motor vehicle that it was "an innovation in modes of travel which
must be accepted."[10]

It also seems doubtful that a candidate's identification with the automobile was ever
inexpedient in most rural areas. William Jennings Bryan, the last politician one would
expect to misinterpret or be insensitive to rural sympathies, was a pioneer in the use
of the motor vehicle for political campaigning. He used a Benz touring car owned by
A. O. Mueller to campaign in southern Illinois in 1896 and used the motor vehicle
more extensively in the campaign of 1900. By 1904 the motor vehicle was commonly
used by politicians for campaign purposes throughout the United States and had
proven particularly useful for stumping tours of rural districts, where its novelty
was considered "an effective aid to the oratorical talents of the spellbinder in drawing
a crowd." The fear of campaign managers that the use of the touring car might be
damaging had been demonstrated to be groundless: "The conclusion seems to have
been reached that by showing the ordinary courtesy (or even a little more) to farmers
in passing teams on the road, the auto might even be made a means of gaining their
friendship and esteem, and thus prove doubly useful for campaign purposes."[11]

Each year farmers become more familiar with the motor vehicle, aware of its advantages over the horse, and anxious to purchase cars themselves. The increasing

[10]Cited in "Farmer's Wise Words," *Motor Age*, 8:33 (November 23, 1905), and "Farmers Coming Around," ibid.,
8:11 (November 30, 1905).
[11]"Automobiles in the Campaign," *Horseless Age*, 14:412 (October 26, 1904).

prosperity of farmers, combined with the appearance of rugged, moderately priced cars such as the Ford Model N and Model T, led to the rapid development of a substantial rural market for motor vehicles after 1906. The hostility toward the automobile that had arisen in rural areas diminished appreciably.

The general attitude of the farmer toward the automobile by 1908 was expressed well by G. W. F. Gaunt, New Jersey State Grange Master, to his fellow delegates at a good roads convention. Before introducing a resolution asking that New Jersey adopt a reciprocal motor vehicle registration agreement with other states and channel its entire income from motor vehicle registration fees and fines into road repair, Gaunt stated: "We farmers are not opposed to the motorcar . . . it will be an important feature in making farm life more attractive. When the motorcar becomes cheaper in price through more general use the farmer will be the first to adopt it for business and pleasure. I stand ready to promise the motorists that the grangers of this state will cooperate with them in bettering not only the condition of the roads but the lot of the motorists, who it appears, have been legislated against too severely."[12] With such active involvement of the farmer in the automobile movement, the last important vestige of opposition to the diffusion of the motor vehicle in the United States disappeared.

Early Owners
The expense of buying and operating a car had initially restricted automobile ownership to persons with much higher than average incomes — although not necessarily to the exceptionally affluent. Ralph C. Epstein gathered data showing that early purchasers of motor vehicles were mainly moneyed businessmen, ranging from self-designated "capitalists" to dry-goods merchants, but physicians and engineers were

[12] "Farmers Are Not Foes," *Motor Age*, 14:36 (October 1, 1908).

also well represented. The first twenty purchasers of Steamobiles at the Detroit salesroom of William E. Metzger in 1898–1899 were listed as four capitalists, four physicians, two manufacturers, four merchants, one broker, one printer, one plumber, and three general businessmen. The purchasers of the first twenty Winton automobiles in 1898 included one capitalist, eight manufacturers, two coal operators, one coal dealer, one flour miller, one brewer, one physician, two dry-goods merchants, and three engineers. About the same types of individuals purchased the first twenty Waverley electric cars, except that six were women, including the wives of two bankers. Early purchasers of curved-dash Oldsmobiles also showed "about the same distribution, except that no 'capitalists' nor manufacturers are listed; merchants and physicians predominate."[13]

The fact that medical doctors constituted the group best represented in proportion to size among early automobile owners establishes physicians as the most innovative single group in the adoption of the automobile in the United States. The local doctors were invariably among the first persons to purchase cars in any community. By 1905 in large and medium-sized cities the number of automobiles used by local physicians in their practices was usually greater than the combined total of all commercial vehicles, excluding public cab fleets. *Automobile* explained in 1908 that "the automobile has no more consistent and more loyal set of users than the medical fraternity. First and foremost, the doctor invests in an automobile for business use; it will take him where he wants to go — where he is needed, often very urgently — in a fraction of the time any other method of transportation at his command can possibly do. . . . So that it is scarcely to be wondered at that doctors comprise a very large portion of the total number of auto users."[14]

[13] Ralph C. Epstein, *The Automobile Industry* (Chicago and New York: A. W. Shaw Co., 1928), pp. 94–97.
[14] "Physicians Tell of Their Great Use of Automobiles," *Automobile*, 18:676 (May 14, 1908).

What appears striking in retrospect is how quickly automobile ownership became more general — not its initial restriction to a few high-prestige groups. As early as 1903, George A. Banker, one of the largest eastern automobile dealers, reported the apparent beginnings of a middle-class market for cars to a representative of *Motor World:* "Of course the wealthy classes are still our chief customers. . . . But they are no longer the exclusive buyers, even of moderately expensive cars, as was the case a year ago. The bank clerk and similar young men with plenty of time and earning good salaries are now found among our customers."[15] Data presented in the Lynds' classic study of Muncie, Indiana, illustrate how rapidly automobile ownership by the middle classes became a reality: "A local carriage manufacturer of the early days estimates that about 125 families owned a horse and buggy in 1890, practically all of them business folk. . . . The first real automobile appeared in Middletown in 1900. About 1906 it was estimated that 'there are probably 200 in the city and country.' "[16] There can be no doubt that the automobile movement in the United States had already developed into a broadly based middle-class movement even before Henry Ford came out with his legendary Model T. Evidence of the high middle-class demand for secondhand cars in Pittsburgh by the summer of 1907 is typical: "Every concern in the city that makes any specialty of this line of trade is reported to be having more calls than it can attend to. Motoring has taken hold of the suburbanites this year as never before and hundreds of clerks and small businessmen who have never afforded a machine before are now to be seen in small cars going to and from their work instead of being packed in musty streetcars or walking a mile to and from the railroad station."[17] The rural market had blossomed, and many dealers in large and medium-sized cities sold more new cars to farmers from the surrounding country-

[15]"One Car for Many," *Motor World*, 5:865 (March 5, 1903).
[16]Robert S. Lynd and Helen M. Lynd, *Middletown* (New York: Harcourt, Brace & World, 1929), pp. 251–253.
[17]"Demand for Second-Hand Cars," *Motor Age*, 12:25 (September 5, 1907).

side than to city people during 1907. One writer commented at the end of that year: "The editor of a country paper in the West wrote four columns describing 'Our New Auto,' after he had purchased a machine. It was not necessary. Out of his two thousand subscribers probably one-tenth knew more about motorcars than he did himself; one-twentieth owned cars, and as many more will by next spring."[18] Industry spokesmen such as Alfred E. Reeves of the American Motor Car Manufacturers' Association were impressed by 1909 that "manufacturers are relying on two great new purchasing factors — the farmer and the man with the middle-class income."[19]

One can only conjecture how much more rapidly automobile ownership would have become common among all segments of American society had cars been easier to purchase at an earlier date. The initial price of an automobile involved a staggering expenditure for the man of average means until well after 1910, and installment selling of automobiles did not become established until the 1920s. A few feeble attempts were made to sell automobiles on time before 1910, but the prevailing sentiment of dealers and manufacturers was then adamantly against the practice. As *Motor World* reported opinion in the trade at the end of 1904, "There is no excess of cars, and customers are to be found for all of reputable make that are produced. To deviate from the cash system now in universal use is to invite disaster without any corresponding gain in the unlikely event of success. No sane businessman will bring himself to do this."[20]

The fact that automobile ownership quickly became common among those segments of the population who could afford it, even at a great sacrifice, at any given point in time in the United States does suggest that the main motives that predisposed an

[18] Charles M. Harger, "The Automobile in Western Country Towns," *World Today*, 13:1280 (December 1907).
[19] Quoted in William B. Meloney, "The Marvelous Growth of the Automobile Industry in America," *Munsey's Magazine*, 42:21 (October 1909).
[20] "Installment Sales," *Motor World*, 9:461 (December 15, 1904).

individual to adopt the automobile were widely held in American society and that differential propensity to buy an automobile was mainly a function of financial ability. This is not to deny that some groups, independently of generally held motives or income, were especially innovative for other reasons. Regarding the innovativeness shown by medical doctors and engineers in adoption of the automobile, for example, it is undoubtedly significant that a highly favorable attitude toward technological innovation and a rationalistic-scientific outlook were institutionalized characteristics of both professions. These characteristics have been demonstrated to be conducive to an individual's propensity to innovate. So has the cosmopolitan frame of reference one can associate with the higher level of education, increased exposure to other than local information media, and travel and change of residence characteristic of professions in general.[21] It might be relevant to compare innovators and laggards in the adoption of the automobile within American society on these criteria, but unfortunately the data that would allow one to do so in any systematic way appear to be nonexistent. However, since the automobile had great appeal for Americans of all social classes and occupations and was rapidly adopted by all segments of society as soon as ownership became financially feasible, the loss is probably not appreciable.

Geographic Distribution

The existence of a comparatively large domestic market, relative affluence, and the lack of tariff barriers among the states undoubtedly encouraged the development of a mass market for motor vehicles in the United States to an extent not possible in Europe. Differences in income distribution and degree of involvement in an emergent urban-industrial social order also made some states and regions more innovative than others in the adoption of the motor vehicle within the United States.

[21] See, for example, Everett M. Rogers, *Diffusion of Innovations* (New York: Free Press, 1962), passim.

The geographic distribution of automobiles by states is shown in Table 2.1, which gives registration figures for each state and the District of Columbia for 1900, 1905, and 1910. The leading twenty-five states in motor vehicle registrations are then rank ordered for each of these years in Table 2.2. Remarkable continuity over the 1900–

Table 2.1 Motor Vehicle Registrations, by State (1900, 1905, and 1910)

	1900	1905	1910		1900	1905	1910
Alabama	40	300	1,780	Nevada	10	70	460
Arizona	20	160	840	New Hampshire	50	500	3,510
Arkansas	20	210	1,150	New Jersey	300	3,640	16,520
California	780	8,020	44,120	New Mexico	10	80	470
Colorado	90	800	4,680	New York	500	9,230	62,660
Connecticut	160	1,650	9,380	North Carolina	50	550	3,220
Delaware	30	190	960	North Dakota	80	790	4,650
Florida	10	100	680	Ohio	480	4,860	32,940
Georgia	80	780	4,490	Oklahoma	10	100	680
Idaho	10	80	470	Oregon	80	910	5,310
Illinois	600	6,160	35,560	Pennsylvania	1,480	9,130	37,350
Indiana	170	1,640	10,110	Rhode Island	130	1,430	5,910
Iowa	40	800	10,410	South Carolina	40	360	2,250
Kansas	220	1,750	10,490	South Dakota	50	550	3,240
Kentucky	40	450	2,680	Tennessee	40	370	2,230
Louisiana	60	630	3,650	Texas	180	1,250	7,180
Maine	70	690	4,040	Utah	20	240	1,350
Maryland	80	850	5,590	Vermont	30	360	2,180
Massachusetts	600	4,880	31,250	Virginia	40	500	3,010
Michigan	360	3,610	20,670	Washington	130	1,260	7,310
Minnesota	260	2,630	15,150	West Virginia	20	190	880
Mississippi	20	260	1,520	Wisconsin	160	1,600	14,200
Missouri	180	2,300	12,270	Wyoming	10	50	360
Montana	20	180	1,030	District of Columbia	80	1,090	6,320
Nebraska	60	570	11,340				

Source: U.S., Department of Commerce, *Highway Statistics, Summary to 1955* (Washington, D.C.: Government Printing Office, 1957), pp. 18-27.

1910 period in the geographic distribution of automobiles among the states on the criterion of registrations is obvious. The only states among the top twenty-five in motor vehicle registrations in 1900 that were not among them five years later were

Table 2.2　Rank Order of the Twenty-five States Leading in Number of Motor Vehicles Registered (1900, 1905, and 1910)

1900	1905	1910
1. Pennsylvania (1,480)	1. New York (9,230)	1. New York (62,660)
2. California (780)	2. Pennsylvania (9,130)	2. California (44,120)
3. Illinois (600)	3. California (8,020)	3. Pennsylvania (37,350)
4. Massachusetts (600)	4. Illinois (6,160)	4. Illinois (35,560)
5. New York (500)	5. Massachusetts (4,880)	5. Ohio (32,940)
6. Ohio (480)	6. Ohio (4,860)	6. Massachusetts (31,250)
7. Michigan (360)	7. New Jersey (3,640)	7. Michigan (20,670)
8. New Jersey (300)	8. Michigan (3,610)	8. New Jersey (16,520)
9. Minnesota (260)	9. Minnesota (2,630)	9. Minnesota (15,150)
10. Kansas (220)	10. Missouri (2,300)	10. Wisconsin (14,200)
11. Missouri (180)	11. Kansas (1,750)	11. Missouri (12,270)
12. Texas (180)	12. Connecticut (1,650)	12. Nebraska (11,340)
13. Indiana (170)	13. Indiana (1,640)	13. Kansas (10,490)
14. Connecticut (160)	14. Wisconsin (1,600)	14. Iowa (10,410)
15. Wisconsin (160)	15. Rhode Island (1,430)	15. Indiana (10,110)
16. Rhode Island (130)	16. Washington (1,260)	16. Connecticut (9,380)
17. Washington (130)	17. Texas (1,250)	17. Washington (7,310)
18. Colorado (90)	18. District of Columbia (1,090)	18. Texas (7,180)
19. District of Columbia (80)	19. Oregon (910)	19. District of Columbia (6,320)
20. Georgia (80)	20. Maryland (850)	20. Rhode Island (5,910)
21. Maryland (80)	21. Colorado (800)	21. Maryland (5,590)
22. North Dakota (80)	22. Iowa (800)	22. Oregon (5,310)
23. Oregon (80)	23. North Dakota (790)	23. Colorado (4,680)
24. Maine (70)	24. Georgia (780)	24. North Dakota (4,650)
25. Louisiana (60)	25. Maine (690)	25. Georgia (4,490)
26. Nebraska (60)		

Note: District of Columbia is included as a state. States having the same number of registrations are listed alphabetically.

Louisiana and Nebraska. These states tied for twenty-fifth place in 1900 and ranked, respectively, twenty-sixth and twenty-seventh in 1905. Iowa, the sole newcomer among the top twenty-five in 1905, ranked twenty-second that year. Maine, the only state among the top twenty-five in 1905 not also among them in 1910, dropped to twenty-sixth and was replaced by Nebraska, which made a spectacular climb to twelfth place. Moreover, there was a close correspondence in the rank order of the top twenty-five states on the basis of motor vehicle registrations for the three years given. Nebraska's thirteen-place rise in rank in five years is unique. In the decade 1900–1910, sixteen states shifted two places or less in rank, seven of these remaining in the same position, while only six states moved up or down in rank three or more places. Other than Nebraska, the most dramatic individual change was New York's rise from fifth place in 1900 to first in 1905 and 1910.

The rank order of states on the basis of the number of motor vehicle registrations does not, however, provide a meaningful index for comparing the extent of diffusion of the motor vehicle in the various states because this measure reflects relative populousness as well as the distribution of motor vehicles. Extensiveness of diffusion is therefore more properly expressed in terms of the ratio of motor vehicles to population. Furthermore, on the common-sense assumption that motor vehicles were purchased almost without exception by adults, the most meaningful comparative index of diffusion is undoubtedly the ratio of motor vehicles registered to persons eighteen years of age and over shown in Table 2.3.

The twenty-one states with higher ratios of automobiles to persons eighteen years of age and over than the United States average of 1 registered automobile for every 125.2 such persons can be considered the "innovative" states in the adoption of the motor vehicle. The thirty-eight states that had lower ratios than the United States average can correspondingly be termed the "laggard" states in the diffusion of the

Table 2.3 Rank Order of States in Ratio of Total Automobiles Registered to Persons Eighteen Years of Age and Over in 1910 (United States Average = 1:125.2)

States with Ratio Higher than U.S. Average		States with Ratio Lower than U.S. Average	
State	Ratio = 1:	State	Ratio = 1:
1. District of Columbia	38.8	22. Maine	126.8
2. California	40.3	23. Pennsylvania	135.0
3. Rhode Island	62.9	24. Nevada	137.8
4. Nebraska	65.9	25. Delaware	141.1
5. North Dakota	72.5	26. Iowa	141.7
6. Massachusetts	74.7	27. Maryland	149.8
7. Connecticut	81.6	28. Arizona	159.4
8. New Hampshire	85.7	29. Utah	162.1
9. Minnesota	87.1	30. Missouri	173.2
10. Oregon	89.7	31. Indiana	177.5
11. Michigan	90.5	32. Montana	256.6
12. Ohio	98.5	33. Louisiana	257.1
13. New York	100.4	34. Wyoming	289.2
14. Kansas	102.5	35. Texas	305.9
15. New Jersey	103.3	36. Georgia	319.3
16. Wisconsin	104.0	37. South Carolina	357.0
17. Illinois	105.4	38. North Carolina	371.5
18. Washington	109.8	39. Virginia	397.5
19. South Dakota	110.9	40. New Mexico	408.8
20. Vermont	111.9	41. Idaho	437.7
21. Colorado	116.1	42. Kentucky	505.5
		43. Tennessee	565.4
		44. Mississippi	641.4
		45. Alabama	663.5
		46. Florida	669.4
		47. Arkansas	742.9
		48. West Virginia	819.0
		49. Oklahoma	1,387.0

automobile. In Table 2.3 the states are listed in descending order of innovativeness. The extensiveness of diffusion in any given state is indicated both by its rank relative to other states and by how much higher or lower its ratio was than the United States average. (The apparent stability of the various states for rank order on size of population as well as on number of motor vehicles registered during the decade 1900–1910 obviates the necessity of ranking the states for previous years, too.)

Table 2.3 illustrates strikingly that innovativeness in adoption of the motor vehicle varied significantly among the different geographic regions of the United States. The diffusion of the motor vehicle was most extensive in the regions generally designated Pacific, West North Central, East North Central, New England, and Middle Atlantic. All three Pacific states were among the twenty-one states with higher ratios than the United States average. Only Maine, which ranked twenty-second with a ratio of 1:126.8, and Indiana, a poor thirty-first, were among the six New England and five East North Central states that fell below the United States ratio of 1:125.2. Pennsylvania, twenty-third with a ratio of 1:135.0, and Iowa and Missouri, which ranked, respectively, twenty-sixth and thirtieth, were excluded from the twenty-one innovative automobile states among the three Middle Atlantic and seven West North Central states. Conversely, none of the four East South Central or four West South Central states ranked high as an area of automotive innovation; Louisiana, thirty-third with a low ratio of 1:257.1, ranked the highest of any of these eight states. Colorado and the District of Columbia were unique in their innovative status among the eight Mountain and nine South Atlantic states.

The exceptions that show deviation from their geographic regional patterns can be explained. Indiana and Missouri were border states, much more "southern" in sociocultural orientation than the other East North Central and West North Central states at this time. Although undoubtedly to a lesser degree, a case can be made that local culture in Iowa had been influenced by the in-migration of a comparatively large number of Southerners in the nineteenth century. As the national capital, the District of Columbia was more cosmopolitan and had a more transient population than any other South Atlantic city and was a wholly urbanized area. Colorado was an unrepresentative Mountain state because the comparative accessibility of the great scenic beauty of the Denver area to eastern tourists had made Colorado a mecca among the Mountain states for wealthy vacationers, who found the automobile delightful for sight-seeing trips. Maine and Pennsylvania, the two remaining states that might be considered exceptions, differed so minimally from the general patterns of their geographic regions that they do not need explanation. Maine ranked twenty-second and Pennsylvania twenty-third with ratios just below the United States average. Thus although these two states ranked below the other New England and Middle Atlantic states, they ranked higher than any East South Central or West South Central state and above all of the South Atlantic and Mountain states except the District of Columbia and Colorado, which were atypical of these regions.

Regional innovativeness in the adoption of the motor vehicle does not seem to be directly related in any important way to either terrain or climate. To be sure, the Mountain states were laggards in automotive innovativeness, but so were several extremely flat southern states, such as Florida. Extremely hilly or mountainous terrain in Colorado and many parts of the Pacific, New England, and Middle Atlantic states did not keep these areas from becoming important centers for the diffusion of the motor vehicle. Had climate been a major determinant, the seasonal limitations upon use of motor vehicles imposed by the combination of relatively severe northern winters and the prevalent open car of the period should have resulted in comparatively more widespread adoption of the automobile in the southern than in the northern states — the opposite of what in fact occurred.

Statistical correlations were made using Kendall's "tau," a measure of association for ordinal (ranked) variables that varies from -1.0 to $+1.0$, to determine the significance of the relationship of several other variables to the ratio of total automobiles registered to persons eighteen years of age and over in 1910.[22] These variables were road conditions, net intercensal migration, population density (a measure of urbanization), and income distribution. On the basis of available indices of these variables, only income distribution emerged as a significant determinant of the pattern of diffusion of the motor vehicle in the United States by 1910. Since reliable figures for income distribution in the United States are not available for the years before 1913, the first reporting of the federal income tax, the 1913 figures on persons reporting net income in excess of $2,500 for the ten months ended December 31, 1913, were used. It was assumed that the relative number of such persons in the various states remained fairly constant from 1910 to 1913. A measure of income distribution for 1910 was then obtained by rank ordering the states on the basis of the ratio of the number of persons in each state reporting net income in excess of $2,500 for the ten months ended December 31, 1913, to the state's total population in 1910. This correlated with the rank order of states on the basis of ratio of total number of automobiles registered to persons eighteen years of age and over at +.48, by far the highest correlation of any variable measured. Since automobile ownership by 1910 was possible for persons with incomes considerably below $2,500, the correlation undoubtedly understates the true importance of income distribution.

The fundamental importance of income distribution to the diffusion of the motor

---

[22] $\mathrm{Tau} = \dfrac{P - Q}{\frac{1}{2}n(n-1)}$. The correlations were done by Robert A. Jones, one of my graduate students. The sources for data other than motor vehicle registrations used in these correlations were various editions of U.S., Bureau of Foreign and Domestic Commerce, *Statistical Abstract of the United States* (Washington, D.C.: Government Printing Office).

vehicle is also evident in the available qualitative data. Almost without exception, contemporary observers attributed the rapid diffusion of the motor vehicle into rural areas after 1905 chiefly to the rising prosperity of the American farmer during the first decade of the twentieth century. As Thomas B. Jeffery, manufacturer of the Rambler automobile, observed, "The mortgage has gone from the middle western farm, and to take its place there is the telephone, the heating system, the water supply, improved farm machinery, and the automobile."[23]

The lag in adoption of the motor vehicle in the South was also generally attributed to the relatively poor financial condition of that section of the United States. For example, when it appeared to a writer in *Motor* in late 1909 that "Southerners have finally awakened to the importance of the automobile," he explained the automobile industry's tardiness in exploiting the southern market: "Following the education of the public in the large centers, it was natural that makers looked for new fields to conquer and turned their attention to the cities of the Middle West. With the increased manufacturing facilities of motorcar makers . . . it has become possible to care for old territories and at the same time to open up new fields." The development of the southern market had been undertaken last by the manufacturer because, "since the Civil War, which devastated the South and left that country in a comparatively poor financial condition, the Southerners have not as a mass been in a position to purchase automobiles. Recent years have put the South on a firmer financial basis . . . and, in brief, a large proportion of the Southerners are [now] in a position to and will buy motorcars."[24] This projection was very optimistic given that, relative to other sections of the United States in 1910, a large number of Southerners enjoyed marginal incomes at best. Nevertheless, the general points made are credible.

[23] "Farmers Taking to Automobiles," *Motor World*, 20:68 (April 8, 1909).
[24] Samuel A. Miles, "The Motor Car in the South," *Motor*, 13:49 (November 1909).

Taking population density (persons per square mile in 1910) as the index of urbanization, rural-urban differences appear at first glance to have been insignificant for the distribution of motor vehicles by states in 1910. The rank order of states in ratio of total automobiles registered to persons eighteen years of age and over correlates with the rank order of states on the basis of persons per square mile in 1910 at only +.16. Ten states that ranked below the United States average of 30.9 persons per square mile in 1910 were among the twenty-one states with higher ratios of automobiles registered to persons eighteen years of age and over than the United States average of 1:125.2, while sixteen states with higher population densities than the United States average were among the laggards in the adoption of the motor vehicle.

Dealing with the diffusion of the motor vehicle solely from the perspective of population density by states in 1910, however, can be misleading. Other data suggest that even in innovative states with low population densities the motor vehicle first diffused into the larger cities, where population was concentrated, and only later spread to the outlying rural countryside. Until 1906 the rural market for motor vehicles was extremely limited. Viewed from this perspective, the comparative lag in adoption of the automobile in the South and the Mountain states may well reflect in part at least the relative absence of a sufficient number of cities large enough to act as initial centers for diffusion in these areas.

There can be little doubt that the motor vehicle was common in cities several years before it ceased being a rarity in most rural areas. *Outing Magazine* observed in 1902 that "in every city of any size there is, at least, one automobile agency, and it is a poor town indeed to which the automobile is a stranger."[25] In sharp contrast, conditions in rural areas a year later were described by a correspondent with *Motor World*: "Although I have traveled nearly four thousand miles in my automobile, it is curious

[25] William J. Lampton, "The Meaning of the Automobile," *Outing Magazine*, 40:696 (September 1902).

to note that I have never yet met another machine traveling over country roads. While they are numerous in every city and large town I have visited, they are evidently not used extensively for road work yet."[26]

By late 1905 progress in the diffusion of the motor vehicle into rural areas outside the South and the Mountain states was apparent. A letter to the editor of *Automobile* from a Michigan farmer in August 1905 reported that "Coldwater, Mich., with a population of about 6,000 has over 50 cars. While southern Michigan is noted for miserable roads, new cars are constantly appearing. In driving my touring car from Clear Lake, Ind., Sunday, a distance of fifteen miles, I saw five other machines on the road."[27] The following spring *Automobile* noted a widespread awakening of interest in the motor vehicle in small towns, evidenced by the fact that "garages are being opened in towns where two years ago it would have been thought folly to attempt such a thing."[28]

Between 1905 and 1908 the major market for motor vehicles shifted from the big city to the country town. Among the eastern states, Pennsylvania may be taken as representative of the general trend. *Automobile* reported: "A careful investigation of automobile conditions in Pennsylvania shows that a majority of the 8,717 cars now in use in the state [in March 1908] are owned by people living in the so-called country towns. It is in these towns that the automobile has come into general use for real service, while in the larger cities it is still a luxury and kept for show. There is not a good-sized town in the Keystone State which has not now from one to a half-dozen flourishing automobile agencies, and this year promises to be a much better season

[26] "Met Few Cars in Country," *Motor World*, 7:63 (October 8, 1903).
[27] "Michigan Farmer Enthusiast," *Automobile*, 13:220 (August 24, 1905).
[28] "Small Cities Awakening," ibid., 14:650 (April 12, 1906).

for these dealers than for the agencies in the big cities of Pittsburgh and Philadelphia."[29]

Developments in the East North Central and West North Central states were even more impressive. Regarding conditions in the trans-Mississippi farm country, *Motor Age* published a picture of the main street of Garden City, Kansas, which showed the street crowded with the automobiles of beet growers, who were in town to do their Saturday shopping. The periodical pointed out that "this is not an isolated condition. Nearly every town in Kansas can make a showing that would rival this. Garden City is the capital of what is properly known as the short grass region and no one is more proud of its motoring population than the farmers themselves, who delight not only in the sporting side of motoring but in the utility of the vehicle as well."[30] The United States Bureau of the Census estimates that there were already 50,000 automobiles and 1,000 tractors on American farms by 1910.[31] Thus the motor vehicle was rapidly losing its early association with the city, and a truly mass market for automobiles was emerging in the United States except in the South and in the Mountain states.

While the importance of income distribution to the development of this mass market for motor vehicles cannot be overemphasized, the explanatory value of this variable is limited. At best, adequate income distribution to permit widespread purchase was a crucial, necessary condition for American adoption of the automobile. The still unanswered questions are: Why, when sufficient money became available to them, did various segments of the American population use this money to purchase auto-

[29] "Pennsylvania Autoists in Country Towns," ibid., 18:369 (March 12, 1908).
[30] "Motoring Farmers in Short Grass Region," *Motor Age*, 14:17 (July 16, 1908).
[31] U.S., Bureau of the Census, *Historical Statistics of the United States: Colonial Times to 1957* (Washington, D.C.: Government Printing Office, 1960), p. 285.

mobiles rather than for other purposes? Why did the few relatively wealthy southern states lag behind every northern state, including some fairly poor ones, in the adoption of the automobile? The answers to these questions are to be found in the compelling motives for the adoption of the automobile, which will be elaborated in the next chapter. Here it is necessary only to note that the automobile was conceived by its proponents as an ideal response to some of the basic problems in American life that had resulted from the rapid rise of an urban-industrial society. One might expect, given that all other motives were equally appealing throughout the country, that the adoption of the motor vehicle would be retarded in those sections of the United States that had been least affected by urbanization and industrialization, namely, the South and the Mountain states.

3
Motives for Adoption

Economy

From its introduction in the United States, the motor vehicle appeared to offer substantial utilitarian advantages over the horse-drawn vehicle. Almost all early comparisons found the automobile more economical. Even before the 1895 *Times-Herald* race, *Scientific American* ventured this opinion: "The first cost of an automobile carriage is about $1,000, not much more than a good carriage. Hardly anyone would care to run a machine carriage more than ten hours a day, the cost being 50 cents a day for fuel or $15 per month. Under favorable circumstances a good horse cannot be kept in a large city like New York or Chicago for less than about $30 to $35 per month."[1] By 1899 a rumor that "automobile stages" would soon be put into service on Fifth Avenue promised to *Harper's Weekly* "the beginning of a lavish use of horseless vehicles as a means of cheap transportation in New York" because the horse "eats from infancy to old age, he is apt to be of inferior quality, and even when good he is very perishable."[2] The motor vehicle was expected to have an infinitely longer useful life than the short-lived dray horse and do much more work for the same amount in operating expenses. Economy was also anticipated from obviating the cost to taxpayers of the daily removal of tons of excreta from city streets.

  The best case for economy over the horse-drawn vehicle probably could be made for the commercial motor vehicle, the form of automobile slowest to be adopted. Professor Robert H. Thurston of Cornell University wrote in early 1900, for instance, that "the economy of the automobile system comes out in high relief when the working of the heavy classes of machines for business purposes is studied." He pointed out that "the fuel account of the machine and that of the animal differ so enormously in favor of the former as to decide any question of profit quite apart from the con-

[1] "New Prizes for Motor Carriage Competition," *Scientific American*, 73:66 (August 3, 1895).
[2] "The Spreading Automobile," *Harper's Weekly*, 43:655 (July 1, 1899).

sideration of the rapid deterioration of the horse in heavy work. The fact that street-car horses have but two to four years of profitable employment and meantime depreciate 50 percent and more in value gives sufficient evidence that the machine may not be relatively, even if absolutely, short-lived." Thurston further noted that by analogy with the railroad locomotive the truck should have a long, useful life and comparatively small depreciation; the best available evidence from the 1899 Liverpool trials of heavy motor vehicles indicated annual depreciation of 15 percent and maintenance costs of 20 to 30 percent. This meant that the capital invested in motortrucks had to be replaced every three years, but meanwhile they did so much more work than horses that there was "a very considerable net return on the investment" compared with a horse-drawn system.[3] Thurston's conclusions were those generally reached. As another writer stated later in the year, "Experts all agree that for hauling lumber, coal, stone, and farmers' produce, etc., over reasonably good roads, the automobile insures a saving of from 25 percent to 40 percent as against horse and wagon."[4]

Large-scale commercial users of the motor vehicle could expect to realize several economies. Rental for fleet storage space, wages for drivers, and fuel bills, as well as depreciation on equipment, were less for a motorized delivery system than for a horse-drawn system because the motortruck took up only half the storage space of a wagon and team, fewer motortrucks than horses were needed to do the same amount of work, and gasoline was cheaper than oats. The reason for the lag in the commercial adoption of the motor vehicle was not that the motortruck seemed less economical initially than the horse and wagon; rather, large-scale adoption was necessary to realize any appreciable economies, and large-scale adoption involved substantial commitment to an innovation not yet perfected and familiar, with the atten-

[3] "The Automobile in Traction," *Review of Reviews*, 21:225 (February 1900).
[4] Cleveland Moffett, "Automobiles for the Average Man," ibid., 21:710 (June 1900).

dant problem of securing the competent drivers and mechanics upon whom any efficient and economical operation of a motorized system in large part depended.

Further experience with commercial motor vehicles indicated that early expectations about their relative economy had been a bit too optimistic, but a good argument could still be made that the motor vehicle was more economical than the horse for commercial use. A 1909 article in *Scientific American*, for example, pointed out that "while the daily cost of the horse-drawn trucks is less than that of the automobiles, the cost per ton-mile, which is the measure of the work done, is much higher." On this basis, tests showed that the saving in favor of the motortruck was 23 percent. The businessman was urged, in addition, to consider "the increase in the volume of his business that will come with the extension of the district through which he can make deliveries, and also the quicker service that the automobile makes possible." It was felt that such considerations "make the adoption of automobiles an economic necessity" for the businessman.[5]

Motor vehicles were also expected to result in great economies in public transportation systems. High fixed costs for urban rapid-transit systems had already overtaxed the resources of many municipalities to the point where the systems could not feasibly be extended to outlying areas where the volume of traffic was slight. *World's Work* believed in 1901 that motor bus lines offered an economical solution to the public rapid-transit problem, especially for suburban service and in medium-sized cities: "The small amount of capital required and the ease and cheapness of operation make the establishment of such lines seem possible. There is of course none of the expense of surveying and building a special roadbed, the laying of tracks and erection of poles and wires, the installation of costly machinery in a properly arranged building. All it demands is a reasonably good highway, a place to be housed and ordinary

[5] Benjamin Rogers, "The Commercial Truck versus the Horse," *Scientific American*, 100:42 (January 16, 1909).

care."[6] Economy tests of motor omnibuses had demonstrated by 1906 that operating costs were "very low indeed, one motor omnibus carrying passengers for less than one-half cent per mile . . . [and] with all the items charged, including interest, depreciation and repairs, a profit can be shown over railroad transportation cost, where the highway is improved and suited to travel in all kinds of weather."[7]

Beginning at the turn of the century, motor buses were tried in a number of localities on an experimental basis and generally proved popular; then in 1907 scheduled motor bus service was inaugurated in New York City and Philadelphia. However, both municipal authorities and private entrepreneurs understandably remained fairly reluctant, despite promised or proven economies, to make substantial financial commitments to introduce motor bus lines in areas where the volume of traffic was negligible or where trolley lines had already been built. In either instance, demand for bus service was apt to be insufficient to warrant the risk involved, at least until the innovation was securely established.

The solution to the rapid-transit problem in the United States therefore came to be mass ownership of private motorcars by individuals—a characteristically American solution in that collective action was, for the time at least, evaded and the burden placed squarely on the shoulders of the individual. Such an individualistic solution to the transportation problems posed by the rise of an urban-industrial society had not been feasible with the horse. Even if the cost of ownership of a horse-drawn rig could have been put within the reach of every citizen, the mass ownership of horses in cities would have compounded in short order already grave problems of sanitation and street cleaning to a point beyond tolerance and required more than twice the parking and storage space of a corresponding number of motor vehicles. The massive

[6] "The Automobile in Rapid Transit," *World's Work*, 5:3308 (April 1903).
[7] Augustus Post, "The Advance of the Automobile," *Independent*, 60:1337 (June 7, 1906).

public expenditures for streets and highways and the problem of air pollution that the mass ownership of motor vehicles would ultimately entail were not foreseen at the time. Nor was it evident then that the worst case for the relative economy of the motor vehicle from the perspective of either the transportation system as a whole or the individual could be made for the widespread adoption of private passenger cars. No one visualized that the mass ownership of automobiles by individuals would necessarily involve a total per capita expenditure for cars, fuel, road building, and maintenance considerably in excess of the cost of any conceivable mass-transit trolley and railroad system. Moreover, it was generally overlooked that the average family did not use a horse and buggy enough to realize a saving from switching to the automobile, the relative economy of which became apparent only when a substantial amount of driving was done.

One group of individual owners who could reasonably expect substantial economies to result from adopting the automobile were physicians, who drove their horses exceptionally hard when making professional calls. Medical doctors consequently found the automobile cheaper to own than horses. Comments in the January 1903 *Horseless Age* illustrate the experience of physicians. One country doctor felt that "any man who can afford a horse can better afford an automobile. Any service which a driving horse can give can be better rendered with an automobile, more quickly and more economically." Another doctor with a large practice explained that "the physician whose business requires him to keep two or three horses certainly will find a well made automobile a good investment; not only because it cuts out the expense of the horses, but in the saving of time [on calls] to devote to the office, and no physician can estimate what this is worth to him in this age of sharp competition."[8]

[8] Dr. C. A. Shepard, "The Country Doctor's Automobile," *Horseless Age*, 11:18 (January 7, 1903), and Dr. D. H. Dean, "My Experience and Some Reflections," ibid., 11:94 (January 14, 1903).

Farmers who used the automobile to transport products to market and as a mobile power plant could also anticipate economies from the adoption of the motorcar. The automobile reduced the farmers' dependence upon the railroad and allowed them to market agricultural products directly over a much wider geographic area. A common observation by 1908 was that "throughout the farming districts of the central West one meets motor-carried loads of hay or milk cans, crates of chickens or a calf, and if of sufficient power, the car will be towing a loaded spring wagon." By then the farmers had also learned that "it means economy to be able to run the cider press in the orchard, the churn in the dairy, and the hay baler in the field, rather than to carry the apples, the milk and the fodder to the horse treadmill or stationary engine."[9]

Lacking adverse experience with the motor vehicle, early commentators were extremely optimistic about the relative economies of the automobile over the horse that the average individual owner could anticipate. *Automobile* summed up common opinion in 1899: "For the automobile, reduced cost is generally claimed, whether it be an electric, gasoline, or steam-propelled vehicle. Were it not for the fact that many of the vehicles are as yet untried, and the cost of maintenance, therefore, not as yet determined, the operating expense could be very closely estimated."[10] Early reports from automobile owners almost always confirmed that the automobile was cheaper than the horse in both initial cost and upkeep. Statistics presented in *Scientific American* in May 1903 were typical: it was estimated that a horse-drawn light driving outfit would cost from $660 to $1,630 initially, and "the monthly cost of maintenance would be about $40. A steam carriage capable of covering several times the daily mileage of the horse would cost from $600 to $950, or a gasoline runabout from $650 to $1,300, and the monthly cost of maintenance should not exceed $25."[11] The con-

[9] Roger B. Whitman, "The Automobile in New Roles," *Country Life in America*, 15:53 (November 1908).
[10] "The Operating Expense of the Automobile," *Automobile*, 1:7 (September 1899).
[11] "Automobile News," *Scientific American*, 88:354 (May 9, 1903).

clusion reached by the *Independent* from such data seemed sound at the time: "So far as we can at present see, the displacement of the horse will cheapen living and travel, certainly not increase them."[12]

Not until about 1906 did the actual experience of automobile owners begin to indicate that for the average man the automobile was most likely to be far more expensive to own than a horse and buggy. A tendency then developed to overlook actual comparative costs and to emphasize solely the economies that might be gained from the automobile's larger radius of operation, superior endurance, and speed. Harry B. Haines reported in the March 1906 *World's Work*, for example, that "according to my experience and that of my friends it is impossible to maintain an automobile as cheaply as horses, though mile for mile, considering the great distances that an automobile will travel, it is cheaper."[13] Haines spelled out what he meant in the January 1907 *Review of Reviews*. He estimated that "it may be possible for a man with a small car who motors modestly to get along with an expense of $20 to $30 a month if he has good luck and handles his car carefully and considerately, but the average cost of maintenance will be from $50 to $300 and even more a month." His own expenses for seven months (nearly 10,000 miles of travel) for an 8-horsepower automobile had been $817.70, including depreciation of 25 percent and $50 for insurance. After giving comparative estimates for two types of automobiles and horse-drawn vehicles, Haines stated that, depending on the specific car, the cost of an automobile was between one-third and double that of a horse. He concluded, however, that the automobile, because it did at least three times the work the horse did, was at least 33⅓ percent more economical than the horse.[14]

Haines's conclusions were those generally reached by automobile owners after

[12]"One More Revolution," *Independent*, 55:1163 (May 14, 1903).
[13]Harry B. Haines, "Automobiles for Everybody," *World's Work*, 11:7347 (March 1906).
[14]Harry B. Haines, "The Automobile and the Average Man," *Review of Reviews*, 35:74–83 (January 1907).

about 1906. But reports of substantial economies over the horse and buggy were still made. For example, an owner whose new automobile cost only half as much to maintain as his horse had concluded in 1909 that depreciation was negligible because an automobile "may be regarded as an investment. . . . Few cars become so worn or decrepit that they are actually thrown on the junk heap. The point is that a great many people feel that they must have a new car every year or two, simply to keep up with the style, although the old one is in running condition."[15] This was undoubtedly true; the estimate of depreciation generally accepted at the time gave five years as the average life of a car. Another owner found that his secondhand car cost less than $12.50 a month to maintain, while his horse had cost $100 a year. The first cost of the secondhand car had been about equal to that of a good horse. Taking into account the increased service given by the automobile, he was "fully persuaded that it was wise economy and not wild extravagance that secured to us our fleet friend, the automobile."[16]

Efficiency, Reliability, and Speed

The motor vehicle appeared to be more efficient than the horse in several respects. J. Frank Duryea spoke the mind of the automobilist in 1897 when he commented that "the horse is a willful, unreliable brute. The ever recurring accidents due to horses which are daily set forth in the papers prove that the horse is a dangerous motor and not the docile pet of the poet. The mechanical motor is his superior in many respects, and when its superiority has become better known his inferiority will be more apparent."[17] Within just a few years, Duryea's sentiments that the motorcar was safer than the horse were widely held. As *Harper's Weekly* said in 1899, "a good

[15] C. O. Morris, "The Truth about the Automobile," *Country Life in America*, 15:259–260 (January 1909).
[16] A. J. Cook, "The Automobile Universal," *Outlook*, 89:988–989 (August 29, 1908).
[17] "The Horse an Unruly Motor," *Horseless Age*, 2:2 (July 1897).

many folks to whom every horse is a wild beast feel much safer on a machine than behind a quadruped, who has a mind of his own, and emotions which may not always be forestalled or controlled."[18]

The opinion that the automobile was safer than the horse rested on two beliefs. First, it was generally held that "between automobiles and horse-drawn vehicles the braking facilities of the former are usually far superior to those of the latter. The average American-built motor vehicle of whatever type may be brought to a stand-still from a twenty mile an hour rate of speed in less space than can a team being driven at a moderate trot—say, seven miles an hour."[19] The second assumption related to the basic difference between organisms and mechanisms: "An automobile does not, like a horse, feel better one day than another, or under some conditions than under others. . . . The element of uncertainty is not furnished by the machine as a rule, but by the individual who is controlling it. For the automobile has not, like the horse, a will of its own, which may act uncertainly. It is sensitive and responsive— acting in exact accordance with the principles upon which it is constructed. The accident which happens to the automobile is seldom due to the machine itself, but almost wholly to the loss of control or presence of mind of the operator."[20]

Other major advantages of the motor vehicle over the horse that came to be increasingly recognized after the turn of the century were its superior maneuverability and imperviousness to weather conditions and fatigue. The horse-drawn vehicle required considerably more space than an automobile to turn around because of its longer length. During summer heat waves, horses quickly became exhausted, and large numbers of animals became ill or died from overexertion, frequently dropping in their tracks and tying up traffic until removed. In the winter, the horse easily lost

[18] "The Status of the Horse at the End of the Century," *Harper's Weekly*, 43:1172 (November 18, 1899).
[19] "Automobile News," *Scientific American*, 86:123 (February 22, 1902).
[20] G. F. Baright, "Automobiles and Automobile Racing at Newport," *Independent*, 54:1368 (June 5, 1902).

his footing on slick streets, and broken legs, which necessitated destruction of the animal, were a common occurrence. The automobile appeared much more adaptable: "Where the horse would drop from fatigue, the automobile knows no weariness. Where the horse would slip and flounder over impassable roads, the automobile will carry its human burden safe and dry-shod."[21] These advantages of the automobile came to be widely appreciated.

Shortsighted as it may now seem, it was even argued at the time that the widespread adoption of the motor vehicle would relieve traffic congestion on city streets. According to an 1896 article in *Scientific American*, for example, "a motorcar of the same length as the ordinary cable car would carry the same number of passengers but would carry them at a considerably greater speed. . . . The existence of a double line of cars moving on a fixed track and claiming the right of way over other vehicles is a hindrance to traffic and is itself delayed." The opinion was expressed that if these rails were removed, the street asphalted from curb to curb, and the streetcars replaced by motor vehicles that could pass one another at will, "the whole volume of traffic would move with less interruption than at present, and . . . the cars themselves would make faster time."[22] It was considered a mark of progress by 1907 that the adoption of the motor vehicle in large cities had "crowded out several thousand horses in the past year, increasing thereby the possibilities of traffic and reducing the amount of space required for each vehicle."[23]

The degree to which the motor vehicle was ever considered less reliable and efficient than the horse, all factors taken into account, is a moot question. The evidence indicates that at any given time after its introduction the motor vehicle was compared quite favorably with the horse-drawn vehicle but that a slight advantage was not

[21] George E. Latham, "The Automobile and Automobiling," *Munsey's Magazine*, 29:164 (May 1903).
[22] "The Motor Car in England," *Scientific American*, 75:423 (December 12, 1896).
[23] George E. Walsh, "The Novelties of Motoring," *Independent*, 62:710 (March 28, 1907).

sufficient to induce most people to innovate. From the beginning, the motor vehicle had been judged on tougher criteria than the horse, and people generally anticipated that the automobile would be substantially improved and sold at a much lower price in the near future. Thus one might well wait a few years until the motor vehicle had outclassed the horse completely and could be purchased for much less money before adopting the innovation. *Motor Age* explained in 1903: "In one way the automobile is its own enemy. It has accomplished so much and has become able to do so much, that the public has reached a point of unlimited expectation. For instance take the man who asks for automobiles at about $400 or less. What does he want for the price of a good horse and buggy outfit? A car equal in capabilities to the horse and buggy? Not by any means. He wants a car which will go from four to six times as fast, and travel twice or three times as far at the same expense. . . . [The public] puts the automobile in a class by itself out of comparison with other means of travel — and then kicks because the first cost is greater than that of a side bar runabout and a spavined gray mare."[24]

Serious mechanical breakdowns, the most substantial defect of the early automobile that might deter purchase, ceased to be a formidable problem in about 1906. As we have seen, the performance of the automobile during the 1906 San Francisco earthquake conclusively demonstrated this: "Never did the machines falter. . . . As fresh and ready for further duty after twenty-four hours continuous service as at the start, they accomplished what no beast of burden in the world could have accomplished. Speed, reliability, endurance, were theirs in the highest degree. Even experienced chauffeurs were astonished at the small amount of repairs needed by machines of popular makes after not only days, but weeks of the severest strain."[25] Winthrop E.

[24] "Unfair Public Demands," *Motor Age*, 3:4 (June 18, 1903).
[25] Arthur H. Dutton, "The Triumph of the Automobile," *Overland Monthly*, n.s. 48:145 (September 1906).

Scarritt in 1907 voiced well the general observation that "five years ago it was a very common occurrence to see the driver of an automobile with his car by the roadside and he himself prone upon the ground underneath it endeavoring to ascertain why it would not go or trying to make the necessary repairs. Although the number of automobiles in use has increased enormously, yet it is only occasionally that one sees a car laid up for repairs."[26]

From the outset, of course, the automobile offered an unparalleled combination of high speed and flexibility of operation — the speed of the locomotive without its disadvantage of being confined to operation on a fixed track. The high speed of the automobile was undoubtedly one of the main advantages that helped promote its adoption, especially for emergency services. It was also considered to be an economy feature "because time is money, and in this country especially the saving of time is a desideratum devoutly to be sought."[27] However, beyond a point that remained vaguely defined, the high speed of the automobile became a liability that negated another touted advantage of the motor vehicle, its supposed safety. So speed was somewhat underplayed as a motive for adoption, generally being ranked as the least important quality of the ideal automobile.

Reconciling the contradiction between the speed and the safety of the automobile posed an awkward problem for supporters of the innovation. *Horseless Age* still insisted in 1908, despite the sharply rising automobile accident rate, that "the well built automobile is inherently a very safe vehicle" and predicted that "when the speed craze dies out . . . accidents will become so rare as to stamp the automobile the very safest of road vehicles."[28] But the periodical was forced to admit the follow-

[26] Winthrop E. Scarritt, "The Horse of the Future and the Future of the Horse," *Harper's Weekly*, 51:383 (March 16, 1907).
[27] "The Automobile in 1905," *Country Life in America*, 7:379 (February 1905).
[28] "The Safety of the Automobile," *Horseless Age*, 22:580 (October 28, 1908).

ing year that "the 'automobile hazard' is not likely to decline in frequency." At a meeting of the International Association of Accident Underwriters, some interesting statistics on automobile accidents during 1908 were reported. The companies had received 1,663 claims for damages arising from automobile accidents that year. One in every sixty-four of these accidents involved a fatality, and the injuries sustained in them resulted in 3,798 weeks of total disability and 4,307 weeks of partial disability—a poor record compared with what was considered normal for policies on horse-drawn vehicles.[29]

Nonutilitarian Attractions

Although the motor vehicle undoubtedly never would have been widely adopted in the United States had it not appeared to offer substantial practical advantages over other types of transportation, nonutilitarian motives greatly enhanced the attractiveness of the innovation to Americans. To begin with, motoring had a hedonistic appeal rooted in basic human drives. *Motor World* phrased this nicely: "To take control of this materialized energy, to draw the reins over this monster with its steel muscles and fiery heart—there is something in the idea which appeals to an almost universal sense, the love of power. Add the element of danger, and the fascination inherent in motovehiclism as a sport is not difficult to understand."[30] Frank A. Munsey similarly explained that "it is in the running of a car, the handling of it, and its obedience to one's will, that the keenest enjoyment of automobiling is found."[31] And a writer in *World's Work* felt that "the sensation which arouses enthusiasm for the automobile comes almost solely from the introduction of the superlative degree

[29] J. E. Jennings, "Automobile Insurance," ibid., 24:153 (August 11, 1909).
[30] *Motor World*, 2:168 (May 30, 1901).
[31] Frank A. Munsey, "The Automobile in America," *Munsey's Magazine*, 34:404 (January 1906).

of speed and from the absence of effort or fatigue. The automobile is a vehicle that touches a sympathetic chord in most of us."[32]

The automobile was also congruent with some core values of American culture. One of these was the high value traditionally placed upon geographic mobility. Among others, Everett S. Lee has pointed out that geographic mobility has been the most pervasive characteristic of American society and that "migration has been phenomenally successful for Americans. . . . Within our country the major flows of migration have been from areas of lower to higher economic returns, or from areas in which the amenities were less well developed to those in which they were better developed. The natural interpretation by the migrant is that migration has been a good thing."[33] The automobile, which tremendously increased the geographic mobility of the individual, was certain to be prized by Americans. The point should also not be lost that the automobile was an ideal symbol of status in our migrant society because, like cash in the pocket, it could be taken with the individual wherever he went as an immediately recognizable sign of his worth.

Individualism was another core value of American culture that supported the adoption of the automobile. *Harper's Weekly* expressed well a common theme that one of the chief attractions of the automobile was "the feeling of independence — the freedom from timetables, from fixed and inflexible routes, from the proximity of other human beings than one's chosen companions; the ability to go where and when one wills, to linger and stop where the country is beautiful and the way pleasant, or to rush through unattractive surroundings, to select the best places to eat and sleep; and the satisfaction that comes from a knowledge that one need ask favors or accommodation

[32] M. C. Krarup, "Automobiles for Every Use," *World's Work*, 13:8170 (November 1906).
[33] Everett S. Lee, "The Turner Thesis Reexamined," *American Quarterly*, 13:83 (Spring 1961). See also George W. Pierson, "The M-Factor in American History," ibid., 14:275–289 (Summer 1962).

from no one nor trespass on anybody's property or privacy."[34] As *Motor World* said, "In the case of a motor vehicle you have a method of moving from place to place as tireless as a train, one which for short journeys and cross journeys is as quick as the train, and yet one which is individualistic and independent, hence its charm."[35]

The automobile was furthermore viewed as a means by which the individual could significantly enrich his social relationships and experiences: "Every friend within 3,000 square miles can be visited, any place of worship or lectures or concert attended, and business appointment kept, the train met at the railway station, every post and physician accessible, any place reached for golf or tennis or fishing or shooting, and with it all fresh air inhaled under exhilarating conditions. It is a revolution in daily life. With an automobile one lives three times as much in the same span of years, and one's life, therefore, becomes to that extent wider and more interesting."[36] There can be no doubt that the average automobile owner found this to be true. One new owner commented in 1907: "I was perfectly content to have my horizon bounded by the ten- or twelve-mile circle that my horses could go in a day and get back in good shape. I now make exploring trips of five times the distance. I can call on friends living thirty miles away who have been asking me to come for twenty years."[37]

Thus the automobile appeared to offer the individual substantially more than mere transportation, and it is no wonder, given the general recognition of these advantages, that the automobile came to be the most prized material object in American culture. The sacrifices that many Americans were willing to make to become automobile owners began to be a source of concern by the end of the first decade of the twentieth century. One critic of the automobile complained at the end of 1908, for

---

[34] Larry McKilwin, "Keeping the Land Yacht Shipshape," *Harper's Weekly*, 53:10 (January 2, 1909).
[35] "Where the Charm Is," *Motor World*, 2:127 (May 16, 1901).
[36] Henry Norman, "The Coming of the Automobile," *World's Work*, 5:3307 (April 1903).
[37] C. M. d'Enville, "The Confessions of an Anti-Motorist," *Country Life in America*, 13:40 (November 1907).

example, that "many who never felt that they were in a position to purchase a horse and carriage . . . now indulge in automobiles costing several thousand dollars originally. . . . A resident of Boston said a year ago that one would be astonished to know the number of second mortgages that had been placed upon houses in the vicinity of his city to enable the owners to procure cars, and a lawyer of New York is responsible for the statement that in his office during the past winter there have been over 200 foreclosures of New York mortgages which had been created with the same end in view."[38] Even *Horseless Age* became concerned that many purchasers of high-priced cars could ill afford them and cited a report by a committee of Pittsburgh clubwomen condemning automobile purchases by social climbers: "So mad has the race for social supremacy become in the East End that owners of houses are mortgaging them in order to buy as many and as speedy automobiles as their neighbors. Extravagance is reckless and something must be done before utter ruin follows in the wake of folly. . . . Many owners of houses worth from $5,000 to $15,000, which they have acquired after years of toil, are mortgaging them in order to buy automobiles."[39] This was indeed a strange outcome from the adoption of an innovation whose advocates had praised economy as one of its main advantages.

  Still another paradox was that the automobile became simultaneously an item of unprecedented mass consumption as well as the most important symbol of status in American society. As a monumental example of the American tendency toward upward social leveling, the solution to this paradox, one seen at the time and ultimately true in fact, was that the use of the automobile as a status symbol would be restricted to the type of car one owned rather than to automobile ownership per se. From the introduction of the innovation, it appeared that mass ownership of motor

[38] Frederick Dwight, "Automobiles: The Other Side of the Shield," *Independent*, 65:1302 (December 3, 1908).
[39] "Social Ambitions as a Factor in the Automobile Market," *Horseless Age*, 20:105 (July 24, 1907).

vehicles was both desirable and inevitable. Like many other modern items of material culture, such as the telephone and the radio, the advantages of automobile ownership to each individual were enhanced as the innovation became more widely adopted. Better service facilities and roads, for example, could be expected to follow from an increase in the number of cars in use and popular support for motoring. Early upper-class owners were anxious, therefore, to have automobile ownership be as widespread as possible, despite the knowledge that the value of their own machines as badges of status would decrease appreciably. As Dave H. Morris, president of the Automobile Club of America, said on behalf of that aristocratic organization of motorists in 1905, "Our real purpose is the development of the automobile as a reliable method of transportation for all the world and not simply for the rich. . . . It is our hope and belief that the automobile will ultimately be made so cheap, reliable and useful that it will be a necessity and not a luxury. It is not too much to say that this tendency is now in full swing, and should soon be visible, even to the casual observer."[40]

A Panacea for Urban and Rural Problems

Proponents predicted that the widespread adoption of the automobile would obviate several of the more pressing problems of our developing urban-industrial society. The degree to which some of these altruistic expectations influenced individuals to purchase motorcars may be a moot question, but they were all reiterated enough to have had some influence upon the image of the automobile movement held by informed people. Therefore, they deserve to be made explicit. The specific problems that the adoption of the automobile was expected to solve were overwhelmingly related to physical and psychological health.

Statements urging the general adoption of the automobile so that the modern city

[40] "A.C.A. President's Views," *Automobile*, 12:40 (January 14, 1905).

could be rid of the unsightly and unsanitary conditions attributable to the horse were a major manifestation of this. An article in the January 1896 *Scientific American* that applauded the possible disappearance of the horse stable is illustrative: "The stable pit filled with the defiled bedding of our obedient and faithful four-legged servant would be known no more to our senses. The contagia bred in its midst and scattered in the dry dust of summer air, to find their way within our sleeping and sitting rooms, would be only the remembered signs of a past and primitive civilization. The germs of glanders would not harbor and be hatched, as they still occasionally are, in the stalls of overcrowded mews."[41] The average man could appreciate that, "in contradistinction to a horse stable, an automobile house can always be made attractive. There are no sanitary devices that need to be put in for the purpose of rendering the place bearable, as there would be if horses were kept in it. Consequently its proximity to the house is an advantage rather than a drawback."[42]

The conclusion reached by the Chicago health commissioner in an endorsement of the automobile as an aid to public health was inescapable by the turn of the century: "Ideal health conditions cannot prevail so long as horses are in the city."[43] Medical authorities stated that tetanus was introduced into cities in horse fodder and that an important cause of diarrhea, a serious health problem among city children at the time, was street dust consisting in the main of germ-laden dried horse dung. Everyone knew that excreta accounted for about two-thirds of the filth that littered city streets. In the form of dried dust during the summer they irritated nasal passages and lungs and prevented windows from being opened to allow proper ventilation, then became a syrupy mass to wade through and track into the home whenever it rained. Insurance actuaries for some New York companies had established by the turn of the century

---

[41] "Horseless Carriages and Sanitation," *Scientific American*, 74:36 (January 18, 1896).
[42] "Not Utilitarian Only," *Motor World*, 5:113 (October 23, 1902).
[43] "Merely a Matter of Time," *Motor Age*, 5:n.p. (December 5, 1901).

that infectious diseases were much more frequently contracted by livery stable keepers and employees than other occupational groups. An appeal to the Brooklyn Board of Health to investigate resulted in the institution of new municipal regulations on stables, compelling more frequent removal of excreta and disinfecting of premises. But *Horseless Age* urged that "the nuisance will not be wholly abated until the great beasts whose refuse litters the streets and fouls the atmosphere in our populous centers, are banished from the cities to the agricultural districts, where they will find temporary harborage."[44]

On a more positive note, motoring itself was widely praised as a restorative for the frayed nerves that resulted from the increasingly hectic pace of life in an urban-industrial society. Frank A. Munsey became as ecstatic about this as a medicine show pitchman: "It is the greatest health giving invention of a thousand years. The cubic feet of fresh air that are literally forced into one while automobiling rehabilitate worn-out nerves and drive out worry, insomnia, and indigestion. It will renew the life and youth of the overworked man or woman, and will make the thin fat and the fat—but I forbear."[45] Or, as a writer in *Outlook* more modestly phrased this theme, "After a day of hard mental effort in study or office, it is better than any medicine to push forward the lever and fly away with the ever faithful and obedient automobile. . . . The restful pleasure and exhilaration that come as we speed away with our unwearying servant are the best cure for the tired nerves."[46] Pneumatic-tired automobiles running on asphalt streets were also expected to cut down appreciably on city noise, which was viewed as a cause of "nervous diseases" and attributed to the iron wheels of horse-drawn vehicles clattering on the cobblestones that horses required for a foothold. "Specialists have many times expressed an opinion that the nervous diseases

[44] "Stable Breeders of Disease," *Horseless Age*, 4:6 (May 3, 1899).
[45] Frank A. Munsey, "Impressions by the Way," *Munsey's Magazine*, 29:183 (May 1903).
[46] Cook, "Automobile Universal," p. 991.

which exist in the city are aggravated, if not caused, in many cases, by noises incident to a great city's traffic. The bells of the new [motor] vehicles will of course be somewhat annoying at first."[47]

The most direct way in which the automobile contributed to the health of the community, however, was by enabling prompter care of the injured and ill and extending the physicians' services more fully into outlying districts. We have already noted that physicians were in the forefront of the automobile movement. Many hospitals in major cities also switched to motorized ambulances quite early. The benefit of the automobile to the country doctor was particularly notable: "The county-seat doctors have a clientage that reaches out twenty miles in every direction, and with teams and buggies, they find it almost impossible to cover it. With a runabout they make their seventy-five to one hundred miles a day and are satisfied."[48] Periodicals recounted many instances of farmers in a district becoming converts to the automobile after someone's life had been saved in the locality by the use of a motor vehicle.

The extension and enhancement of rural life were anticipated to be other major accomplishments of the automobile movement. Almost always, discussion of this facet was cast in terms of the promotion of physical and psychological health and involved invocation of the "agrarian myth." The city had many recognized advantages over the farm, but urban living nevertheless basically repelled Americans. Most middle-class city dwellers were anxious to escape as far into the surrounding countryside as they could without giving up the economic and educational opportunities, services, and amusements of the metropolis. The automobile, which appeared to make it possible for everyone to enjoy the best of both rural and urban environments in everyday life, was viewed by its supporters as the ultimate instrument to reform

[47] "The Horseless Carriage and Public Health," *Scientific American*, 80:98 (February 18, 1899).
[48] Charles M. Harger, "The Automobile in Western Country Towns," *World Today*, 13:1280 (December 1907).

American society into a suburban utopia. This theme of the reconciliation of the country and the city was well expressed by *Motor Age* in 1905: "For the past couple of decades there has been an alarming tendency on the part of the country youth and the country maiden to drift toward more settled portions of the country and to surround themselves with such luxuries as city life naturally brings. No man or woman can be blamed for disliking isolation. It has been the cause of more insanity than any other one thing. . . . When the day has come when motorcars . . . shall pass over all the highways and byways of the country, the tendency to flock to cities will have passed away, to a large extent, and the man who today is living in crowded tenements will see his way clear to live as nature provided he should live, to see comforts and blessings which now are largely found in cities alone."[49]

The automobile was expected to stimulate the exodus of the upper and upper-middle classes to the suburbs that had begun with the introduction of the trolley. It was expected also, given the anticipated imminent lowering of the price of cars, ultimately to involve the lower-middle and lower classes in the suburban movement. The *Independent* accordingly predicted in 1903: "The automobile will hurry this tide [begun by the trolley] countryward with accelerated speed. It will begin its work with the well-to-do—those who are capable of keeping up a private establishment. This is the class which is now in the van of the movement to escape from the city."[50] A year later the periodical voiced the expectation that "the time is not far distant when the inevitable slump in price will come, and it [the automobile] will then become the vehicle, not only of the few, but of the many, bringing with it a relief from city life . . . opening up the country for modest homes, to which city workers may daily escape." The utopian effects of suburbia for the individual and society seemed obvious:

[49]"Get Near to Nature and Really Live," *Motor Age*, 8:19 (November 2, 1905).
[50]"One More Revolution," pp. 1162–1163.

"Imagine a healthier race of workingmen, toiling in cheerful and sanitary factories, with mechanical skill and trade-craft developed to the highest, as the machinery grows more delicate and perfect, who, in the late afternoon, glide away in their own comfortable vehicles to their little farms or homes in the country or by the sea twenty or thirty miles distant! They will be healthier, happier, more intelligent and self-respecting citizens because of the chance to live among the meadows and flowers of the country instead of in crowded city streets."[51]

As a matter of fact, by 1906 the automobile was already beginning to encourage middle-class movement to the suburbs. *Automobile* reported that "places fortunately situated, and blessed with healthful surroundings, which formerly were undesirable because of their inaccessibility, are rapidly developing, according to the leading real estate authorities, who are free to admit that they mention the automobile as the means of transportation when soliciting the patronage of purchasers. . . . Numbers of people with moderate-sized incomes are reported to be buying outside sites for homes, and expending the money they save on their lots in the purchase of cars with which to make the journey to their places of business."[52]

Just as the movement of population from the city to the suburb was hailed as social progress, the reverse movement of population from the country to the city was condemned as social disaster. The automobile was expected to halt the latter as effectively as it advanced the former. A writer in *Outing Magazine* predicted in 1902, for example, that with the adoption of the automobile "the millions of our rural population will be brought into closer relations with the towns and with neighbors, and the loneliness of farm life, which drives so many to the cities, with detriment to all, will no longer retard our agricultural growth, nor prevent a proper distribution of pop-

[51]William F. Dix, "The Automobile as a Vacation Agent," *Independent*, 56:1259–1260 (June 2, 1904).
[52]"Automobiles and Real Estate Development," *Automobile*, 15:120 (July 26, 1906).

ulation for the national welfare."[53] By 1907 it seemed obvious that the automobile would "remove the last serious obstacle to the farmer's success. It will market his surplus product, restore the value of his lands, and greatly extend the scope and pleasure of all phases of country life."[54]

A predominant fear, unallayed by memories of chronic overproduction of agricultural commodities during the late nineteenth century, was that the siphoning of the rural population into the cities would soon deplete the number of farmers to the point where a critical food shortage would result. Mounting evidence of soil depletion in many agricultural regions made the outlook appear even grimmer. Rising prices for farm products during the first decade of the twentieth century disturbed city consumers, who were confronted with higher prices for food. Although the economic condition of the farmer had improved substantially during the decade, the financial rewards of an agricultural occupation were still not sufficient to keep talented and ambitious young men tied to a life of isolated drudgery. Should these young men move to the city en masse, as they appeared to be doing, it was feared that food would become critically short in supply and prohibitive in price, and overproduction of manufactured goods might saturate markets, driving down wages and prices to a ruinous level.

The adoption of the automobile by farmers appeared to offer an ideal solution to this foreboding social problem. It was assumed that the automobile would break down the isolation of rural life and allow the farmer the amenities that had drawn him to the city, lighten farm labor through its use as a mobile power plant, and significantly reduce the cost of transportation of farm products to market, thus raising the farmers' profits while lowering the food prices paid by consumers. Proponents

[53] William J. Lampton, "The Meaning of the Automobile," *Outing Magazine*, 40:699 (September 1902).
[54] G. W. Atterbury, "The Commercial Car as a Necessity," *Harper's Weekly*, 51:1925 (December 28, 1907).

of the automobile as the key to the "back to the farm movement" spoke with conviction. Two responses to a 1909 speech on the farm problem by James J. Hill before the Bankers' Association of Chicago are illustrative. Hayden Eames, the general manager of Studebaker, said that the automobile "develops a sense of community in agricultural districts which was utterly impossible with the former methods of transportation. It makes the farmer's life and surroundings much more liberal, and, under many conditions, far more attractive even to the young people than the life of the city." Eames was so convinced he was right that he erroneously predicted that the 1920 census would show a movement of population from the city to the country because of what the automobile had done for rural life.[55] Writing in *Motor*, Thomas L. White also erroneously predicted that the adoption of the automobile by farmers would lower food prices and relieve population congestion in cities. He argued: "Whether we look to the importance of attracting to or retaining on the farms the class of intellect which is capable of solving agricultural problems presented by the impaired resources of the soil, or whether we look to the importance of checking the growth of the cities by such a revolution of agricultural conditions as will encourage the settlement of the rural districts, the question of better communications is in each case fundamental."[56]

That the automobile was soon going to solve the problems of rural life in the United States did seem unquestionable in 1910. Henry Ford had introduced his rugged, popularly priced Model T, and farmers had come to be a mainstay of the phenomenally developing market for cars. The conditions that *Horseless Age* reported to exist in Kansas were typical: "Now the farmer scurries up and down the roads to town and back in an hour or two, to his neighbors, to his church and over his place. The farm-

[55]Hayden Eames, "Influence of Auto on 'Back to the Farm Movement,'" *Automobile*, 21:554 (September 30, 1909).
[56]Thomas L. White, "The Motor Car and the Cost of Living," *Motor*, 13:65 (March 1910).

er's wife is in town almost every day. She does her shopping as would a suburbanite of the cities."[57] It was not foreseen that the contribution of the tractor to the mechanization of agriculture would lead by the 1920s to considerably higher fixed costs for farm equipment, combined with ruinous overproduction of staple farm products. Nor was it foreseen that the automobile would ultimately make the small family farm obsolete.

Thus the adoption of the automobile seemed, to proponents of the innovation, to afford a simple solution to some of the more formidable problems of American life associated with the emergence of an urban-industrial society. The motorcar seemed to be a panacea for the social ills of the day, one that necessitated minimal collective action or governmental expenditure. Best of all, perhaps, the individual did not need to wait for others to act; by buying a car, he could immediately improve his own life appreciably. The inherent appeal of the motorists' paradigm for social betterment soon became evident. By the 1920s there was every indication that the residents of Middletown had internalized the suggestion of an automobile advertisement of the day, "Hit the road to better times!"

[57] E. H. Smith, "The Use of Automobiles on Kansas Farms," *Horseless Age*, 25:240 (February 7, 1909).

4

Institutional Response:
Government and the Press

Governmental Apathy

Prior to the inauguration of President William Howard Taft in 1909, when the automobile finally displaced the White House horses, the federal government's interest in the motor vehicle was confined to some halfhearted experiments undertaken by the United States army and the Post Office Department and the purchase of a few electric cars by the Library of Congress, the Bureau of Standards, and the Government Printing Office. This neglect stood in sharp contrast with the very active role that European governments played in the diffusion of the motor vehicle. Advocates of the automobile still complained in 1909 that "the Washington government has not given to the motorcar that support which a new method of transportation deserves, or has that government given even a semblance of support compared with the financial and legislative aid that have been rendered by many of the governments of Europe to their motoring interests."[1]

Lacking our decentralized federal political system and tradition of minimal government, European countries early developed national legislation regulating the operation of motor vehicles. England's infamous Locomotives on Highways Act, passed by Parliament in 1865 and not repealed until 1896, is an example of such legislation at its worst. It has been appropriately damned as an anachronistic restraint that severely hampered the initial development of motoring in Great Britain. This legislation limited the speed of self-propelled road vehicles to 2 mph in towns and 4 mph on the open road and required that each "road locomotive" be attended by three persons, one of whom had to walk 60 yards ahead of the vehicle carrying a red flag by day or a red lantern by night.

In their more typical functioning, however, the national automobile laws common

[1] "Government Recognition of Motor Cars," *Motor Age*, 15:6 (March 25, 1909).

in Europe during the first decade of the twentieth century had the advantage of imposing uniform, reasonable standards upon all of a nation's motorists and ensured the competence of everyone who drove an automobile on the public roads. The American motorist lacked these benefits because the national government remained reluctant to assume any regulatory power over the motor vehicle that would supersede the prerogatives of municipal and state authorities. Despite strong pressure to do so from automobile interests, Congress failed to enact any national motor vehicle legislation. As we shall see in Chapter 6, the outcome was a rather chaotic, inadequate, and minimally restrictive system of municipal and state regulation that neither pleased the motorist nor sufficiently protected the general public.

Governmental regulation here was also notably absent in the supervision of automobile construction standards. *Horseless Age* applauded the fact that the automobile laws of European countries placed the construction of motor vehicles under the control of government and that "every type of automobile that is placed upon the market must be submitted to inspection by a department of the government and must satisfy certain requirements of law." American practice, on the other hand, was strictly laissez-faire. Consequently, many American manufacturers turned out cars that did not meet even the extremely low minimal safety requirements of the period. *Horseless Age* believed that "when the enthusiasm [of automobile purchasers] is at its height safety appliances are often thought of lightly, and government supervision of this matter would be quite to the point."[2] But no action was taken beyond municipal and state requirements, by no means universal even by 1910, that motor vehicles be equipped with headlights and taillights, a horn or some other warning device, and brakes.

[2] "Government Inspection and Approval of Vehicles," *Horseless Age*, 10:492 (November 5, 1902).

War Department

The governments of France, Germany, and England also realized the military potential of the motor vehicle by the mid-1890s. They offered substantial subsidies to encourage the development of motor vehicles suitable for military purposes and conducted extensive military experiments with motor vehicles. One result was to discourage the manufacture of light cars in Europe in favor of heavier touring cars, trucks, and tractors that would be better suited for use as officers' staff cars, weapon carriers, and the transport of troops and supplies. Although this emphasis retarded the development of a low-cost car for the average man, it did have the benefits of giving European countries leadership in the development of practical motorized trucks and buses and of increasing the military effectiveness of these countries.

French interest in the military use of the motor vehicle dated from governmental support for Nicholas Cugnot's experiments with heavy steam vehicles in the late eighteenth century. Sustained support for the development of the military automobile, however, did not begin in France until October 1897, when a technical commission of the army, headed by artillery officers, was charged with conducting experiments with motor vehicles at the yearly maneuvers. Within a decade a special budget equivalent to about $200,000 had been set aside in France for subsidies averaging about $1,400, payable over four years, to automobile owners who agreed to place their cars at the disposal of the army in event of mobilization. The German army began its experiments with eight motor vehicles during the grand maneuvers of 1899; after this an imperial volunteer automobile squad became a feature of the annual maneuvers in Germany. The German military budget by 1908 included an appropriation of approximately $250,000 to be paid out in subsidies amounting to as much as $2,250 each over a five-year period to owners or manufacturers of automobiles with more than 30 horsepower who agreed to turn over their vehicles to the government if a national emergency occurred. The British War Office offered prizes up to £1,000 for the development of a military tractor and conducted extensive trials of the vehicles entered in competition in 1903. Military motor vehicles were shortly thereafter introduced in the colonial service by the British army and were used in the Boer War. Subsidies in England amounted to about $584 for each motor vehicle earmarked for possible military use.

Although these European experiments with military motor vehicles received adequate coverage in American periodicals, our War Department was slow to respond by making tests of its own, and it offered neither prizes nor subsidies to encourage the development of suitable cars. Two light electric supply wagons and an officers' staff car were purchased by the Signal Corps from the Woods Motor Vehicle Company in late 1899. These were the worst possible types of cars for military use. Automobiles were also cursorily examined by the Ambulance Corps the following year. But the United States army showed no interest in a light automobile gun carriage that the Duryea Manufacturing Company built in 1899 for Major R. P. Davidson of the Northwestern Military Academy. The official position of the army toward the motor vehicle at the turn of the century was expressed to a reporter from the Associated Press by Major J. B. Mott, who had represented the United States as an observer at the 1899 French military maneuvers: "I do not believe they [motor vehicles] would be of sufficient value on the rough American roads, and over enormous tracts of country in the United States, to justify the heavy expense of their introduction and maintenance in the American army. Our needs differ considerably from those of the European countries. The latter must always prepare for possible war on their own soil, and their conditions favor the use of autocars while the possibility of hostilities within the United States are remote, and their utility is highly problematical."[3]

The pleas of a few progressive officers were ignored by their superiors and, lacking the incentive of subsidization, by the American automobile industry as well. General Nelson A. Miles was one of the few American officers who saw the military potential of the automobile from the outset. Upon his retirement in 1903, Miles urged Secretary of War Elihu Root to replace five regiments of cavalry with troops using motor vehicles and bicycles and to establish a road-building corps of at least 5,000 men. He was unsuccessful. Miles believed that the conditions encountered in the Spanish-American War indicated that the horse was obsolete in warfare. He also felt that the large preponderance of cavalry to infantry in the American army compared with European armies was both useless and more expensive to maintain than motorized units would be. General A. W. Greely, chief signal officer, was another pro-automobile American military man. In his annual report to the Secretary of War in 1902, Greely stated that the limited experience of the Signal Corps with the automobile as well as experiments conducted by European armies indicated the great potential of the motor vehicle for military purposes. But he complained that "despite repeated and urgent requests . . . it has been impossible to find an American manufacturer of acknowledged standing who would consent to construct for the Signal Corps an automobile along such indicated lines of structure, fuel and fittings as are deemed necessary for efficient use as self-propelling vehicles forming part of flying telegraph trains or balloon trains."[4]

The early pattern of apathy remained characteristic of the War Department until

[3] "The Automobile in War," *Motor Age*, 3:199–200 (October 11, 1900).
[4] "Autos for U.S. Signal Corps," *Automobile*, 7:15 (November 15, 1902).

Plate 18.   1904 Winton Signal
Corps wagonette standing in front
of an early Washington, D.C.,
public garage. This was one of the
first motor vehicles specially designed for the United States army.
Courtesy Smithsonian Institution.

at least 1909. In 1904 the Signal Corps obtained two specially designed Winton touring cars for testing in maneuvers. The only other specially built military motor vehicle then owned by our government was a car built in 1903 by the Standard Motor Construction Company of New Jersey under War Department supervision; it was being tested at Fort Leavenworth, Kansas, for use as a field repair shop. The army also bought its first automobile ambulance, a White steamer with a lengthened chassis, in the spring of 1906 for trials at Fort Meyer, Virginia. Despite the success of these vehicles, reports praising the work done by the automobile during the San Francisco earthquake from army officers on the scene, and some successful tests by state militias, little was done to introduce motor vehicles more widely into military service in the United States until August 1909, when, a decade behind European armies, the first major field test of military motor vehicles in the United States occurred at the annual war games of the American army — that year a mock invasion of Massachusetts umpired by General Leonard Wood in a White steamer.

Post Office

The Post Office Department was initially more alert than the War Department to the potential value of the automobile. Nevertheless, the postal authorities remained cautious and did very little about adopting the innovation until it had been unquestionably established as reliable and accepted by the public.

The interest of the Post Office Department in the motor vehicle was evident as early as 1896, when the Railway Mail Service, which had charge of mail collection in New York City, began to experiment with motor vehicles for the collection of mail from street boxes. The second assistant postmaster general stated in his 1896 annual report that "it is hoped that the experiments with the horseless wagons, which will be tried during this fall, will be successful, and will enable the department to put these collection wagons in service at a greatly reduced expense, the theory being that the horseless wagon will be very much less expensive to operate than the horse wagon."[5]

Following this lead, experiments were conducted by the postmasters in several cities before the turn of the century. They demonstrated that the automobile was superior to the horse-drawn vehicle for the collection of mail. The most noted experiment, conducted in Buffalo, New York, in 1899, showed that the mail from forty boxes along a six-mile route could be collected by automobile in half the time necessary with a horse and wagon. This result was soon replicated in another test in Washington, D.C. The postmasters of Brooklyn, Chicago, and Boston consequently became anxious to initiate automobile mail collection in their jurisdictions.

But while the postal authorities in Washington continued to express optimism about the long-range potential of the motor vehicle for postal service, they remained unwilling to commit themselves to immediate adoption. Regarding the Buffalo experiment, the first assistant postmaster general concluded that "valuable improvements to the collection branch through this new departure in locomotion are limited at present by requisite conditions, which seem to demand either asphalt or other smooth pavements. These deterrent conditions may and doubtless will be eliminated by further improvement in the carriages in the near future, when the substitution of motors for the horse and wagon will possibly become universal."[6]

Standard practice at the time was for the postal authorities to negotiate four-year contracts with private carriers for the collection and transfer of mail. In a few instances firms were allowed or induced to attempt limited experiments with motor vehicles under short-term contracts. Such contracts were negotiated for Minneapolis in 1901, for Philadelphia in 1903, and for the 1904 St. Louis Exposition. An im-

[5]"Horseless Carriage for Mail Service," *Scientific American*, 75:375 (November 21, 1896).
[6]"Autos to Carry the Mails," *Motor Age*, 1:209 (November 23, 1899).

promptu test under severe winter driving conditions also took place in 1902, when the Cleveland post office used several curved-dash Oldsmobiles to help transport mail during the Christmas holiday rush.

As the terms of the Minneapolis contract clearly illustrate, the Post Office Department hardly could have expected to encourage private entrepreneurs to haul mail by automobile. The Post Office Department advertised in October 1901 for bids to put motor vehicles in trial service in the Minneapolis business district. The carrier was required to put up a discouragingly high $20,000 bond and furnish five motor vehicles for service at any given time, with an additional car in reserve. In addition, he had to assume full responsibility for the maintenance and operation of the vehicles in a rough schedule of daily service that included both collection from letter boxes and transfer of mail between the main post office, postal stations, and substations. For this the contract ultimately negotiated paid just $17,313, for service from January 1, 1902, to June 30, 1903. It is not surprising that the Post Office Department found only one firm, the Republic Motor Vehicle Company, that was willing to assume the risk.

These early trials demonstrated that the motor vehicle cut collection time in half, cost less than horses and wagons to operate, and was reliable enough even in deep snow and extremely cold weather. Yet progress toward more general adoption continued at a slow pace. Plans were made in 1906 to initiate motor vehicle mail collection and transfer in several more cities. Baltimore was chosen as a test site because of the severe conditions imposed by that city's many steep grades and large amount of heavy, cobblestone pavement. The two Columbia gasoline cars put into experimental service under a short-term contract in Baltimore on October 1, 1906, were widely hailed as a great success, but in the short run the Baltimore trial merely led to more trials in other cities. The first vans built specially for the Post Office Department were put into service in Milwaukee in March 1907. Limited experiments were soon initiated in Indianapolis, Detroit, and Washington, D.C., which proved on balance highly favorable to the motor vehicle, even if they did not allow its unequivocal endorsement. However, as late as April 1908, *Horseless Age* complained that "at the present time the United States Post Office has no automobiles officially in service." The motor vehicles that had been tried had been declared unsuitable by the postal authorities, and the periodical found that "commercial auto builders are making no effort in this direction."[7]

Not until mid-1909 did the Post Office Department make its first substantial commitment to the use of the motor vehicle. Acting upon the strong recommendation of the New York City postmaster, Edward M. Morgan, the postal authorities in Washington permitted fourteen electric mail vans to displace and supersede horses and wagons entirely for the collection and transfer of mail among nineteen post offices in Manhattan and the Bronx on a year's trial basis beginning July 1, 1909. Thus meaningful adoption of the motor vehicle by the Post Office Department came about a decade after the first successful experiments indicating the worth of the innovation for postal service.

The Post Office Department was more active in encouraging the use of the automobile for rural free delivery. But since rural carriers had to purchase their own vehicles out of comparatively meager salaries, the practical outcome was that few RFD routes were served by motor vehicles until after 1910. The first instances of Post Office Department interest in the automobile for rural free delivery date from only shortly after the inauguration of RFD service in November 1901. The postmaster general gave a Hagerstown, Maryland, RFD carrier the first special permission to use an automobile on his route in July 1902. The following month he approved an

[7] "Automobiles in the Postal Service," *Horseless Age*, 21:475 (April 22, 1908).

automobile mail wagon designed by George F. DeGroot, a New Jersey letter carrier, for RFD use. An experimental RFD automobile route was also established between Portland and Pennville, Indiana, before the year was out. A policy of general sanction for the use of the automobile in RFD service was established when Postmaster General G. B. Cortelyou ruled in January 1906 that the automobile could now be adopted by RFD carriers without special permission. Tests conducted by the Post Office Department from June 27 to July 3, 1906, resulted in official approval of an Orient Buckboard expressly designed for rural mail delivery. However, the formidable problem remained that, although the Orient car sold for a low $400 and cost about one cent a mile in fuel to operate, the maximal annual salary of an RFD carrier was only $720. Consequently, in spite of the fact that great interest in the automobile was expressed in the correspondence column of the *R.F.D. News*, relatively few rural mail carriers were able to switch over from the horse to the motorcar. As one disgruntled RFD carrier wrote to *Motor* in April 1908, "Although I have spent a year trying to find a car suitable for rural service, as yet I have been unable to find one that would negotiate my hills, ford my creeks, and be at a price that I could pay."[8]

Municipal Government

Municipal governments in the United States, with a few notable exceptions, were slow to adopt motor vehicles until after about 1905. Heavy, steam-propelled fire engines were introduced in the United States as early as 1867 in Boston and 1871 in New York City, but the use of these vehicles was soon discontinued because they were difficult to steer and unreliable, especially in winter. By the end of 1903, however, self-propelled fire engines were again being tried in Boston, New Orleans, Pittsburgh, Hartford, Connecticut, and Portland, Maine. The first automobile patrol

[8] "Motor Cars for Rural Mail Carriers," *Motor*, 10:53 (April 1908).

wagon in the United States was built for the Akron, Ohio, police department in 1898 and, despite hard use, was still performing well in 1905. Hartford, Connecticut, adopted a specially designed electric police ambulance in 1902; Boston replaced four mounted police with a Stanley Steamer to patrol its Back Bay section in the summer of 1903; and Milwaukee began to use an automobile "Black Maria" in 1904. New York City, with twenty-one municipal automobiles (it had over 5,000 municipally owned horses), led the nation by a wide margin in 1905. The New York City municipal cars included four used by the mayor and borough presidents, six owned by the Department of Street Cleaning, three Police Department motor bicycles, and two automobiles each in service with the Fire Department, Department of Health, Department of Docks, and Department of Public Works. *Horseless Age* summed up at the end of 1905: "Although several of the most progressive cities in the country employed motor vehicles for some particular branch of work as long as three years ago, it is only during the past year that the automobile has found extensive application in this field." The periodical explained that this conservatism had been due to a lack of reliable commercial vehicles but anticipated that more extensive adoption of motor vehicles by municipalities could be expected in the near future.[9]

About 1905 the advantages of the motor vehicle began to impress municipal authorities, and plans were being made in many cities to use motor vehicles more extensively in the near future. The attitude of New York City officials, who by mid-1905 had scheduled for immediate purchase twenty-four additional municipal automobiles, is illustrative. The New York Department of Street Cleaning claimed: "The automobile is not only a great help to a city department, but in ours, at least, is now an absolute necessity, as all our work is based upon our ability to use automobiles. Without them we could not do one-tenth of the work of inspection with our present staff." Fire Chief

[9] "The Automobile in Municipal Service," *Horseless Age*, 16:821 (December 27, 1905).

Richard Crocker similarly praised his new red touring car, saying "there is no comparison . . . horses could not begin to do the work for a single day. The only trouble is that I am unable to keep a mechanic on account of the long and irregular hours which are required." Dr. Thomas Darlington, president of the Board of Health, planned to obtain four automobile ambulances as soon as he could because "their need is a matter of life and death, on account of the time which could be saved in taking a patient to a hospital in an emergency."[10] The New York City Police Department budget for 1906 included an appropriation for the purchase of twenty more police motor bicycles: "The means of rapid locomotion obviously should be in the hands of the police as well as of the citizens, whether they be honest or dishonest. The fact that there are some twenty-three thousand automobiles in New York State alone at the present time renders such considerations of the greatest importance."[11]

As pointed out earlier, the 1906 San Francisco earthquake demonstrated conclusively the superiority of the motor vehicle for emergency services to municipal authorities throughout the United States. *Overland Monthly* reported, for example, that, when the earthquake struck, "it took but the first glance to see that the street railway systems were paralyzed. Horses were few and of little value for rapid transit. The automobile was the only solution to the problem." The magazine estimated that during the crisis countless lives and at least $100 worth of property had been saved through the use of motor vehicles for every dollar that had been invested in automobiles by San Franciscans. The value of the automobile during the disaster was well publicized and proved to be a stimulus to the adoption of motor vehicles by other municipalities: "The fire and emergency hospital services of various cities are favorably considering the substitution of automobiles for horse-drawn vehicles, as a result of the lessons

[10] "Automobiles Used by New York City," *Automobile*, 12:741–744 and 13:11–13 (June 22 and July 6, 1905).
[11] "For the Motor Police," *Motor World*, 11:283 (November 2, 1905).

taught in San Francisco since April 18, 1906. Some cities, it is true, have already secured automobile fire engines and automobile ambulances. These propose to get more, and those without them propose to get some right away."[12]

The rapid general acceptance of the self-propelled fire engine by municipalities illustrates well the progress made in municipal adoption of the motor vehicle during the next few years. Specially equipped, motorized fire engines were being sold even to many small cities and towns by 1908. Wherever the motorized fire engine was adopted, its excellent performance in actual service, compared with that of the horse-drawn fire engine, elicited orders from neighboring communities. Two Rambler fire engines bought by Long Beach, California, in late 1907 immediately proved so efficient, for example, that by January 1908 seven other cities in southern California had opened negotiations for fire engines with Thomas B. Jeffery & Company. Enthusiastic testimonials solicited from fire chiefs were an excellent sales pitch for the manufacturers of fire engines. For example, George W. Kerr, a representative of the Knox Automobile Company, used testimonials to good effect in a paper he read before the New York State Association of Fire Chiefs in 1908. The secretary of the Radnor, Pennsylvania, Fire Company had written that, after two years of service, Radnor's Knox fire engine had "horses beaten to a standstill, not only from the saving standpoint, that is in maintenance, but in actual use. . . . We have come to the conclusion that for suburban fire companies there is nothing better than the auto for getting there, and it is only a question of time when horses will be done away with in the country districts." Similarly, the chairman of the fire committee of the Springfield, Massachusetts, City Council claimed yearly maintenance costs of only $327.82 for its auxiliary squad's Knox fire engine versus $617.00 in yearly maintenance for the

---

[12] Arthur H. Dutton, "The Triumph of the Automobile," *Overland Monthly*, n.s. 48:154 (September 1906).

squad's three-horse hitch. The Springfield fire chief declared the Knox so efficient and reliable that "unless something unforeseen happens, we will never go back to the horse-drawn vehicle." Kerr himself felt confident that "the era of motor fire apparatus is at hand": the innovation had been substantially adopted in Europe, where several cities had already gone over entirely to motorized fire engines, great strides had also been made in adoption of the motor vehicle by American fire departments since 1906, and the Knox company's daily mail showed "an intense interest in the subject throughout the United States."[13]

Although municipal services in all American cities were still overwhelmingly dependent upon the horse-drawn vehicle in 1910, the rapid progress made after 1905 in adopting the motor vehicle in many cities, and the enthusiasm of municipal authorities wherever the automobile had been tried, left little doubt by 1909 about the imminent displacement of the municipally owned horse-drawn vehicle. By late 1908, New York City was spending about $25,000 a month in maintenance and depreciation on its municipal automobiles — enough to justify the construction of the first municipal garage in the United States. In New York City, automobiles had by then been "supplied to municipal officials wherever the need for them was shown — and indeed in several instances when the need was but vaguely defined."[14] The same situation was evident in most large and medium-sized American cities within just a few years.

The Press
The early apathy of government toward the motor vehicle was counterbalanced by the enthusiasm of the American press. Newspapers and magazines played a signif-

[13] George W. Kerr, "Motor Propulsion for Fire Apparatus," *Motor*, 11:61–63 (October 1908).
[14] "The First Municipal Garage," *Motor World*, 18:911 (September 24, 1908).

Plate 19.   Sales catalog illustration
of a 1910 Knox truck. Courtesy
Free Library of Philadelphia.

The Proof of Efficiency and Durability lies in
REPEAT ORDERS
You can afford to investigate a means of transportation which has long since superseded horse traffic.
Solves the short haul freight and express problem and eclipses all in economy.

Plate 20. Sales catalog illustrations and specifications of 1910 Knox fire engines. Courtesy Free Library of Philadelphia.

MODEL M-4, 2-TON CIVIC AND FIRE VEHICLE, "FIRST SIZE"

SPECIFICATIONS

MAXIMUM ROAD SPEED, 40 miles per hour.

WHEEL BASE, 128".

WHEEL TREAD, 60".

FRONT TIRES, 40" x 6" ⎫ Fisk bolted-on heavy car type
REAR TIRES, 40" x 6" ⎭ Fisk demountable rims.

STEERING, screw and nut.

BRAKES, foot brake, contracting bands on ends of jack shaft. Hand brake, internal expanding in rear wheel drums.

DRIVE, by universally jointed propeller shaft, jack shaft and double side chains to the rear wheels.

GASOLINE CAPACITY, to suit class of service.

FRAME, 5" section rolled channel steel.

SPRINGS, semi-elliptic, front 2" x 42"; rear 2" x 52".

MOTOR, 5½" x 5½", 48 H. P. Model "M." (See page 6.)

TRANSMISSION, Model 14. (See page 12.)

PRICE CHASSIS, $4,300 in the lead.

DIMENSIONS OF CARRYING BODY, 7' 1" x 44".

Price open express body mounted on chassis, including painting of complete vehicle, $200.00.

Price of fire bodies and equipment on application.

Rear wheels can be fitted with dual pneumatic or solid rubber tires.

MODEL M-4, 2-TON FIRE VEHICLE

KNOX MODEL 64, 1-TON CHASSIS FOR AMBULANCE AND PATROL WAGONS

SPECIFICATIONS

MAXIMUM ROAD SPEED, 40 miles per hour.

WHEEL BASE, 134¼″.

TREAD, 56″.

TIRES, 38 x 5½ Fisk bolted-on heavy car type, on Fisk demountable rims.

FRONT AXLE, "I" beam construction, special heat treated open hearth steel.

REAR AXLE, KNOX full floating type, running on imported Hess-Bright ball bearings; nickel steel shafts and gears.

STEERING GEAR, of the celebrated Gemmer manufacture.

FRAME, cold pressed of special heavy carbon steel, reinforced by heavy inverted truss. Frame has 1½″ drop at the rear and is inswept in front to improve steering.

UNIT POWER PLANT, including the KNOX famous Model "R" four-cylinder water cooled motor, see page 7, and Model 4, three speed selective transmission, see page 11, joined to the motor by the KNOX patented unit construction.

BRAKES, both brakes act on rear wheel drums.

SPRINGS, nickel steel, 40 inch semi-elliptic front, 54″ ¾ scroll elliptic rear, with oil cups on all hangers and pins.

LUBRICATION, the well known De Dion system.

PRICE

Chassis as above, painted with two coats of lead and fitted with front fenders and running board, bonnet over motor, dash, side oil lamps and oil tail lamp, battery and tool boxes, battery, coil, gasoline tank, and all necessary tools and extra parts, $3,100.00.

MODEL 64 CHASSIS

KNOX AMBULANCES

USING CHASSIS 64 DESCRIBED ON PAGE 29

Prices, according to specifications, on application

HOLYOKE CITY AMBULANCE

CHICAGO AMBULANCE

icant role in encouraging the diffusion of motor vehicles in the United States. As we have already observed, interest in the automobile was initially engendered by newspaper and magazine coverage of the 1895 Paris-Bordeaux-Paris race; the first American automobile races were sponsored by the *Chicago Times-Herald* and *Cosmopolitan Magazine*; and Charles B. Shanks's press coverage of Alexander Winton's 1899 Cleveland to New York run did much to stimulate popular interest in the automobile. Newspapers were also among the first commercial users of motor vehicles. Probably the first instance of note occurred when two Philadelphia papers, the *North American* and the *Inquirer*, began using automobiles to deliver Sunday editions to the New Jersey shore in 1901.

By the turn of the century, it was obvious that press coverage of the motor vehicle had been well out of proportion to the innovation's apparent importance at the time and that this had been a major stimulus to diffusion. *Automobile*, for instance, stated in August 1900 that "the unprecedented and well nigh incredible rapidity with which the automobile industry has developed . . . is largely due to the fact that every detail of the subject has been popularized by the technical and daily press . . . groundless conservatism and petty jealousy have been foreign elements from the beginning, and could not therefore exert their retarding influence."[15] Two years later, *Outing Magazine* reported that "at present a dozen publications thrive in the interests of the industry, while every newspaper of repute has its automobile department, hundreds of special articles are to be found in periodicals of general circulation, the advertisements of makers and dealers find places in almost every high-class publication, and numerous books have come from the publishers."[16]

Articles on the automobile that appeared in the popular press were overwhelmingly

[15]"Our Correspondence Column," *Automobile*, 2:137 (August 1900).
[16]William J. Lampton, "The Meaning of the Automobile," *Outing Magazine*, 40:696 (September 1902).

favorable. Indeed, one of the major early criticisms of the daily-newspaper coverage voiced by the trade journals and spokesmen for the automobile industry was that it was dangerously overoptimistic. The Oakman Automobile Company's New York representative, for example, told *Motor Age* in 1900: "The lay press is doing a lot of injury to the automobile industry by filling the public full of a lot of inflated nonsense, so that all an automobilist has to do is to get into his wagon, press the button and the vehicle will do the rest until the end of time."[17] The following year *Motor Age* classed as "enemies" of the automobile industry "those newspapers which, without knowledge of the facts, attack manufacturers on the ground that their prices are too high and which encourage the public to expect and demand prices at which it is impossible to make a good vehicle. The ultimate effect of the outcry of such papers will be an attempt by some irresponsible maker to place on the market a machine which will reflect discredit on the whole industry."[18]

Newspaper and magazine coverage of the automobile became so enthusiastic that critics of the motor vehicle began to object. One writer, who considered it necessary to give "a reasonable counterblast to motor eulogies," complained in 1908: "The proceedings of motor clubs are set forth at length. Our magazines teem with 'motor flights' and astonishing tours and articles upon the romance of motoring. All is harmony and enthusiasm. Only at rare intervals does some 'Pro Bono Publico' or 'Indignant Citizen' raise an anonymous howl in the correspondence column of his favorite paper, cursing automobiles and wishing they had never been invented."[19]

The trade journals were overly defensive and frequently misinterpreted, as indications of hostility to the motor vehicle, constructive criticism and legitimate concern

[17]"Foes of the Industry," *Motor Age*, 2:151 (April 12, 1900).
[18]"Your Friends and Your Enemies," ibid., 5:n.p. (October 10, 1901).
[19]Frederick Dwight, "Automobiles: The Other Side of the Shield," *Independent*, 65:1299 (December 3, 1908).

for the public interest voiced by popular periodicals of more general circulation. Too often the specialized automobile periodical was unwilling to recognize that speeding, reckless driving, and accidents were proper matters for the daily newspaper to report and criticize editorially. During a feud with the *New York Times*, for example, *Automobile* objected to the *Times*'s stand against speeding and the utility of the Vanderbilt Cup race. This supposedly made the *Times* "motorphobic," despite the newspaper's editorial statement on June 26, 1905, that "from the first appearance of those [motor] vehicles the *Times* has fully and cordially recognized all their great possibilities for both business and pleasure, and its hostility has been, not to automobiles or auto-mobiling, but to the abuses of them both — not to the manufacturers or owners of automobiles, but to the frequent misapplication of ingenuity of the first and the too frequent lawlessness and discourtesy of the second."[20]

On occasion, the trade journals were apt to make absurdly paranoid statements about so-called motorphobia in the daily press. But upon further investigation and in more rational moments, such comments were generally disavowed. *Motor Age* conducted extensive interviews during 1903 with the managing editors of metro-politan dailies throughout the country and found little newspaper prejudice against the automobile: "Nine-tenths of the editors expressed the belief that the automobile was the vehicle of the future. They professed a desire to deal fairly with automo-bilists, and when speaking of legislation they, in nearly every case, said that their editorial comments in favor of restrictive measures were meant more for the protec-tion of automobiling than for its limitations."[21] Assessments by other trade journals agreed. *Horseless Age* in 1903 found that "fanatical opposition to the automobile is on the whole very rare in this country. The metropolitan dailies occasionally print

[20] "The Same Old *Times*" and "The *Times* Still Unconverted," *Automobile*, 13:22–23 (July 6, 1905).
[21] "Editors on Automobiling," *Motor Age*, 3:6 (May 7, 1903).

strong editorials denouncing speed excesses and careless driving, but the whole press is practically unanimous in recognizing the automobile as a legitimate pleasure vehicle and as destined to a great future in the commercial world." The periodical expressed regret that sensationalistic journalism overplayed reports of "furious driving" but admitted that the newspapers had been "fair minded." It was noted that "the widely circulated and influential publications usually take a broad view of such matters, and the motorphobic articles which occasionally meet our eye generally originate in country papers." The reason given for these "occasional outbursts of country papers" was "the narrowmindedness of their editors, who base their views upon isolated experiences of their own or their neighbors and generalize upon too slender data."[22]

Neither the trade journals nor the automobile manufacturers were seriously concerned about the many seemingly hostile cartoons and jokes about the automobile that appeared in popular periodicals of the day. Rather, automobile cartoons and jokes were looked upon as being truly humerous and ultimately beneficial to the diffusion of the motor vehicle. *Life*, the most important humor magazine of the period, printed many cartoons and jokes based on the presumption that the motor vehicle was either dangerous or unreliable. But the advertising manager of *Life* defended the magazine's policy of publishing so much automobile humor on the basis that it stimulated the automobile industry by helping to bring an automobile consciousness to the public. The indications are that many manufacturers agreed. Henry Ford liked and encouraged jokes about his product to the point that he collected and published them in a book, *Ford Smiles*. Peerless went so far as to advertise its 1904 car by a series of cartoons showing Buster Brown driving an automobile with reckless disregard for the safety and rights of other users of the road.

[22] "Motorphobia," *Horseless Age*, 12:348–349 (September 30, 1903).

What antagonized the automobile interests most about the lay press was that the daily papers exhibited a growing (and legitimate) concern about the abuses of motorists and automobile accidents. The motor vehicle undoubtedly was given so much attention by the newspapers in the first place because it made for interesting and exciting copy with broad popular appeal. Quite naturally then, the newspapers could also have been expected to play up accounts of accidents that had sensationalistic news value and helped to sell papers. As more motor vehicles came into use, the automobile accident rate inevitably rose; responding to public interest and concern, the press appeared, from the standpoint of the motorist whose reputation and "sport" seemed at stake, to become motorphobic.

Reluctant to admit the need for stronger laws and law enforcement to curb the irresponsible motorist, automobile interests urged the launching of a propaganda campaign to win over the newspapers. *Automobile* recommended "a campaign of education among the newspaper men," consisting of demonstration rides sponsored by automobile clubs. The periodical found "nothing ulterior in the motives of a club that undertakes a campaign along the line suggested — it is merely placing the moulders of public opinion in a position to weigh the subject with unbiased minds." As an additional method of persuasion, *Automobile* went on to suggest that "the club should make a practice of furnishing a good news 'copy' to the papers. Any one who is a good source of news is beloved by the reporters and sporting and city editors."[23]

In areas other than the emphasis given to speeding, reckless driving, and automobile accidents, close cooperation between automobile interests and the popular press was evident. Lacking the requisite technical expertise to interpret developments themselves, reporters and editors had necessarily turned to the automotive expert for information. The automobile manufacturer, the automobile clubs, and the trade

[23] "Unfavorable Newspaper Influence and How to Counteract It," *Automobile*, 13:544 (November 9, 1905).

journals, realizing the value of favorable publicity, were eager to oblige. Consequently, a large proportion of the information on the automobile that appeared in newspapers and popular magazines was either written or influenced by ardent automobilists. It is unquestionable that this in no small part accounted for the overwhelmingly favorable image of the motor vehicle in the popular press of the day.

On May 13, 1897, Colonel Albert A. Pope initiated the custom of the press interview as an established part of introducing new models of automobiles to the public. Pope invited representatives of the press to a private showing of his first electric cars, allowed them to operate the vehicles, and supplied pictures for publication. The press interview was soon institutionalized and became more elaborate. Manufacturers did not hesitate to bring reporters long distances at company expense to be entertained and given a preview of new models in the hope that "free" publicity would follow. Alexander Winton, who after his experience with Shanks remained impressed with the value of favorable newspaper coverage, was one of the more conspicuous manufacturers in his attempts to court the press. He was commended by *Automobile* for his "characteristic enterprise and liberality," for example, when in January 1904 he brought representatives of both the trade and the lay press from the East and Chicago to the Winton factory at Cleveland in a special Pullman with a private dining car attached. A banquet was held after the reporters had been shown around the Winton plant. The result was "as well fed and happy a lot of newspaper men as ever were assembled . . . with the single regret that Winton excursions did not come every Saturday."[24]

Trade journals undertook to serve as sources of information about the automobile for periodicals of more general circulation. The contributions of *Motor Age* and *Automobile* were most notable. Louis R. Smith and W. J. Morgan, New York reporters

[24] "Journalistic Excursion to Cleveland Factory," ibid., 10:59–60 (January 16, 1904).

for *Motor Age*, made what was probably the first attempt to form a press bureau for automobile news at a 1901 endurance run sponsored by the Automobile Club of America. Smith and Morgan took it upon themselves to interpret events for the reporters from the daily papers who were present so that incidents that seemed at face value unfavorable to some manufacturers would be seen in proper perspective. They also acted as correspondents for three dailies. But the most ambitious attempt to found an automobile press bureau occurred in January 1907, when the Technical Press Bureau, under the management of Harry W. Perry, associate editor of *Automobile*, was established in New York. The goal of this organization was "to supply articles on the design, construction, sale and use of automobiles to the automobile and popular press. . . . with a corps of experienced writers to prepare such matter upon demand, so that the requirements of an editor in any phase of the subject can be filled in short notice."[25]

Automobile clubs often engaged in similar activities. For example, in 1907 the recently formed Missouri Automobile Association announced plans "to dispel the prejudice which exists in the rural districts against motoring by the dissemination of accurate information concerning the power-propelled vehicle and the men who operate it." The club's major tactic was to set up "a bureau where all motor literature printed in this country. . . will be maintained. That part of it which we think will be most interesting and instructive to the country reader will be sent out to the weekly newspapers with requests to print as much of it as possible. We shall endeavor to establish friendly relations with the country press, so that we will get proper treatment."[26]

But there were definite limits upon the type and amount of influence that could be

[25]"A Technical News Bureau Established," ibid., 16:52 (January 10, 1907).
[26]"Ink to Educate Them," *Motor Age*, 11:9 (May 9, 1907).

exerted on the American press. European journalistic ethics had often allowed the automobile manufacturer to purchase outright favorable publicity for his car in news articles. The endorsement of the American press could not be so crudely gained. Regarding French journalistic practice, *Motor Age* reported: "As to the importance of the Parisian press eulogies it is to be regretted that acquaintance with journalistic methods in the French metropolis compels the observation that press notices . . . are broadly for sale. It is customary to hire certain writers who make a specialty of this kind of work to furnish signed articles in such manner that only the initiated can distinguish them from legitimate news matter."[27]

However, newspapers and magazines in the United States refused to tout specific makes of cars in news articles: "It is one of the unwritten laws of the daily paper office that stories relative to automobiling must not contain the names of the automobiles figuring in the news occurrences. The daily paper refuses to print words, phrases or sentences which in any way possess advertising value. It is a good press agent, indeed, which can get the large dailies of the large cities to publish a story in which appear the names of the cars about which the story is written."[28] This rule did not seem to apply to the names of foreign cars, which did not advertise extensively in American periodicals. Consequently, the Panhard came to be the favorite make of car in the magazine fiction of the day.

American periodicals avoided the endorsement of specific makes of cars for understandable reasons. More dependent than their European counterparts upon advertising revenue, American periodicals could not afford the space to give free plugs to all in news articles; neither could they favor one or a few advertisers. Since a large number of companies were apt to advertise motor vehicles in any given periodical,

[27] "About Imported Enthusiasm," ibid., 1:129–130 (October 24, 1899).
[28] "Attitude of the Daily Press," ibid., 8:6 (August 31, 1905).

no single account was overly important; therefore none could demand special consideration. The risk inherent in appearing to favor unduly the car of any advertiser was that one might antagonize dozens of others.

Finally, the quantity and type of coverage given the automobile by American newspapers and magazines were undoubtedly not directly influenced very much by consideration of the interests of advertisers, despite the importance of advertising revenue. Before 1905, periodicals received little automobile advertising compared with that from the horse-and-carriage trade, yet the predominant attitude of the press was that the automobile would soon displace the horse. As the amount of automobile advertising increased, so too did the publication of sensationalistic reports and editorials denouncing the excesses of motorists and calling public attention to automobile accidents. The total amount of automobile advertising carried by any popular periodical was simply not appreciable enough yet to be used as an effective sanction on editorial policy.

Thus American popular periodicals maintained an enthusiastic attitude toward the motor vehicle and were willing to be advised by automobile interests on matters requiring technical expertise. But the press still insisted that automobile speeding, recklessness, and accidents were legitimate topics for sensationalistic reports and editorial comment. The questionable complaint of motorists that this constituted "motorphobia" was finally ended once automobile ownership became sufficiently widespread and the motor vehicle securely enough established that motorists were no longer a defensive minority.

5

Automobile Clubs

The automobile club became the most important institution championing the diffusion of the automobile in the United States. Voluntary associations of motorists propagandized to encourage a favorable image of the automobile and automobilists; lobbied for liberal motor vehicle legislation and defended automobile owners in both civil and criminal suits; worked for the improvement of streets and highways; organized races, tours, tests, and exhibits; provided storage and repair facilities; and contributed to the development of mechanical expertise among automobile drivers and mechanics. Since these activities are dealt with in other chapters, our immediate concerns will be the origin of the automobile club and the changes in its membership policies and functions.[1]

Beginnings

The first automobile club in the United States was the American Motor League. Charles B. King suggested its organization in a letter of October 8, 1895, to the *Chicago Times-Herald*, and it was founded on November 1, 1895, shortly before the *Times-Herald* race. Charter members included King, the Duryeas, Elwood P. Haynes, and several other industrial pioneers. This attempt to organize American motorists was premature, and the American Motor League failed to get off the ground.

By the turn of the century, the number of automobile owners in a few big cities was sufficient to warrant the formation of several local automobile clubs. Drawing their membership almost exclusively from the affluent and socially prominent, these first clubs placed great emphasis upon social functions. Application for the state charter for the Chicago Automobile Club was made in December 1899 by J. Ogden Armour, E. Walter Herrick, Samuel Insull, F. K. Pulsifer, and Andrew R. Sheriff. The Auto-

---

[1]Although it is somewhat sketchy, probably the best general account of the rise of the automobile club in the United States is contained in Bellamy Partridge, *Fill 'er Up: The Story of Fifty Years of Motoring* (New York: McGraw-Hill, 1952), especially chap. 8, "The Coming of the A.A.A."

mobile Club of America, organized in New York City a few months before, soon was said to have more millionaire members than any social club in the world. August Belmont, Alfred G. Vanderbilt, Henry Clay Frick, John W. Gates, A. W. Rossiter, J. F. O'Shaughnessy, and Frederick Southtack were all admitted at one 1902 meeting. The ACA fully lived up to its reputation as "an ultra-fashionable coterie of millionaires, who have taken up the new and expensive fad of auto-locomotion and banded themselves together for its pursuit and the incidental notoriety attributed to all the functions of upper swelldom."[2]

Automobile Club of America

The Automobile Club of America was founded at the Waldorf-Astoria in New York City on June 7, 1899, by nine prominent New York automobilists and soon became the most powerful as well as the first successfully organized local automobile club in the United States. At its first regular meeting on October 16, 1899, the membership committee reported that 85 applications for membership had been received, 35 of which had been accepted. The ACA constitution provided for four classes of membership—honorary, life, active, and associate (that is, nonresident). Honorary members were limited to 25 and active members to 400, but no limits were set for the number of associate or life members. Committees were soon formed to initiate action on virtually every matter of importance having to do with motor vehicles.

  The club at first provided minimal facilities for members at its clubrooms on the second floor of the Plaza Bank Building at Fifth Avenue and Fifty-eighth Street. The apparent reason was that "the millionaire and socially prominent contingent which gives the club its standing as an adjunct to swelldom enjoys membership in the Metropolitan, Union, and other leading social clubs, and asks naught of the ACA in the way

[2] "The Automobile Club of America," *Motor Age*, 2:553 (June 28, 1900).

of club facilities." But the majority of members were comparatively less affluent, upper-middle-class individuals who soon began to agitate for a clubhouse with bar, restaurant, and garage to justify the cost of membership. One club official explained in behalf of this faction late in 1902 that "exclusiveness should not be carried to the extreme and . . . if the club is to continue to be a power in automobiling the prominence can best be maintained by a club that shall offer club facilities which will attract all desirable followers of the automobile. Were they given club facilities there are scores of automobilists to whom the hundred dollar initiation fee and the fifty dollar annual dues would be no bar to joining."[3] Not until 1905, however, was a resolution to build such a clubhouse passed. The new clubhouse, an eight-story building on West Fifty-fourth Street between Broadway and Eighth Avenue, was finally completed in April 1907, several years after the new facilities could hope to attract new members. By then, adequate garage facilities were available to the general public, and automobile ownership had become far too widespread to serve as the basis for an exclusive social club.

Through its membership roster of nationally prominent figures, the Automobile Club of America expected to transcend being merely another local organization of motorists. The New York club had ambitions to be the national voice and conscience of motorists. One of its later presidents explained: "The Automobile Club of America was formed, as its name suggests, as a national organization . . . with its headquarters in New York City. It was promptly accorded recognition by the national automobile clubs of France and Great Britain, and has always taken a prominent part in national and even international affairs pertaining to automobiling. . . . through its various committees it touches the interests of automobile owners and builders in so many

[3] "A.C.A. Members Propose Club House," ibid., 2:7 (December 4, 1902).

Plate 22. The Automobile Club
of America clubhouse and garage.
Courtesy Free Library of Philadelphia.

CLUB HOUSE AND GARAGE
54TH STREET WEST OF BROADWAY
NEW YORK

Plate 23.   Main assembly hall of
the Automobile Club of America
clubhouse. Courtesy Free Library
of Philadelphia.

directions that its influence has been felt throughout the country."[4] News of the formation of the American Automobile Association, a national federation of local clubs, in 1902 was received with enthusiasm in New York City "when it became known that the Automobile Club of America had been practically presented with supreme power in regard to the affairs of the new body by its holding not only the presidency, the treasuryship and the secretaryship, but also a position on the board of directors." To New York's self-appointed automobile elite, this demonstrated "that those who attended the convention favored a proper recognition of the New York Club's prestige and leadership."[5]

Big-City Clubs

The pretentions of the ACA proved unrealistic in a democratic, localistic society. Speaking out for many motorists, the editors of *Motor World* with foresight declared in January 1901 that, "We regret to see a decided tendency on the part of some American automobile clubs to declare themselves organizations of the elect; self-constituted arbiters of all automobilism and an aristocracy or autocracy to whose sacred membership no man without cerulian sanguinaceousness or millionairish pretentions is to be eligible. . . . Aristocracy never has survived a transplanting to American soil, and this automobile club idea will not be an exception to the rule of failure. No club, no matter how rich or exclusive its membership may be, can arrogate to itself the right to pose in any way as supreme ruler of the present or future of the motor vehicle."[6]

The hegemony of the ACA was challenged by a mushrooming of local automobile clubs throughout the United States. At least twenty-two separate local organizations

[4] Colgate Hoyt, "The Automobile Club of America," *Motor*, 8:50 (June 1907).
[5] *Motor Age*, 1:7 (March 13, 1902).
[6] "Blood and Boodle," *Motor World*, 1:246 (January 10, 1901).

had been formed by early 1901. Among those operative by then in the ACA's own Middle Atlantic regional bailiwick were the Long Island Automobile Club, the Automobile Club of Brooklyn, the North Jersey Automobile Club, the New Jersey Automobile Club, the Philadelphia Automobile Club, the Pennsylvania Automobile Club, the Automobile Club of Rochester, the Buffalo Automobile Club, and the Troy Automobile Club. By early 1904 nearly one hundred automobile clubs were active in the United States. It was "as difficult to find a number of motorists in one locality who have not formed a club, as it is to find an individual motorist who is not a member of some such body."[7] These clubs could not be expected to accept passively a secondary role under the dominance of an elite group of New York City automobilists. They collectively represented a much broader constituency of interests and the overwhelming majority of the nation's motorists. Moreover, most problems were local in scope, and in solving local problems a club had to depend almost entirely upon its own resources.

The most obvious early rivals for the position of national leadership assumed by the ACA were probably the Massachusetts Automobile Club and the Chicago Automobile Club. Both clubs were founded early, located in principal cities, and boasted of illustrious membership rosters. They were also well ahead of the ACA in providing elaborate clubhouse facilities for their members. However, neither exhibited as much aggressive drive and ability to mobilize resources for practical accomplishment.

The Massachusetts Automobile Club received its charter in Boston on October 31, 1900, and soon absorbed the New England Automobile Club, an early rival with whom it had differed over the trivial issue of a suburban versus a downtown location for a clubhouse. The three-story MAC clubhouse on Boylston Street in Boston, the first of its kind in the United States, opened on January 1, 1902, and featured a garage

[7] "Automobile Club Life and Work in the United States," *Horseless Age*, 13:196–197 (February 17, 1904).

for the storage of members' cars, club parlors, billiard rooms, dining rooms, and a large repair room. Facilities were greatly expanded in 1904, when the clubhouse was enlarged to three times its original size. However, by 1906 the MAC was unable to maintain leadership even over the local automobile movement. The Bay State Automobile Association, founded in January 1905, soon proved to be an energetic competitor, opening its five-story clubhouse at 283 Delmonico Street with a membership of 600, almost double that of the MAC.

Reasons for the failure of the Massachusetts Automobile Club, after a promising start, to assume a more prominent role in the automobile club movement are not far to seek. The MAC remained snobbish to the point of neglecting public relations almost entirely, disdained attempting to influence motor vehicle legislation, and rather exclusively emphasized social functions and providing services for a small, select body of members. President Frank E. Peabody reported in 1907: "The club has taken little active part in the promoting of automobile legislation or in organizing racing events. . . . it has always taken a moderate and conservative view of its duties and is perhaps less indebted to the press than any other club of its scope and kind." Great continuity in the leadership of the MAC is evident: Peabody was only its third president. Active membership as late as mid-1907 was still conservatively limited to 350, and 35 applications were then on a waiting list. Peabody explained that "the main objects of the club are, as may be gathered, social, and it is intended primarily as a general rendezvous and headquarters for the members, who are all private car owners."[8]

The Chicago Automobile Club, on the other hand, suffered less from exclusivity in its early years than from apathy, factionalism, and ineffective leadership. First incorporated in December 1899, the CAC had to be organized anew in August 1900

[8] Frank E. Peabody, "Massachusetts Automobile Club," *Motor*, 8:56 (July 1907).

because the club had initially "failed to meet the expectations of its promoters. Its organizers, though among the most enthusiastic devotees of automobilism, were too actively engaged in business to spare the necessary time to push the club to the front and it remained active in name only." The reorganized club, following the practice of the ACA, limited the number of active members to 400 and allowed an unlimited number of associate memberships. Provision was also made for 35 honorary memberships — to include ex officio the president of the United States, the governor of Illinois, and the mayor of Chicago. In a shrewd move, five "advisory" memberships were created for the Chicago commissioner of public works, who controlled city motor vehicle registration, and the members of the Chicago Board of Examination for automobile drivers' licenses. The CAC's comparative lack of exclusivity is indicated both by its welcoming representatives of the automobile industry and retail trade as members and by the temporary suspension of its initiation fee during 1901–1902 in order to attract members. Despite these efforts and still another change in leadership, the CAC had attracted only 60 active members by early 1902. By the end of that year, it was evident that "club runs have not been entirely successful. . . . Especially, no plan of entertainment has been found of sufficient interest to regularly draw good attendances."[9] A fine clubhouse replete with all the facilities a motorist could wish for was purchased at 243 Michigan Avenue, but the CAC still had only 150 active and 25 associate members at the beginning of 1903. Factionalism within the club became so rampant that another president was forced to resign. Only after 1904, under the leadership of John Farson and Ira M. Cobe, did the CAC patch up its internal dissensions and become, far too late, sufficiently energetic to be capable of any national influence whatever. Even then the club's emphasis remained on the provision of services that were fast coming to be considered superfluous. A new, luxurious

[9]"The Chicago Automobile Club," *Motor Age*, 2:1 (November 20, 1902).

six-story clubhouse was opened in Plymouth Place just south of Jackson Boulevard in the spring of 1907, necessitating an increase in dues and initiation fees that had previously seemed an unwarranted expense to most of Chicago's middle-class motorists.

The Chicago Automobile Club's early difficulties were not unique. Many big-city automobile clubs whose membership rosters boasted names of socially prominent and affluent automobilists found that only a handful of these select people were willing to assume responsibilities for club activities and that the majority of local motorists remained apathetic about the club's existence. As *Motor Age* complained in January 1903, "Clubs flourish — on paper — in many large cities and some small ones. But, in fact, there is not a genuine automobile club in the United States. . . . A few — a very few — enthusiasts carry on the work. The rooms or clubhouses are practically deserted."[10]

Local Clubs

The prominent early big-city clubs generally failed to realize the need to attract as many members as possible. They also failed to see that the social activities and elaborate clubhouse facilities, which necessitated both a restricted membership and high fees, would cease to attract many motorists once automobile ownership became fairly widespread, motoring came to be considered utilitarian rather than a "sport," and the public garage became an established institution. Developments by 1905 made clear that a club's influence depended more on the quantity than on the quality of its members; most motorists were more interested in practical accomplishments than in social functions and storage facilities for their cars.

Few local automobile clubs were more successful by 1905 than the New Jersey

[10] "Personal Interest," ibid., 3:4 (January 8, 1903).

Automobile and Motor Club. Organized at Newark in 1903 for the mutual protection of motorists from legal harassment, this club increased its membership to 450 in two years, although it had no clubhouse. The New Jersey Automobile and Motor Club gained recognition for the victories scored by its attorneys in several court cases and for its ability to influence the passage of model motor vehicle legislation in New Jersey. Similarly, the Automobile Club of California, founded as the San Francisco Automobile Club at the Cliff House in 1900, enjoyed a boom in membership in early 1905 despite its lack of clubhouse facilities. The club had an excellent record of accomplishment in influencing motor vehicle legislation, local road improvement, and community relations. The Chicago Motor Club, organized in August 1906 with solely utilitarian goals, no clubhouse, and no social features, also experienced rapid growth in both number of members and influence in the automobile movement.

The formula for a successful association of local motorists was first and best exemplified by the militant Automobile Club of Buffalo, New York. It neared its temporary and flexible limit of 500 members only a year after it took over from the more exclusive Buffalo Automobile Club in June 1903 and welcomed to membership "anyone interested in motoring." William H. Hotchkiss, president of both the Automobile Club of Buffalo and the New York State Automobile Association, explained in 1904: "Such another organization does not, perhaps, exist. As yet it has no home, though one is preparing; its dues are nominal . . . it rarely meets, yet it has wielded an influence for the good of pleasure-motoring . . . that is far reaching, not the least exploit being its recent agitation for a state fair motor vehicle law." Rather than being a social club, the Automobile Club of Buffalo was "a rallying point for those causes that motorists favor. . . . Its mission is selfish, not social. So continuing, Buffalo will continue enthusiastic."[11]

[11] William H. Hotchkiss, "The Motor-Mad Bisons of Buffalo," *Motor*, 2:27 (May 1904).

The elite character, formal organization, and social and service functions of the early metropolitan automobile clubs were particularly ill suited to associations of motorists in smaller cities and rural areas, where a local club had to draw from a wide cross section of the population to recruit even a modicum of members and could not afford to build a clubhouse. *Automobile* pointed out in 1903: "A formal automobile organization is no easy matter to keep up outside of the leading centers. The need is rather for some different sort of local association, better suited to the semirural environment and less expensive to a smaller [and less affluent] membership."[12] The small-city automobile club thus developed into a democratic organization with limited practical goals. Reports from club secretaries received by *Automobile* in 1905 are illustrative. Members of the Bloomington (Illinois) Automobile Club agreed that "in order to give our club an excuse for existence, it should aim to accomplish, and should accomplish, some definite result. . . . in the very nature of the club, it could not very well become a social affair." The 64 members of the Rockford (Illinois) Automobile Club represented "all interests from bankers to clerks," as did the Automobile Club of Wayne County (Richmond), Indiana, which was "composed of two professors, one rector, three railway engineers, one broker, four doctors, two students, seven manufacturers, one farmer, three machinists, three clerks, one bookkeeper, and two bank directors."[13]

National Organization

As early as 1901, many automobilists began to feel that a national association of local automobile clubs to deal with matters of more than local concern would be beneficial. Still others believed that the large number of motorists unattached to any local club

[12] "Informal Local Situations," *Automobile*, 8:576 (May 30, 1903).
[13] "Automobile Club Movement in America," ibid., 12:720–724 (June 15, 1905).

might be induced to join a national body with an open membership and only nominal dues, one that would eschew social functions to concentrate solely upon practical problems affecting all users of automobiles. The Automobile Club of America, the best organized and most influential local club at this time, circulated a plan for affiliation. The response indicated that most clubs favored affiliation but were reluctant to give the ACA any position that would ensure its continuing domination and control over the automobile club movement in the United States.

Two competing national automobile associations emerged in Chicago within four days, March 3–6, 1902: the American Automobile Association (AAA) and the American Motor League (AML). On February 21, 1902, five local automobile clubs — the Automobile Club of America, the Philadelphia Automobile Club, the Long Island Automobile Club, the Rhode Island Automobile Club, and the Chicago Automobile Club — sent out a circular letter calling for a meeting in Chicago on March 3 and 4 to discuss affiliation. Delegates from eight clubs consequently met and founded the American Automobile Association. Then on March 6, 1902, at a meeting in the Chicago Coliseum, with Charles E. Duryea presiding as president, the American Motor League was revived by some of its original (1895) organizers and representatives of the League of American Wheelmen and the National Cycling Association.

Conceived as a national organization that would attempt to form branches in the states, the American Motor League tried to enlist individual motorists as members. The AML constitution welcomed any "man or woman 18 years of age and over, of good moral character and respectable standing" to become a member for a nominal $1 initiation fee and $1 annual dues. It stated that the AML goals were "the advancement of the interests and the use of motor vehicles . . . by reports and discussions of the mechanical features, by education and agitation, by directing and correcting legislation, by mutual defense of the rights of said vehicles . . . by assisting in the work of constructing better roads, better sanitary and humane conditions, and in any other proper way which will assist to hasten the use and add to the value of motor vehicles as a means of transit." The officers consisted of a president, three vice-presidents, and a secretary, treasurer, and club attorney, "to be elected by the active membership," and an official board of state consuls who were to be elected in states with over 100 members and appointed by the president in others. Standing committees were also elected to oversee membership, legislation, finance, highways, tours and runs, and racing. Handicapped from the outset both by lack of funds and prestige and by weak organizational structure, the AML never developed a position of influence comparable to that of its rival, the American Automobile Association.

Unlike the AML, the American Automobile Association began as an association of local automobile clubs. At the AAA organizing convention, opinion was at first about equally divided on whether or not to admit motorists unattached to any local club as individual members. Some delegates, aware of the impending revival of the AML, worried about competition from a rival association organized on an individual basis. H. H. Rice, a delegate from the Automobile Club of Rhode Island, argued: "There are cases where clubs cannot be formed. We will gain enthusiasm from a big individual membership. We do not want competition from an individual league. Should we limit our power?" Winthrop E. Scarritt, the ACA representative who was to become first president of the AAA, expressed the position that won out: "The automobile microbus is spreading in all directions and individual membership will weaken the influence of a club federation. I am heartily opposed to the idea. Let individuals in the absence of local clubs get a hustle and then join us."[14]

The AAA constitution provided for local automobile clubs to join the association for an initiation fee of $10 for each club and $3 for every active, associate, and life

[14] "Birth of the American Automobile Association," *Motor Age*, 1:39 (March 6, 1902).

member on its roster. The affiliated clubs were to be represented at the AAA annual and special meetings by delegates entitled to cast one vote for each active, associate, and life member in their respective clubs. This democratic principle gave the elite ACA an initial but ephemeral preponderance of representation among the national officers and of influence upon policy because the New York City club at this time had a disproportionately large membership roster relative to the combined membership strength of the few other local clubs that had formed the AAA. However, it was inevitable that, as more local clubs joined the association and other local clubs became less restrictive than the ACA about admitting new members, the power of the New York club within the AAA would wane; control and policy would come to reflect a broader spectrum of interests, especially the interests of the middle-class automobilist. Officers provided for in the AAA constitution were a president, three vice-presidents, a treasurer, a paid secretary, and a seven-man board of directors that was to meet monthly. The objectives of the AAA were stated to be "securing rational legislation . . . to protect the interests of owners and users of all forms of self-propelled pleasure vehicles. . . . To promote and encourage in all ways the construction and maintenance of good roads and the improvement of existing highways, and generally to maintain a national organization devoted to automobilism."

  The rapid decline of conservative influence in the AAA became evident in June 1903, when the exclusive club basis of affiliation was dropped at a meeting in New York and the constitution was amended to provide for the admission of unattached, individual motorists. This new "open door" policy declared that "individual owners and those in any way interested in the sport shall be eligible." Individual members would be entitled to one vote at any regular or special AAA meeting and, as in the AML, would pay a nominal $1 initiation fee and $1 annual dues. *Motor World* further reported: "It was the sentiment of the meeting that the adoption of these amendments should be followed up by the institution of an aggressive recruiting campaign, and it was resolved to issue blanks for membership application and distribute them everywhere."[15]

The first few years of the American Automobile Association's existence proved to be trying ones, marked by little practical accomplishment. An attempt was made to amalgamate the faltering AML into the AAA during the spring of 1904, but the two national associations could not reach agreement on the question of representation in club elections, and the proposed merger was abandoned in July. Dissension also developed within the AAA, and several officials resigned. By early 1906, dissatisfaction with the AAA's accomplishments was rampant, and local clubs began to withdraw. Only the racing committee had shown signs of activity, and here a quarrel over the control of racing had developed with the ACA. Since motor vehicle legislation and road improvement were matters for state and local governments, the national association had been able to do little in these areas beyond what aggressive local clubs could do on their own. Consequently, the local clubs began to believe that they had "received little in return for their money." *Horseless Age* felt "it is no wonder that the practical minded members are becoming dissatisfied."[16] The Pennsylvania clubs withdrew first, and by early 1908 they had been joined by many of the Massachusetts, New York, and Missouri clubs. A particularly notable withdrawal was that of the ACA on March 12, 1908, at a meeting of the New York State Automobile Association in Buffalo.

Motor Age reported that the withdrawal of the ACA from the AAA was "the culmination of a series of differences that have existed for some time, with a strong feeling of unpleasantness, between the New York Club and the state body of the national association." Having progressively lost power in the AAA to faster-growing clubs

[15] "Admits Individuals," *Motor World*, 6:374 (June 4, 1903).
[16] "Disintegration of the A.A.A.," *Horseless Age*, 17:471–472 (March 28, 1906).

in smaller cities, the ACA had been "chafing under the restraint of the national and state body with which it is affiliated." The immediate cause of dissension was an attempt by the ACA to undermine a legislative proposal for $2 to $11 motor vehicle registration fees backed by the New York State Automobile Association. Representing a much wealthier constituency than the thirty-four other New York local clubs and wishing to increase state revenues for highways as much as possible, the ACA opposed the bill on the basis that the recommended fees were "too cheap for a motorcar, and . . . [they] would stand for a yearly tax of from $4 to $40, according to the weight of the car." After the ACA resignation was offered and accepted, Oliver A. Quagle of Albany, president of the New York State Automobile Association, declared on behalf of the state's less affluent automobile owners "that before any law is enacted taxing a motorcar any $40 a year, it will have to pass over his dead body."[17]

The withdrawal of the ACA thus clearly drew the issue of whether the AAA was to reflect the interests of the New York City upper-class automobilist or the interests of the great majority of middle-class motorists. William H. Hotchkiss of Buffalo, by then president of the American Automobile Association, gave an unequivocal answer: "I do not regret the resignation, but welcome it. It is high time that motorists understand whether a mere name adopted in the infancy of the motor vehicle in this country, and which has since become a misnomer, entitles any local club in any city, no matter how great, to lord it over hundreds of other clubs in other parts of the country. . . . whether the American Automobile Association represents those motorists or whether they are to be represented by a small clique of gentlemen who manage a local social club. I, therefore, hail the issue and have no doubt of the results."[18]

[17]"A.C.A. Is Out of A.A.A.," *Motor Age*, 13:11 (March 19, 1908).
[18]Ibid.

   The decline in power of the ACA was inherent in its inability to respond to changes in the character of the American automobile movement. The New York club had been unable either to absorb as members or to control the increasingly larger number of middle-class motorists dispersed throughout the United States. As early as December 1903, the officers of the ACA became concerned enough to announce their intention "to make that organization more democratic and extend its sphere of activity." The ACA faced the danger of "lapsing into the role of a mere social organization," and the fear was that "it would soon cease to be a factor in the automobile movement."[19] The limit on the number of members was consequently raised several times — to 1,000 active and 300 associate members by 1907 — but there was still a long waiting list of applicants. In a last-ditch attempt to recruit members from among the many middle-class motorists throughout the country, without having to grant them corresponding clubhouse privileges, the ACA in 1908 initiated a new class of members, called "subscribers to the bureau of tours." The number of active members was again raised in 1909 — to 1,600. But these measures were not sufficient to give the club a broad popular basis of appeal or support. Despite its attempts at democratization, the ACA had retained its identification as a millionaires' social club. *Harper's Weekly* pointed out in January 1909, for example, that "prominent among the active members may be mentioned Colonel John Jacob Astor, Cornelius Vanderbilt, George J. Gould, William Rockefeller, E. H. Harriman, John T. Havemeyer, August Belmont, C. K. G. Billings, P. E. Collier, Paul D. Cravath, Hon. Chauncy M. Depew, J. B. Duke, Alfred I. du Pont, Stuyvessant Fish, John H. Flagler, John W. Gates, Robert Goelet, and others."[20]

   Notwithstanding the ACA's excellent record of practical accomplishment within

[19]"To Be More Democratic," *Horseless Age*, 12:614 (December 16, 1903).
[20] Harry W. Perry, "Motor Clubs of Five Nations," *Harper's Weekly*, 53:13–14 (January 2, 1909).

New York State, the club had failed to transplant the European pattern of highly centralized control over a national automobile movement by an elite group of automobilists, exemplified by the Automobile Club of France, in the American environment. To exercise effective national influence in the United States, any automobile association had to reckon with the predominant democratic ethos of American culture and the facts of widespread automobile ownership and our federal political system, with its decentralized governmental powers. Under these conditions, a national automobile association in the United States had to be able to accommodate a mass membership at low cost, which in turn meant providing only very limited and depersonalized services, and it had to have an organizational form that would allow considerable initiative and power to remain at the local and state levels. Moreover, once automobile ownership became fairly widespread, there was considerably less need for the status conferred or lobbying pressure that could be exerted by a club membership roster of prominent names. As *Horseless Age* pointed out in 1908, "Now, both automobile legislation and road building are entirely state matters, and the majority of motorists, therefore, do not see how a national association can accomplish much in these directions. . . . Also, as the use of the automobile is becoming general, the inducements for its users to combine and to defend their rights are no longer as strong as when the machines were used only by a small class."[21]

The American Automobile Association, a loose federation of local and state clubs, began to mend its fences and expand as these inevitable limitations upon the role of a national automobile club in the United States came to be accepted. On September 16, 1908, the AAA reached a compromise with the ACA in which the New York club agreed that it would not encourage other local clubs to withdraw from the AAA. The serious financial loss suffered in the large-scale withdrawal of local clubs was

[21] "The Finances of the American Automobile Association," *Horseless Age*, 22:831 (December 9, 1908).

bridged by an agreement with the National Association of Automobile Manufacturers whereby the trade association contributed $5,000 to the AAA treasury in return for three seats on its board of directors, thus establishing a firm relationship between the AAA and the automobile industry. In addition, the annual dues of individual members were raised to $3. A number of new clubs were also admitted, most being dominated by local automobile dealers who were primarily interested in obtaining sanctions for local races. Growth was marked during 1908–1909. At the AAA annual meeting in November 1909 it was reported that membership had increased 50 percent during the past year and that six new state associations had been formed. Total AAA membership was 25,759, representing thirty state associations that comprised 225 affiliated clubs. Thus by 1910 the AAA had emerged as the principal spokesman for the American motorist.

6

Regulating the Motor Vehicle

No issue affecting the automobile stirred more controversy at the time or has since been more misunderstood than early attempts to regulate the motor vehicle. Regulation pitted the motorists against the general public, who, appalled by speeding and reports of accidents in the daily press, demanded that government take action. Contrary to popular myth, however, early motor vehicle legislation appears in retrospect to have been extremely reasonable. All things considered, little prejudice against the automobile is evident in either early legislative enactments or their enforcement.

At first the few laws regulating the ownership and use of horse-drawn vehicles were merely extended to motor vehicles as well, but, from 1900 on, the passage of special motor vehicle legislation became increasingly necessary. The movement toward regulation of the motor vehicle began at the municipal level about the turn of the century. Local automobile ordinances were passed, which almost invariably required registration, including the display of an identifying numbered tag on the vehicle, so that an automobilist guilty of speeding or reckless driving could be more easily apprehended. After 1903, state laws requiring the registration of motor vehicles rapidly came to replace and supersede this unwieldy and inconvenient system of municipal prerogative.

Automobile Registration

Table 6.1 shows the years in which motor vehicle registration was initiated in the various states and the type of registration required.[1] These data reveal that the first state to require all motor vehicles to be registered was New York in 1901 and that a movement toward compulsory state motor vehicle registration first became evident in 1903, when eight states followed New York's lead. Seventeen additional states

[1] For a general history of the registration fee, see also James W. Martin, "The Motor Vehicle Registration License," *Bulletin of the National Tax Association*, 12:193–208 (April 1927).

Table 6.1 Year of First State Motor Vehicle Registrations, 1901–1921

State	1901	1902	1903	1904	1905	1906	1907	1908	1909	1910	1911	1912	1913	1914	1915	1916	1917	1918	1919	1920	1921
Alabama			P	—	—	—	—	—	—	—	A	—	—	—	—	—	—	—	—	—	—
Arizona												A	—	—	—	—	—	—	—	—	—
Arkansas											A	—	—	—	—	—	—	—	—	—	—
California					P	—	—	—	—	—	—	—	—	A	—	—	—	—	—	—	—
Colorado												A	—	—	—	—	—	—	—	—	—
Connecticut			P	—	—	—	—	—	—	A	—	—	—	—	—	—	—	—	—	—	—
Delaware					P	—	A	—	—	—	—	—	—	—	—	—	—	—	—	—	—
Florida					P	—	—	—	—	—	CA	—	—	—	—	—	—	SA	—	—	—
Georgia										A	—	—	—	—	—	—	—	—	—	—	—
Idaho												A	—	—	—	—	—	—	—	—	—
Illinois							P	—	A	—	—	—	—	—	—	—	—	—	—	—	—
Indiana					P	—	—	—	—	—	—	A	—	—	—	—	—	—	—	—	—
Iowa				P	—	—	—	—	—	—	A	—	—	—	—	—	—	—	—	—	—
Kansas												A	—	—	—	—	—	—	—	—	—
Kentucky										A	—	—	—	—	—	—	—	—	—	—	—
Louisiana															A	—	—	—	—	—	—
Maine					P	—	—	—	—	—	A	—	—	—	—	—	—	—	—	—	—
Maryland				P	—	—	—	—	—	A	—	—	—	—	—	—	—	—	—	—	—
Massachusetts			P	—	—	—	—	A	—	—	—	—	—	—	—	—	—	—	—	—	—
Michigan					P	—	—	—	—	A	—	—	—	—	—	—	—	—	—	—	—
Minnesota			P	—	—	A	—	—	—	—	—	T	—	—	—	—	—	—	—	—	A
Mississippi												A	—	—	—	—	—	—	—	—	—
Missouri			P	—	—	—	—	—	—	—	A	—	—	—	—	—	—	—	—	—	—
Montana													P	—	A	—	—	—	—	—	—
Nebraska					P	—	A	—	—	—	—	—	—	—	—	—	—	—	—	—	—
Nevada												A	—	—	—	—	—	—	—	—	—
New Hampshire					A	—	—	—	—	—	—	—	—	—	—	—	—	—	—	—	—
New Jersey			P	—	—	A	—	—	—	—	—	—	—	—	—	—	—	—	—	—	—
New Mexico												A	—	—	—	—	—	—	—	—	—
New York	P	—	—	—	—	—	—	—	—	A	—	—	—	—	—	—	—	—	—	—	—
North Carolina							P	—	A	—	—	—	—	—	—	—	—	—	—	—	—
North Dakota											A	—	—	—	—	—	—	—	—	—	—
Ohio							P	—	A	—	—	—	—	—	—	—	—	—	—	—	—
Oklahoma											A	—	—	—	—	—	—	—	—	—	—
Oregon					P	—	—	—	—	—	A	—	—	—	—	—	—	—	—	—	—
Pennsylvania			LP	—		SA															
Rhode Island			P	—	—	—	—	A	—	—	—	—	—	—	—	—	—	—	—	—	—
South Carolina						CP	—	—	—	—	—	—	—	—	—	A	—	—	—	—	—
South Dakota					P	—	—	—	—	—	—	—	—	A	—	—	—	—	—	—	—
Tennessee						P	—	—	—	—	—	—	—	—	A	—	—	—	—	—	—
Texas						CP	—	—	—	—	—	—	—	—	—	—	A	—	—	—	—
Utah									P	—	—	—	—	—	A	—	—	—	—	—	—
Vermont				P	—	—	—	—	A	—	—	—	—	—	—	—	—	—	—	—	—
Virginia						P	—	—	—	A	—	—	—	—	—	—	—	—	—	—	—
Washington					A	—	—	—	—	—	—	—	—	—	—	—	—	—	—	—	—
West Virginia					A	—	—	—	—	—	—	—	—	—	—	—	—	—	—	—	—
Wisconsin					P	—	—	—	—	—	A	—	—	—	—	—	—	—	—	—	—
Wyoming													A	—	—	—	—	—	—	—	—
District of Columbia			P	—	—	—	—	—	—	—	—	—	—	—	—	—	—	—	A	—	—

Source: U.S., Department of Commerce, *Highway Statistics, Summary to 1955* (Washington D.C.: Government Printing Office, 1957), p. 16.
A: Annual C: County L: Local P: Perennial S: State T: Triennial

Plate 24.   1905 Michigan license
plate, the first one issued in Detroit.
Courtesy Smithsonian Institution.

had passed motor vehicle registration laws by 1905, and all except three of the twenty-six states that required registration in 1905 allowed motor vehicles to be registered in perpetuity — that is, registration did not have to be renewed each year. As of 1910, thirty-six states required motor vehicle registration — twenty-one annual and fifteen perennial. All states had a motor vehicle registration law by 1915, but not until 1921 did all states require annual registration.

Local automobile clubs at first contested the legality of city ordinances requiring registration, but their opposition soon evaporated. Chicago was one of the first large cities to require motor vehicle registration, and the Chicago Automobile Club voiced a strong protest against the requirement that numbered license plates be displayed, even though the city initially allowed motorists to select their own numbers and charged a fee of only $3. Under the leadership of John Farson, the new club president, about eighty members of the Chicago club waged an ultimately unsuccessful attack against the "numbering ordinance." Many Chicago motorists were arrested for failure to comply with this law until a final decision was handed down against the Farson group by the courts in 1905. Farson, however, never had the complete support of his club, and by 1904 he was representing only a small minority of the members. Some of the affidavits taken in support of the city's case were procured from prominent Chicago club members who thought the city ought to regulate the motor vehicle. Then, during Farson's absence from a meeting on October 17, 1907, the Chicago Automobile Club voted unanimously to abandon its fight and comply with the city numbering ordinance. Some 200 members registered their cars the following day, and several even offered to allow the police to use their cars to help apprehend speeders and violators of the city's numbering ordinance.

Patterns of protest to local registration laws, invariably based on grounds that now seem absurd, were similar in other large cities. Henry Ford and Horace Dodge, for example, lost a 1904 suit that they brought on behalf of Detroit's motorists to test the constitutionality of that city's registration ordinance. They claimed that the $1 fee constituted double taxation of personal property and that the ordinance was unjust "class legislation" because owners of horse-drawn vehicles were neither forced to carry identification tags nor deprived of the right to allow children under sixteen years of age to drive their vehicles. Similarly, the Milwaukee Automobile Club, under the leadership of its president Father J. F. Szukalski, an outspoken priest, threatened to test the constitutionality of the Milwaukee registration ordinance before the Wisconsin Supreme Court on the grounds of "class legislation." But within a few months the Milwaukee motorists "submitted as quietly as you please to the mandates of the great grandstand players of the common council and every machine that may be seen on the streets of the city now has its tag, which stands out behind as the car puts on speed like the tail of an overgrown beaver. . . . according to the Milwaukeean's way of thinking [about the numbering ordinance], it doesn't do the city any harm; it doesn't do the motorist any harm, and it doesn't do anybody else any harm, so 'what's the use' of fighting?"[2]

  Undoubtedly, the most important reasons for motorists' objections to numbering ordinances remained covert. Motorists generally feared that the facilitation of identification of their vehicles would increase chances of arrest, fine, imprisonment, and the payment of damage claims. Also, registration helped tax assessors identify and locate automobile owners who were evading the payment of personal property taxes on their cars. To cite but one example, it was estimated that in Denver one-third of the automobiles in the city had gone untaxed prior to the adoption of a registration ordinance.[3] Since such motives could not be expressed legitimately, motorists were forced

[2]"But What's the Use," *Motor Age*, 6:11 (November 3, 1904).
[3]*Horseless Age*, 11:564 (May 6, 1903).

to cloak their cases in the respectable mantle of the constitutionality of so-called class legislation and the supposed discriminatory taxation of a few dollars' fee. The courts unequivocally rejected this ridiculous line of reasoning with monotonous regularity. As a result, the threatened legal crusade against registration quickly waned. Probably the last such effort worth noting was a halfhearted attempt, undertaken after a year's hesitation, by the National Association of Automobile Manufacturers to test the constitutionality of state motor vehicle registration laws in 1905. By then, however, most motorists had become convinced that "the continual wrangling with authorities was a much greater annoyance than carrying numbers."[4]

Rather than fight registration laws, the automobile clubs began to channel their energies into eliminating the major faults of the existing system of solely local automobile ordinances. Some clubs took the initiative to frame bearable local ordinances themselves. The Cincinnati Automobile Club, for example, drafted and sponsored the Cincinnati automobile ordinance to forestall the more drastic legislation the club feared might be passed by city officials if the club failed to act. Even more important, the automobile clubs began to agitate for state rather than municipal control of registration, for uniform state laws, and for interstate reciprocity provisions. The solution suggested by *Horseless Age* to the Chicago numbering ordinance debacle came to be widely accepted as the proper one by motorists: "Automobilists would do well to take the initiative in the formation of a state association and then work for a reasonable state law, depriving local authorities of the right to regulate the use of automobiles in their own territory."[5]

The prerogative of municipal governments to extract fees from and regulate motorists was by no means completely negated by the state motor vehicle laws that were

[4]"Numbering and Interstate Recognition of License Numbers," ibid., 14:463–464 (November 9, 1904).
[5]"Chicago Ordinance Tangle," ibid., 13:423 (April 20, 1904).

passed, but the threatened growth of a complex and abusive municipal system of motor vehicle laws was effectively checked by superseding state legislation. State motor vehicle registration made sense from the standpoint of both the automobilist and the authorities. Separate registration in each city or county in which an automobile was operated imposed an inconvenience and a prohibitive financial burden on the motorist. A welter of license plates flapping from the rear end of a fleeing automobile made identification of the car, the main reason for registration to begin with, almost impossible. A single state license plate, respected anywhere the motorist traveled, was clearly more desirable. The most exasperating situation existed in Missouri, where state law provided for separate registration in each county in which a motor vehicle was driven. As late as 1906, the motorist who wished to drive legally in every county of Missouri had to pay $295.50 in registration fees; the cost of registration fees alone for a trip from St. Louis to Kansas City was $25, versus only $15 for regular round-trip railroad fare. Due to the agitation of Missouri motorists, the law was finally modified after June 14, 1907, to require a single $5 state registration that expired when either the vehicle was sold or the owner's county of residence changed.

Automobilists ideally wanted regulation of the motor vehicle by the federal government, including a single federal license that would be valid in all states and uniform speed limits throughout the country. With the avowed purpose of forestalling local and state automobile laws, the National Association of Automobile Manufacturers petitioned both the Senate and the House of Representatives as early as 1902 to frame and enact legislation providing for a national automobile license under the power of Congress to regulate interstate commerce. Automobile interests were agreed by 1905 that "recognition of the automobile has become so complete in all sections that it calls for some sort of national regulation, if any regulation is to be had. It is too big an affair for dinky legislatures, county boards or town trustees and supervisors to handle with judgment and fairness to the public and the motorist. It is up to the federal government to take a hand and place the matter where it belongs."[6] The American Automobile Association and the National Association of Automobile Manufacturers therefore jointly undertook a campaign to secure a federal motor vehicle law.

Primary responsibility for this was assumed by Charles T. Terry, a professor of law at Columbia University who acted as both legal council for the NAAM and chairman of the AAA legislative committee. Beginning in 1905 in the Fifty-ninth Congress, several federal automobile bills were introduced, but these bills died in committee because legislators doubted the necessity for and the constitutionality of such an extension of the power of the federal government. A national legislative convention held in Washington, D.C., in February 1910 marked the high point of efforts to secure federal motor vehicle legislation, but by then the need for a single, national license had been fairly well obviated by the general adoption of interstate reciprocity provisions and a trend toward increased uniformity in the motor vehicle laws of the various states.

Automobile interests also came to acknowledge that registration had some definite advantages. *Horseless Age* commented in 1905, for example, that "it is a question whether at the present early period of development of the automobile the numbering and licensing laws are not a blessing in disguise." The periodical believed that carrying numbered identification tags had tended to restrain reckless drivers and thereby had helped to reduce accidents and lessen public opposition to motorists in general. Moreover, since registration had not deterred anyone from buying an automobile, "these laws are not in any way injurious to the industry."[7] Many motorists, because the general practice in most states was to use funds from registration fees for road

---

[6] "National Law Badly Needed," *Motor Age*, 8:8 (July 20, 1905).
[7] "The Constitutionality of Licensing," *Horseless Age*, 15:320 (March 15, 1905).

construction and maintenance, came to favor higher and annual registration fees as one means of securing better roads.

Licensing of Operators

Governmental certification of the competence of automobile operators was well established in Europe by the turn of the century, but the practice was then still virtually nonexistent in the United States. Although New York State theoretically required drivers of steam cars to be licensed engineers, lax enforcement made this law a farce. The police commissioners of New York City, for example, referred the matter to the superintendent of the Street Department, who reported that "he did not believe there was any practical necessity for requiring the employment of a regularly licensed engineer." So the commissioners dodged the issue by adopting a recommendation that "after the petitioner [for permission to operate a steam car] has learned to operate the machine he might himself become licensed, the only expense involved being a fee of $3."[8]

Chicago framed the first meaningful ordinance in the United States that required the examination and licensing of all automobile operators. Several automobile accidents attributable to the incompetence of drivers prompted the mayor in 1899 to direct the Law Department of the city to frame an ordinance similar to that in effect in France. By 1900 a series of eighteen questions relating to the mechanism of the type of car to be driven, the responsibilities involved in operating a motor vehicle on city streets, and the applicant's past driving record had been prepared for use in the examination of automobile operators in Chicago. This examination was given by an appointed board of examiners and had to be retaken every year. The applicant also had to be in good physical condition. The initial fee was $3 and annual renewal

[8] "License Required to Operate Steam Vehicles," ibid., 5:8 (November 1, 1899).

cost $1. A license could be revoked if it was demonstrated after a hearing that a driver had violated local traffic regulations or was otherwise unfit to operate a motor vehicle.

Automobile interests were well ahead of municipal and state governments by 1902 in recognizing that the compulsory examination of all automobile operators would be desirable. *Horseless Age* reported the attitude toward operators' licenses in November 1902: "The general sentiment of the leading automobile organizations and of the public press seems to be favorable to it. A license law will prevent novices from driving to the common danger on public streets before they have acquired the requisite skill in manipulation of their vehicles, and perhaps, still more important, will place automobile drivers under greater responsibility."[9] Officials of both the American Automobile Association and the Automobile Club of America publicly advocated at this time that the states should certify the basic competence of all automobile operators by requiring them to pass examinations before being allowed on the road.

But few cities or states responded immediately with adequate legislation. Most local ordinances, where any existed, were ridiculously lenient regarding the qualifications of drivers. For example, the 1904 Milwaukee automobile ordinance merely required that automobile drivers be at least eighteen years of age and have the use of both arms. After the 1902 Kansas City, Missouri, automobile ordinance had been in effect almost a year, only two or three applicants for operators' licenses had actually been examined. Bills providing for the certification of operators' abilities had been introduced in several state legislatures by 1903, but no meaningful legislation (that is, provision for examination of competence) was passed at the state level until 1906. Among the more progressive states in automobile legislation, New York required that only professional chauffeurs take out a license and carry a badge, and their competence to drive

9"Automobile Legislation," ibid., 10:491–492 (November 5, 1902). See also ibid., pp. 494–495, for the specific views of automobile club officials.

was not examined. Until 1906 New Jersey simply demanded that an automobile owner file with the secretary of state a declaration verified by a notary that he was competent to drive the automobile he desired to register.

Several states began to make more adequate provision for licensing automobile drivers after 1906. One of the first to do so was New Jersey, which began to tighten requirements a bit with the creation of a new Department of Motor Vehicle Regulation and Registration. While motor vehicles could still be registered by mail, a New Jersey operator's license now had to be obtained in person from a state examiner, and the applicant had to make an affidavit on the extent of his driving experience, physical condition, and knowledge of the state's motor vehicle laws. Massachusetts initiated even stricter requirements in 1907: an actual road test to demonstrate competence became mandatory, as well as a written examination on the state's motor vehicle regulations. Two examiners, one at the State House in Boston, the other visiting in rotation eight additional cities throughout the state, examined applicants by appointment. *Motor Age* noted that "this strict examination is commended by the motorists as a whole, who see in it a step in the right direction, in that it will tend to sift out the inexperienced and help in the movement to bring about sane motoring."[10]

Focusing primarily on the qualifications of the professional chauffeur, both associations of chauffeurs in New York City and Philadelphia and prominent members of the Automobile Club of America began to urge more rigid examination procedures for operators' licenses about 1905. The position of the upper-class automobile owner was expressed well by Dave H. Morris, the current president of the ACA, in *Harper's Weekly:* "I would recommend . . . the creation of a state commission of three members to be appointed by the governor, whose duty it would be to issue licenses and institute an examination into the capabilities of chauffeurs. The owners of automobiles,

---

[10] "Strict in Bay State," *Motor Age*, 12:10–11 (August 1, 1907).

particularly those who have wives and children, are entirely dependent upon the skill, caution and general efficiency of their chauffeurs, and it is my view that, with such trust reposed in them, they should be compelled to pass a comprehensive and adequate state examination."[11] Professional chauffeurs, who had become increasingly concerned about competition for jobs, agreed. Joseph Dunn, vice-president of the Philadelphia branch of the Chauffeurs' Association of America, explained: "Nowadays any boy who has worked a day or two in a garage . . . considers himself qualified to handle an automobile. For the safety of the public and the protection of our own interests, we propose to put a stop to this practice."[12]

At least by 1908 the opinion of motorists overwhelmingly favored that all operators of motor vehicles be licensed and required to pass an examination to determine their competence. *Automobile* reported in April 1909: "Upon the question of licensing all operators there is now a striking unanimity that has gained ground rapidly in the past twelvemonth, owing probably to the great increase of automobiles on the road. The inconsiderate must be punished and the incompetent must not be permitted to drive."[13]

Despite the motorists' own desire to have their competence examined and certified, state governments still remained reluctant to take adequate action at the end of the first decade of the twentieth century. As of 1909, only twelve states and the District of Columbia required all automobile drivers to obtain licenses. Except for Missouri, these were all eastern states — Connecticut, Delaware, Maine, Maryland, Massachusetts, New Hampshire, New Jersey, Pennsylvania, Rhode Island, Vermont, and West Virginia. In seven other states, only professional chauffeurs had to obtain operators' licenses — California, Florida, Illinois, Michigan, Minnesota, New York,

[11] Dave H. Morris, "The Automobilist and the Law," *Harper's Weekly*, 50:47 (January 13, 1906).
[12] "C.A.A. in Philadelphia," *Automobile*, 12:230 (February 4, 1905).
[13] "The Licensing of All Operators," ibid., 20:552 (April 1, 1909).

and Ohio. The application forms for operators' licenses in these nineteen states as a rule asked for little more information than the applicant's name, address, age, and the type of automobile he claimed to be competent to drive. This might have to be notarized, but in the vast majority of these states a license to drive an automobile could still be obtained by mail. In the twelve states requiring that all operators be licensed, a combined total of 89,495 licenses were issued between January 1 and October 4, 1909, but only twelve applicants were rejected for incompetency or other reasons during this period—two in Rhode Island and ten in Vermont.[14]

Restrictions on Use

The only notable restriction on the use of streets and highways by motorists was that motor vehicles were at first excluded from parks in most large cities. But this prohibition was in some cases never enforced and in all cases short lived. For example, although automobiles had been excluded from Fairmount Park in Philadelphia, the park police generally did not stop motorists who used the drives. Then in October 1900 the rule banning motorists from Fairmount Park was rescinded, and automobiles were allowed on all drives except West River and Wissahickon Drives, which were set apart for horses. Similarly, Baltimore prohibited all automobiles from Druid Hill Park, but early in 1900 the policy was changed to allow electric cars the use of the park drives. Owners of steam and gasoline automobiles objected to this discrimination and began to agitate for relief through the courts in 1901. Finally, in the spring of 1902 the governor of Maryland signed a bill that prevented the Baltimore park commissioners from prohibiting automobiles from public parks or limiting their speed to less than 6 mph.

[14] The forms used for operators' licenses in the various states were reprinted in "Licenses and Licensing," *Motor*, 13:37–40, 110, 118 (October 1909). The figures given here for the total licenses issued and the number of applicants rejected are from this same periodical, 13:53 (November 1909).

The most talked-about case of park exclusion involved the prohibition of automobiles from Central Park in New York City. By mid-1899, automobiles were allowed in all of the New York City parks except Central Park. Two of the three park commissioners favored admitting automobiles to Central Park too; the third disapproved, so a hearing was held in November 1895. Fifteen persons spoke in favor of the automobile, while ten persons voiced opinions against admission. Among those speaking to allow automobilists the use of Central Park were George F. Chamberlain, vice-president of the Automobile Club of America, and Lawrence N. Fuller, "one of the best-known horsemen in the city." The group opposed to admission was composed of "a livery stable keeper, a number of private persons who are accustomed to drive in the Park, and an attorney for the hackmen who ply their trade therein." The park commissioners reserved decision at the meeting, but several weeks later approval was given to admit motor vehicles to Central Park in limited numbers "until the horses are accustomed to them and the Board considers it safe to remove all disability from the motor carriage." Until then, permits were to be "restricted to those who, in the judgment of the Board, are cautious and competent drivers of motor vehicles." *Horseless Age* advised New York automobilists to be content with the limitations established by the park authorities: "Their complete conversion is only a matter of a little time, and their present attitude of conservatism is dictated by a sense of duty to the public, and is not altogether indefensible."[15]

Legislating Speed

By far the most serious confrontation between motorists and the authorities and the general public occurred over attempts to regulate speed. Motorists claimed that the

[15]"Hearing before the Park Board," *Horseless Age*, 5:10 (November 15, 1899), and "Park Rules Relaxed," ibid., 5:7 (November 22, 1899).

same rule that had governed the speed of horse-drawn vehicles — that speed on the open road be "reasonable and proper" with respect to road and traffic conditions — ought to apply unchanged to motor vehicles, and they denounced any additional restrictions on speed as unwarranted "special legislation." W. Wallace Grant, president of the Long Island Automobile Club, put this bluntly in 1902: "Except in unfamiliar localities the automobilist is always the best judge of his own safe speed. The law should give him the utmost freedom in selecting this speed, and should charge him with corresponding responsibility in case of accident." This position appeared sound to Grant "because the range of speeds attainable with propriety by the automobile is so far in excess of that physically possible to the horse, it follows that no arbitrary schedule of speed limits can possibly be framed which will fit the conditions of highway traffic." To those who were more interested in preventing accidents than in assigning responsibility for them after the fact and who complained that the excessive speeds possible for the motor vehicle were precisely what necessitated legal limits, there was a ready answer: James M. Padget, president of the Topeka Automobile Club, gave the motorist's typical reassurance that "an automobile going at a rate of 20 miles per hour is no more dangerous to life than a horse going at the rate of 10 miles per hour."[16]

However, "special legislation" involving maximum miles-per-hour clauses became increasingly necessary. The top speeds of horse-drawn vehicles ranged from about 8 to 15 miles per hour, and vehicles traveling below these speeds composed the bulk of traffic on both city streets and country roads. The low average and top speeds of horse-drawn vehicles made an established maximum miles-per-hour limit for them superfluous; all that was required for safety with horse-drawn traffic was a general injunction that speed be "reasonable and proper." But motor vehicles were capable

[16] "Views of Clubs and Officials," ibid., 10:496 (November 5, 1902).

of sustained speeds several times in excess of the top speeds of horse-drawn vehicles—speeds that were hazardous on poor roads where slower horse-drawn traffic was predominant. And it was obvious that many motorists were either unwilling or unable to adjust their speeds to existing road and traffic conditions, the only possible criterion of reason and propriety. *Outlook*, a popular periodical especially concerned about speeding and reckless driving by automobilists, expressed the concern of the public well in 1908: "It is difficult to persuade the public, who find in almost every morning's paper a report of one or more automobile accidents of a serious nature, that it is as safe to drive an engine twenty to forty miles an hour over a highway as to drive a pair of horses eight or ten miles an hour. It is certain that the present law is not adequate for the protection of persons traveling on the highway from reckless drivers of automobiles. The automobile has become almost a necessity; it certainly is a permanent method of locomotion to which society must adapt itself, and from the careless use of which society must protect itself."[17]

Public opinion, although overwhelmingly favorable to the new mode of transportation, became aroused very early against speeding and reckless driving. The automobile trade journals were well aware that agitation for restrictions on the speed of motor vehicles stemmed from a legitimate concern for the public safety caused by the motorist's frequent disregard for the rights of other users of the streets and highways. For example, *Motor Age* reported at the end of 1899: "Chicago generally hailed the advent of the horseless carriage with a good deal of rejoicing. The people wanted it. But we doubt if they want it driven over them or over their rights in the public streets, and the warmth of their welcome is going to be a good deal cooled unless automobile owners exercise more care."[18] By 1901 it was apparent that this fear had been war-

[17] "Concerning Automobiling," *Outlook*, 89:632 (July 25, 1908).
[18] "Criticisms Worth Heeding," *Motor Age*, 1:245 (December 7, 1899).

ranted: "Despite laws, warnings, and common sense many automobilists — and club members are not excepted — run their machines over the streets and roads at a pace which cannot be considered fair to other users of the thoroughfares or in keeping with common sense. Leading members of clubs take sufficient interest in the welfare of automobilism to devote their time to the passage of laws which will establish their rights and within a week members of the same clubs give cause to the authorities to wish the laws had been made more stringent."[19]

Antispeed organizations had little difficulty in presenting a convincing case that motorists neither respected existing speed ordinances nor adjusted their speeds to the normal flow of traffic. Horace E. Parker, secretary of the New York Committee of Fifty, one of the more vigilant antispeed organizations, made this clear to *Horseless Age* when he presented data obtained with stopwatches in New York City: "Between 2 p.m. and 3 p.m., Fifth Avenue, between Fifty-seventh and Fifty-eighth Streets, 22 automobiles and 255 horse-drawn vehicles passed in one direction. Nearly all automobiles were going at from 10 to 17 miles an hour. Of the horse-drawn vehicles not more than 6 exceeded 9 miles an hour." Although the city speed limit was 8 mph, one automobile had been clocked at 25.71 mph. Parker had made a canvass of registered voters in the area to determine public opinion about raising the city speed limit to 10 mph. Postcards were sent to some 20,000 persons, and he claimed that 95 percent of those who responded were against the increase. *Horseless Age* was also impressed that "Mr. Parker particularly expressed himself, both personally and on behalf of his society, as being by no means antagonistic to automobiles, and strongly urged that he and they realize the present value of motor vehicles, and the perfectly apparent importance these vehicles will have in future locomotion.

[19] "Excessive Speed in Cities," ibid., 4:n.p. (May 30, 1901).

... [The society's sole] motive is to promote such legislation as will effectually stop fast driving."[20]

Special regulations governing the use of motor vehicles were still notably absent in the United States in 1902, and the little legislation that had been passed by then was minimally restrictive. Only four states—Connecticut, Massachusetts, New York, and Rhode Island—had passed any state motor vehicle legislation, and Rhode Island had failed to pass any miles-per-hour clause establishing a maximum speed limit. The maximum speed limit for motor vehicles outside city limits was a reasonable 15 mph in both Connecticut and Massachusetts and a liberal 20 mph in New York. Dependence upon purely local ordinances everywhere else in the United States meant typically that there were no laws whatever governing speed on the open road outside city limits, the very place where travel at an inordinate rate of speed was most possible for the motorist. The municipal ordinances in effect at the time almost never restricted the automobile to lower speeds than the top speeds for horse-drawn vehicles—that is, 6 to 8 mph speed limits within business sections and 10 to 12 mph in other parts of cities were the rule, with occasional provision that speeds not exceed 4 mph when crossing certain intersections, approaching curves, or meeting other vehicles. Even municipal ordinances were entirely absent in 1902 in Florida, Kentucky, Maryland, Montana, New Mexico, North Dakota, South Carolina, Tennessee, Utah, Virginia, and Wyoming, undoubtedly because automobiles were still extremely rare in these states. The first municipal automobile ordinances had just been introduced, but not yet passed, in Davenport, Iowa, and Portland, Oregon, and no automobile legislation was yet in effect in any other Iowa or Oregon city.

Up to 1902 the automobile clubs had usually been able to forestall restrictive legislation embodying miles-per-hour clauses, even where the number of motor vehicles and

[20] "Opinions of Anti-Speed Organizations," *Horseless Age*, 10:497 (November 5, 1902).

the actions of motorists clearly warranted it, by promises that their members would exercise restraint. Where they had failed, the clubs had often managed to get legislation favorable to the motorist adopted, the prime example being the New York State motor vehicle law of April 25, 1901, with its liberal 20-mph maximum speed limit, that had been drafted by the Automobile Club of America. But it began to appear inevitable to many motorists that the free-and-easy situation they had thus far enjoyed must soon come to an end. *Horseless Age* reluctantly commented at the beginning of 1902, for example: "It is with regret we confess that in numerous and flagrant instances their [automobilists'] conduct has been most disappointing to friends of the industry and irritating to the public at large. . . . A condition so intolerable could not be expected to long exist in the United States, where it is quite generally understood that roads are for the common use of all and not the private property of a few rich enthusiasts." The obvious point was that "the antispeed bills . . . are the natural and necessary result of the lawless acts of automobilists themselves. The provisions of the present law have been found inadequate to abate the nuisance."[21] Later that year, even *Horseless Age* came out in favor of the miles-per-hour clause establishing definite speed limits. Commenting on the position still taken by most motorists, that prescribed speed limits were not necessary, the periodical expressed the opinion that "it is too indefinite, that views as to what is safe and proper differ too much with the individual automobilist. . . . The average automobile driver may not be able to closely gauge his speed, but a definite limit of, say, 20 miles an hour certainly means more to him than the speed where danger begins, the danger limit. . . . A speed limit, therefore, is quite desirable even for the open country, as much for the benefit of the automobilists themselves as for the protection of the outside public."[22]

[21]"The Flurry of Anti-Speed Legislation," ibid., 9:65 (January 15, 1902).
[22]"Automobile Legislation," p. 491.

The automobile clubs were favored in their sustained efforts to prevent reactionary legislation from being passed by the cyclical nature of the public concern over speeding and reckless driving, which reached its high point every year at the climax of the touring season, then dropped to its low in late winter. Serious accidents and minor annoyances accumulated through the summer months, with the result that by the opening of state legislative sessions in the fall a large volume of complaints from indignant citizens demanded that drastic bills be introduced to curb "scorchers." By the time these measures actually had to be voted upon, however, the public's temper had cooled. Meanwhile, the automobile clubs lobbied energetically. The clubs had adequate funds earmarked for the influencing of legislation, employed extremely able representatives, and could count on the influence of their prominent members. Their tactics usually included demonstration rides for the lawmakers, intended to prove that automobiles traveling at high speeds were really quite safe compared with much slower horse-drawn vehicles. As a result the automobile legislation passed was rarely punitive. The severity of the initial bills and the fact that any law had been passed at all satisfied the public that something was being done, while the watered-down legislation actually enacted met with the approval of the automobile clubs.

By 1906 most states had adopted motor vehicle legislation that provided for reasonable maximum speed limits, given the road and traffic conditions of the day, on the open highway (that is, outside incorporated municipalities). Fifteen states then had speed limits of 20 mph, and five states allowed maximum speeds of 24 or 25 mph. Nine states limited speed on the open highway to 15 mph, while only three states had severely restrictive laws—Alabama (8 mph), Maryland (12 mph), and Missouri (9 mph). The remaining three states with automobile laws had no established maximum speed limits: Rhode Island and West Virginia left the setting of speed limits to local authorities, and Florida merely set a 4-mph state speed limit on curves, bridges, fill, and intersections. The 4-mph limit for such places was commonly prescribed by state laws at the time. The 1906 state laws also generally provided for lower maximum speed limits within incorporated municipalities, which ranged from 8 to 15 mph, depending on the particular state and whether the road was in a closely built-up or outlying section of the municipality.

Liberal as the state speed laws generally were in 1906, the 1905–1906 period marked the zenith of restrictive legislation against the speed of motor vehicles. Before this, few speed laws had been in effect, and later, with the rapid diffusion of the motor vehicle, speed laws became progressively more lenient. Among the thirty-four states that had passed state motor vehicle legislation by late 1909, eleven had maximum speed limits of 25 mph on the open highway; fourteen had 20-mph limits, and two of the latter, New Hampshire and Pennsylvania, had passed new laws raising the 20-mph limit that were to go into effect on December 31, 1909; Texas had an 18-mph limit; and five other states had 15-mph limits. Restrictive speed limits of 8 and 12 mph were still retained by Alabama and Maryland, respectively, and Florida merely kept its law requiring a 4-mph limit under specified circumstances. The public had become accustomed to the motor vehicle, and automobile ownership was becoming more widespread, with the result that public demands for severe legislation against speed had lessened appreciably. As *Outing Magazine* summed up the legislative picture late in the summer of 1909, "In the early statutes some antagonism to the automobile perhaps showed itself, but that has all passed away."[23]

Enforcement of Legislation

The effectiveness of motor vehicle legislation lay in its enforcement, and all indications are that enforcement was inadequate, much less severe. Policemen on foot,

[23]T. O. Abbott, "The Lawmaker and the Automobile," *Outing Magazine*, 54:614 (August 1909).

horseback, or bicycles were outmatched by the speeding motorists they pursued, and even after automobile squads were introduced in some large cities the police remained technologically disadvantaged compared with violators of the speed laws. *Automobile* noted in 1905, for example: "Because of the increasing number of high speed automobiles in St. Louis, the police automobile squad is almost unable to catch and arrest offenders against the speed ordinance, and the city authorities will probably replace the police department cars with machines of greater power and speed as soon as an appropriation can be made. About the only chance the police now have to arrest the driver of a machine who exceeds the speed limit is to catch a glimpse of the license number of the fleeing car and take the offender into custody at his home later."[24] The refusal of the motorist to stop on command or to appear before the authorities when identified in a complaint were also grave problems for the police, and lenient police methods were apt to be met with contempt by motorists. The Pittsburgh police found in 1908, for instance, that automobilists identified as speeders or reckless drivers would not respond to warning letters asking them to appear at the station at their convenience "rather than have the strong arm of the law to bring them in." The motorists took "these letters of warning as a joke, and many of them have had the letters framed and hung them up in their offices as so-called diplomas."[25]

Motorists did their best to avoid apprehension by the authorities. As noted earlier, registration laws, the real key to the effective enforcement of laws governing the use of motor vehicles, were at first widely disregarded by motorists in many localities. A road-block examination conducted by the Boston police on July 20, 1904, for example, established that only 126 of the 234 motorists stopped had complied with the Massachusetts state registration and license requirements. It was believed that for the

[24] "St. Louis Auto Police," *Automobile*, 12:688 (June 8, 1905).
[25] "Police Courtesy Abused," *Motor Age*, 13:30 (March 5, 1908).

Boston area "the results are to be considered typical of what would be found by a complete canvass."[26] The most notorious form of evasion was undoubtedly the widespread early practice in Chicago of carrying "bogus license numbers to be used when speeding," which were "judiciously changed at frequent intervals, in order that no one number might become fixed in the minds of the police. . . . Goggles with face masks became quite popular, and all motorists with a love for fast driving came to look uniformly alike when the high gear was in mesh."[27]

To overcome such obstacles to law enforcement, the "speed trap" was devised shortly after the turn of the century and employed in New England, the environs of Chicago, and on Long Island. Generally, a quarter-mile stretch of highway, often a shorter distance, was marked off in an area where speeding had become a problem. Officers equipped with stopwatches were stationed at both terminal points; when a vehicle crossed one terminal point, a signal was passed to the other by hand or by an electric buzzer to begin timing the car's speed. If the automobile exceeded the legal limit, an attempt was made to halt it, arrest the driver, and bring him to trial, immediately in most cases, before a local magistrate. Since many automobilists failed voluntarily to obey the command to stop, it became common practice for the authorities to stretch a rope across the road. The mayors of the towns along Chicago's North Shore found that even this was not sufficient: wire cables had to be substituted for hemp ropes because "the more determined offenders . . . fitted scythelike cutters in front of their machines, which made short work of such ropes." One mayor found that throwing cordwood or logs in the path of speeders was the ideal solution.[28]

Automobilists deeply resented the speed trap. They considered it an expression

[26] "Police Make a Haul," *Motor World*, 8:655 (July 28, 1904).
[27] "Decay of Speed Laws and Ordinances," *Automobile*, 9:499 (November 14, 1904).
[28] "The Automobile War on the North Shore, Chicago," *Horseless Age*, 10:123 (July 30, 1902).

Plate 25. 1903 advertisement for automobilists' clothing. Courtesy Free Library of Philadelphia.

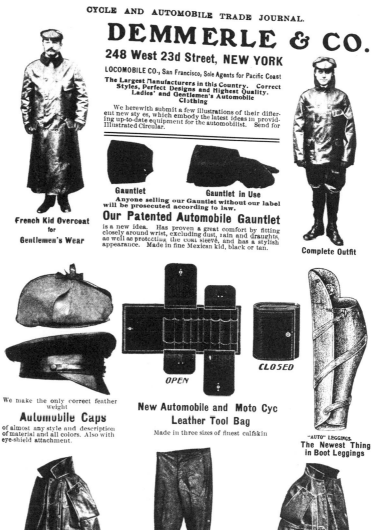

Plate 26.   1903 advertisement for accessories, showing automobilists' goggles and face masks. Courtesy Free Library of Philadelphia.

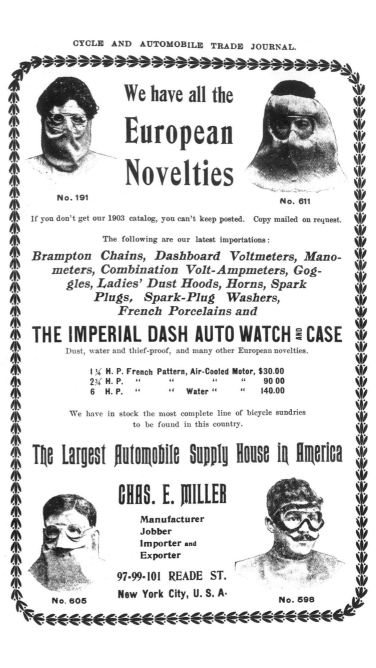

of irrational "motorphobia" intended primarily to provide a rich new source of revenue for rural Dogberrys who indiscriminately convicted the innocent as well as the guilty. Motorists complained that the ropes and other obstacles used to stop violators constituted a hazardous and illegal blocking of the public roads and that stopwatch evidence should be given less credence in court than the driver's own assessment of his speed (which was in most cases based entirely on his biased impression and at best upon one of the erratic speedometers of the day that generally underestimated true speed). The automobilists claimed that many drivers pleaded guilty on the spot and paid stiff fines only because of the inconvenience of returning for a hearing. They further argued that tourists could not always know beforehand where the boundaries of municipalities began or what the local speed limits were.[29]

Cases cited in the automobile trade journals illustrate that motorists' complaints had some merit; in some instances there were flagrant abuses of the legal rights of automobile drivers. But it was erroneous to generalize, as the motorists often did, either from exceptions or from abuses common enough in some localities, and conclude that the speed trap in its normal functioning in most places constituted an unjust, corrupt, and unnecessary practice. The methods advocated and adopted by automobile interests to thwart the effectiveness of the speed trap certainly showed neither a proper respect for the law nor any awareness that speeders needed to be curbed in the interest of automobilists themselves as well as for the safety of the general public. Whenever possible, the automobile clubs placed warning signs or stationed representatives wearing club colors at conspicuous points on the road to inform drivers about the location of speed traps. Some automobile trade journals openly advocated a system of signals among drivers to accomplish the same end.

[29] Good summaries of the respective points of view of the motorist and the constable can be found in Alfred E. Ommen, "The Motorist and the Police," *Motor*, 10:45–48 (May 1908), and Seth Bird, "The Motorist and the Country Constable," ibid., p. 76.

Automobile suggested that the ideal answer to the speed trap was to put blackboards in local garages "in a prominent place for observation by outgoing cars giving in chalk-marks the location and character of well-known local traps and other seasonable warnings. . . . It might almost be said that garage keepers owe such a service as this to their customers and the touring fraternity at large."[30] These actions did not encourage local authorities or the public at large to believe the contention of the automobile clubs and journals that most motorists were law-abiding citizens who were anxious to see the miscreants in their own ranks apprehended.

Action Against Speeders

The emergence of vigilante groups to aid local authorities is evidence of how far the enforcement of speed laws lagged behind public sentiment in many communities. The vigilante antispeed organization was a common phenomenon shortly after the turn of the century; but with the spread of the automobile and the institutionalization of sanctions against its misuse, the role of private citizens' groups in combating speed had declined appreciably by 1910. The most mild means of support for authorities was the posting of rewards by private organizations for evidence leading to the conviction of speeders and reckless drivers. At the other extreme, indignant citizens took illegal measures to stop "scorchers" on roads near their homes.

  The early battle between motorists and the residents of Long Island provides a good illustration of the types of action taken by private citizens. New York motorists from the outset of the diffusion of the automobile had taken excessive liberties on Long Island's comparatively fine roads. After several years of great patience, the Island's residents were finally roused to take action. The Long Island Highway Protective Society was therefore incorporated in September 1901 under the auspices of the

[30] "Autotrap Warning Best Given by Garage Keepers," *Automobile*, 15:318 (September 6, 1906).

leading citizens of Oyster Bay to aid in the apprehension of speeders and reckless drivers. In general, the society's methods were quite reasonable attempts to obtain tougher laws and help authorities to identify and apprehend violators, but some embittered, unidentified residents declared war on all automobilists. As *Horseless Age* reported the situation, "Not considering for the moment the rather extravagant proposition of riddling the pneumatics of fugitive scorchers with bullets, . . . glass and other tire puncturing instruments have of late been distributed over these [Long Island] roads in great quantities, presumably by parties who consider their interests affected by speed excesses." The periodical made certain to add that "it should be borne in mind that the animus of this Long Island hostility can scarcely be regarded as anachronistic or due to a backwoods mode of thought, fanatic opposition to progress, as some have contended, but it is rather a feeling of retaliation for aggression actually committed."[31] The situation in other communities where such acts occurred appears to have been analogous.

Prior provocation notwithstanding, motorists were rightly incensed by the illegal actions taken by some individuals to curb speeders. The motorists' common fault, however, was that they were most often unable or unwilling to discriminate sufficiently between proper and illegal forms of protest against their excesses. Consequently, they failed to support the necessary sanctions exercised by constituted authorities over their activity. Without such support, the legitimate enforcement of reasonable restraints was undercut, making violent reaction appear a viable and necessary alternative to some threatened citizens.

Rather than admit there was a general problem requiring action by the authorities, the automobile clubs insisted that speeding and reckless driving were engaged in by only a very small minority of motorists — mainly by hired chauffeurs — and the

[31] "Retaliatory Measures," *Horseless Age*, 5:326 (July 10,1901).

clubs tried to keep the enforcement of speed laws in their own hands as much as possible. Club officials made pledges to legislators that automobilists would obey reasonable laws and urged members to uphold these promises. Club members who broke the law were to be disciplined by the club itself, and this was considered to be a sufficient deterrent. The Automobile Club of America, for example, consistently reiterated that any member accused of speeding or reckless driving would be given a fair hearing by the club. If found guilty, he was to be warned and suspended; a second offense was to be punished by expulsion from the club. The philosophy behind the expulsion of a club member for traffic violations as an effective sanction was revealed in a letter sent by the Minneapolis Automobile Club to its members: "It would brand him as a reckless operator, and if trouble or accident of any kind should thereafter occur for which he should in any way be responsible, the fact that he had been expelled from the club for reckless driving would strongly prejudice his case, either before a court or in the mind of anyone wishing to place the responsibility for the accident or trouble upon him."[32] Only on rare occasions did the clubs offer their services to the police to help in apprehending violators of the law.

The argument for self-discipline put forth by the automobile clubs proved unworkable in practice. Although the Chicago Automobile Club claimed that most of that city's speeders were nonmembers, the Oak Park police found that most vehicles seen exceeding the speed limit carried the club's emblem. Richard Sylvester, superintendent of police in Washington, D.C., typically found too that "some members of automobile clubs early forget their promises to aid and encourage lawful running, and do not cooperate with the authorities as they agreed."[33] This was an understatement.

[32] "Club Warning to Members," *Automobile*, 8:20 (May 9, 1903).
[33] Richard Sylvester, "The Selfishness of City Speeding," *Harper's Weekly*, 51:384 (March 16, 1907).

An early assessment of club policy given by *Horseless Age* basically continued to hold true: "So far as the moral or deterrent influence of the automobile clubs is concerned, we have yet to hear of a single case of reprimand or expulsion of any member, while examples of law breaking so habitual and defiant as to have become a public scandal have been reported against them."[34] Indeed, it was October 1904 before the Automobile Club of America suspended its first member for speeding. Since this case involved an illegal race that had been given wide publicity, club action here was necessary to make a recent club resolution declaring hired chauffeurs mainly responsible for speeding seem more than an insincere dodge. Chief of Police O'Neill of the Chicago force gave the obvious answer to automobile club pretentions at self-discipline in a letter to John Farson, president of the Chicago Automobile Club. Responding that he was not satisfied with the club's promise to discipline its own members, Chief O'Neill said, "Enforcing the laws is the business of the police department and must be done according to law and not in accordance with social rules formulated by clubs and organizations."[35] Even had the clubs been able to control their own members, restrictive membership policies and the rapid more general adoption of the motor vehicle would clearly have made dependence upon club sanctions against violators of the law insufficient in short order.

Courts versus the Automobilist

Complaints from motorists about arbitrary police methods and summary trials notwithstanding, in general, the courts enforced the law with impartial fairness tempered by leniency. Automobile clubs advised members to plead "not guilty" and often provided defense attorneys with club funds. The motorist stood a good chance

---

[34] "Flurry of Anti-Speed Legislation," p. 65.
[35] "More Trouble in Chicago," *Horseless Age*, 14:381 (October 12, 1904).

of winning his case because judges were reluctant to convict without strong objective evidence. Should the motorist be found guilty, a small fine, usually $10 or $15 for first offenders, and a reprimand were his penalty. It was generally acknowledged that affluent automobilists considered such fines as mere operating expenses: "The wealthy chauffeur cares nothing for a fine of $25. In fact, he finds a certain satisfaction in paying it occasionally. . . . A heavier penalty must therefore be exacted if a law of this kind is to be effective. The millionaire must be brought face to face with a punishment that will deter — a term in jail."[36] But the courts remained reluctant to hand out more severe penalties for traffic offenses. As one commentator complained in 1908, "Courts have not been able so far to persuade themselves that 'overspeeding' is an offense serious enough to warrant imprisonment, and confine themselves to fines and 'reprimands.'"[37]

Even in automobile accidents that involved serious injury or manslaughter, the courts were reluctant to be severe. In the rare instances when they were, automobilists expressed shock. *Automobile*, for example, considered the imprisonment in November 1902 of two professional chauffeurs after very serious accidents to have been "foremost among the subjects which have engrossed the automobile world during the past week. . . . the severity was a complete surprise." The periodical believed that one of the men involved, Herbert A. Marple, "was made a scapegoat for the sins of automobilists as a class and for the failure of society in forming a public opinion strong enough to hold reckless driving in check." Marple was the first man to be convicted of manslaughter with an automobile in Connecticut. He received a $1 fine and a year in the county jail for killing a farmer in an accident. The evidence indicated that the farmer had probably been drinking and might have been driving

---

[36] "Flurry of Anti-Speed Legislation," p. 65.
[37] Frederick Dwight, "Automobiles: The Other Side of the Shield," *Independent*, 65:1300–1301 (December 3, 1908).

on the wrong side of the road; but the accident had occurred on a foggy night when visibility was only five or six feet, and Marple had obviously been going too fast for the driving conditions and had been negligent. The driver involved in the other accident, W. Byrd Raymond, had collided with a trolley car full of women and children in Yonkers, New York, seriously injuring a number of them, after harassing the motorman of the trolley by playing tag with the vehicle. Raymond was sentenced to six months in jail. The editorial position taken by *Automobile* was: "It is after all not very reprehensible on the part of professional automobile drivers to indulge in stunts with the vehicles entrusted to their care, if it must be admitted that examples of similar reckless behavior by persons in higher social standing come under their daily observation. . . . it may be questioned if it is really conforming to our national dignity to seize upon two obscure automobile servants for this purpose while men of higher station have been permitted to settle similar cases with small fines or out of court."[38]

Probably the first case in which a hit-and-run driver was given exemplary punishment in the United States occurred as late as 1908. While recklessly driving his car under the influence of alcohol, Dr. Walter H. Morris, a Newark, New Jersey, dentist, had killed a man descending from a trolley in downtown Newark, then fled the scene at high speed, demolishing a peddler's wagon. Morris turned himself in to the police a few days later and entered a plea of "non vult," which deprived him of the right to appeal the court's sentence of eighteen months in prison in the criminal suit that followed. He was faced, in addition, with civil suits asking $105,000 for damages arising from the accident. During the period the case was considered unique in the severity of the punishment imposed.[39]

[38] "Motorists Sent to Jail Without Option of Paying Fine," *Automobile*, 7:10 – 16 (November 8, 1902), and "Vindictive Court Decision," ibid., p.22.
[39] "Automobilist in Felon's Cell," *Motor World*, 17:845 – 846 (February 6, 1908).

As a sanction against speed and reckless driving, the prospect of a civil suit for damages was apparently as ineffective as the threat of criminal prosecution. By the turn of the century, *Horseless Age* had received a number of letters from persons who said their fear of incurring damage suits prevented them from buying an automobile. The periodical gave its assurance at the close of 1899 that this fear was unrealistic: "While many have been threatened with such procedure, very few cases have come to trial, and in only one case, so far as the editor knows, has an adverse decision been given, and this was for a small amount and the decision could probably have been reversed on appeal." If the motorist obeyed the ordinary rules of the road and extended normal courtesy, he had nothing to fear: "An occasional threat of prosecution may be looked for, but very seldom will a case actually come into court, and when it seems likely to reach that stage communicate at once with the Automobile Club of America, Waldorf-Astoria, New York, one of whose chief objects is to protect the rights of all users of automobiles."[40]

This pattern characterized damage suits against motorists during the ensuing decade. Decisions reported in the automobile trade journals, which kept a vigilant eye on the courts, were mixed but on the whole equitable.[41] Most of the cases mentioned appear justifiably to have been decided against the motorist on the basis of either his negligence or recklessness or the violation of speed laws, and the damages awarded seem to have been reasonable. The few exceptional instances where outlandish damages were awarded were usually remedied upon appeal. The automobilists won a significant proportion of the damage suits brought against them, and the decisions were almost without exception based upon the specific merits of the case, rarely revealing predisposed bias against the motorist or the motor vehicle.

[40]"Damage Suits," *Horseless Age*, 5:7 (December 27, 1899).
[41]See, for example, "Automobile Suits," ibid., 10:512–513 (November 5, 1902).

Why then did early automobilists complain, as they often did, that the courts were prejudiced against them? A writer in *Outlook* perhaps gave the best answer in 1909: "The belief prevailing in the minds of many that no judge or jury will give an unprejudiced decision when an automobilist is brought up before the law is largely due to the little respect shown thereto by most of the [motoring] fraternity."[42]

[42]Montgomery Rollins, "Sane Motoring—Or Insane?" *Outlook*, 92:281 (May 29, 1909).

7
Roads, Services, and Mechanical Expertise

An American automobile culture emerged despite a notable lag in the development of adequate roads, services, and mechanical expertise. By European standards, American roads and provisions for automobile insurance were abominable. European commitment to a limited, upper-class market for cars also obviated the needs for substantial storage and repair facilities and widespread dissemination of mechanical expertise that the American mass market entailed. Although significant progress had been made toward solving these problems in the United States by 1910, accomplishment still lagged far behind the needs of an ever-increasing number of motorists.

Roads

When the automobile was first introduced in the United States, it was widely believed that the comparatively poor condition of roads here might retard its general adoption. *Scientific American* warned in 1895: "Because motor vehicles for common roads are practicable in France and England, it does not follow that they would be in America. The roads in those countries are almost perfection; but in this country a fairly good road is the exception." The periodical had come to the conclusion that "the roads in America are not good enough except in certain localities as yet to permit of a very rapid development of the automobile carriage, but their use in great cities [where some paved streets existed] is likely to be rapid."[1]

 The best roads were to be found in the New England and Middle Atlantic states, the poorest in the South and in rural districts of the Middle West, but everywhere in the United States road conditions were far from satisfactory. To cite an example from only one state, *Overland Monthly* complained in 1896 that "from the standpoint of a road engineer, there are not over one hundred miles of first-class road in California,"

[1]"New Prizes for Motor Carriage Competitions," *Scientific American*, 73:40 (July 20, 1895), and "Automobile Carriages: Prize Winners at the Paris Bordeaux Race," ibid., 73:66 (August 3, 1895).

and of the few wagon roads leading out of San Francisco "there is not one which at some period of the year . . . is not practically impassable for ordinary [horse-drawn] vehicles, either from mud or dust." *Overland Monthly* listed examples throughout the state and concluded that it should not "be taken from the foregoing that the roads of California are exceptionally bad. . . . California roads will compare favorably, in the general average, in those sections where roads have been constructed, with the roads of any state in the Union, excepting, perhaps, states like New York, New Jersey, Ohio, Massachusetts, where organized road work has been prosecuted for some time."[2]

The first census of American roads revealed that in 1904 only 7.14 percent of the roads in the United States were surfaced at all, and most of these just with gravel. There was only about one mile of improved road for every 492 inhabitants, and almost none of even this surfaced road was fit to withstand steady use by motor vehicles. Probably only a few hundred miles of road in the United States were really adequate for automobile traffic in 1904.[3] Colonel Albert A. Pope commented at the time that "the American who buys an automobile finds himself with this great difficulty: he has nowhere to use it."[4]

Public concern over the poor condition of American roads began to grow in the closing years of the nineteenth century. Good roads became a popular political issue, and strong planks for good roads were incorporated in the state platforms of the leading political parties. At the national level, William Jennings Bryan and President Theodore Roosevelt were among the prominent political leaders who attended the

[2]"The Good Roads Movement and the California Bureau of Highways," *Overland Monthly*, n.s. 28:446–448 (October 1896).
[3]Maurice O. Eldridge (Chief of Records, Office of Public Roads), *Public Road Mileage, Revenues, and Expenditures in the United States in 1904*, U.S. Department of Agriculture, Office of Public Roads, Bulletin no. 32 (Washington, D.C.: Government Printing Office, 1907).
[4]Colonel Albert A. Pope, "Automobiles and Good Roads," *Munsey's Magazine*, 29:168 (May 1903).

National Good Roads Convention at St. Louis in April 1903, where resolutions were passed endorsing the principle of state aid to counties and municipalities and the support of the federal government for highway construction.[5]

Propagandists for good roads capitalized upon several themes that had great popular appeal, especially for farmers. One was the high cost of transporting farm products to market, which was attributable to poor roads. *Scientific American* reported that "figures have been assembled to prove that owing to the frightful condition of almost all American roads, it costs 25 cents a ton-mile to haul. The superb roads of the old countries of Europe make possible the hauling of farm products at 12 cents a ton-mile." The higher food prices resulting from poor roads meant that city consumers as well as farmers paid the penalty for this "almost criminally shameful condition of 2,000,000 miles of road."[6] Another important theme was that road improvement increased land values in rural areas. Colonel Albert A. Pope pointed out that reliable statistical data collected among farmers in the Middle West indicated that the increase in land valuation due to the construction and maintenance of good roads averaged about $9 an acre. Pope asked rhetorically: "Is there any granger in the land who would not jump at the chance to meet his share of the tax for good roads, and reap this direct and many indirect benefits therefrom? "[7]

Early leadership of the good roads movement was assumed by bicycle manufacturers, dealers, and owners, who found the streets and highways of the United States generally ill suited to the pneumatic-tired vehicle. From its inception in 1880, the League of American Wheelmen (LAW) adopted the promoting of improved public

[5]*Proceedings of the National Good Roads Convention, St. Louis, Mo., 1903*, U.S. Department of Agriculture, Office of Public Road Inquiries, Bulletin no. 26 (Washington, D.C.: Government Printing Office, 1903).
[6]"The Political Economy of Good Roads," *Scientific American*, 99:451 (December 19, 1908).
[7]Colonel Albert A. Pope, "Good Roads and the Nation's Prosperity," *Harper's Weekly*, 51:370 (March 16, 1907).

roads as a major activity.[8] Colonel Albert A. Pope, the nation's leading bicycle manufacturer, and General Roy Stone headed the crusade for road improvement. Pope's activities included the publication of many propagandistic articles in popular periodicals, numerous public lectures, support for several trade magazines, organizational activity, and work as a legislative lobbyist. Under his leadership, the League of American Wheelmen founded the *Good Roads Magazine* (later to become the *L.A.W. Bulletin of Good Roads)* in 1892 and drafted a petition to Congress that resulted in the creation in 1893 of the Office of Road Inquiry in the Department of Agriculture. General Roy Stone organized the National League for Good Roads, with branches in most states, at the 1893 Columbian Exposition. At the local level, cyclists agitated for the improvement of city streets. For example, the Cycle Dealers' Board of Trade was formed in San Francisco in 1896 for the express purpose of uniting support to get Market Street repaved. In New York, John B. Uhle, a former member of the board of directors of the LAW, was the most active promoter and first president of the New York Highway Alliance, an organization founded in 1902 to coordinate the efforts of cyclists, horsemen, and automobilists to improve that city's streets.

Automobile interests rapidly displaced bicycle organizations as the dominant force in the good roads movement after about 1903. However, this transition was accompanied by great continuity in personnel because bicycle enthusiasts tended to become automobile enthusiasts. Former cyclists continued to agitate for good roads as members of automobile clubs. It is important to note that Colonel Pope, the most important figure in the movement, was the leading automobile as well as bicycle manufacturer in the United States by the turn of the century and that a large proportion of the early

[8] For the most detailed study, see Philip P. Mason, "The League of American Wheelmen and the Good-Roads Movement," Ph.D. dissertation, University of Michigan, 1957.

Plate 27.   1904 Pope-Hartford and
Pope-Toledo cars on a good Vir-
ginia road of the day. Courtesy
Smithsonian Institution.

Plate 28.   Stuck in the mud, an all
too common experience for the
early motorist. Courtesy Smithsonian Institution.

automobile manufacturers, dealers, and mechanics were recruited from the bicycle industry.

The automobile, to a much greater degree than the bicycle, made the public conscious of the need for good roads. Its impact was immediate. Colonel Pope's own assessment of the influence of the automobile upon the good roads movement by 1903 was that "the good roads agitation is now on a footing such as it never had in the past. . . . For this, no doubt, much credit should be given to the various automobile clubs and associations scattered throughout the country. It was none the less creditable to these bodies that their share in the movement has been so unobtrusive that now, for the first time, the demand for better highways may be said to be in every sense a popular one."[9]

The movement for improved roads was led by an alliance of automobilists and farmers by 1910. At the Second Annual Good Roads Convention, held on September 21–23, 1909, in Cleveland, Ohio, "the two dominant influences . . . were the American Automobile Association, representing the autoists and the cities, and the National Grange, representing the farmers. Cooperating with these organizations were the American Road Makers' Association, the National Association of Automobile Manufacturers, and the American Motor Car Manufacturers' Association." George S. Ladd, the special roads lecturer of the National Grange, spoke to the delegates, praising the role of the automobile in bringing about public concern over poor country roads: "We can only say that until the day of the automobile the city resident was not concerned about country roads. . . . And the farmer, before the automobile went spinning through his farm, didn't realize how far he was from his neighbors, how isolated was his life."[10] Through standing roads committees headed by prominent members, local

[9] Pope, "Automobiles and Good Roads," p. 167.
[10] "The Second Annual Good Roads Convention," *Horseless Age*, 24:335 (September 29, 1909).

automobile clubs put much effort into the good roads movement, at first without much public fanfare to avoid associating road improvement too closely with the special needs of the motorist. The activities reported in the automobile trade journals include direct appropriations for signboards, sponsorship of petitions for action and candidates for such positions as county supervisor and road superintendent, direct lobbying at state legislative sessions and meetings of county and city officials, and taking officials who remained adamant for automobile rides over sections of road that needed improvement.

The advocates of road improvement had achieved only limited success by 1910. The most conspicuous failure in the automobile interests' attempts to influence legislation was the 1903 introduction and death in committee of the Brownlow-Latimer Federal Good Roads Bill, the first attempt to involve the federal government in a program of highway construction. The major improvement that could be unequivocally attributed to the motor vehicle was the erection of directional and warnings signs.

The signboard movement was originated in 1901 by the Automobile Club of America and gained rapid momentum in the eastern states. By the end of 1901 the ACA had been joined by the automobile clubs of Buffalo, Rhode Island, Massachusetts, Long Island, and New Jersey in a campaign to mark the routes from New York City to Boston, Philadelphia, and Buffalo (via Albany) as well as the roads on Long Island with iron-strip signs bolted to iron posts. In addition, the New York Highway Alliance cooperated with the ACA to secure the enforcement of a New York state law compelling county authorities to erect guideposts at the crossings of main highways upon the petition of twenty resident taxpayers of a county. A national program for erecting danger signs on roads was initiated in 1903 by the American Motor League (AML), which advertised that it would provide any motorist with stencils and directions for putting up signs. The signboard movement became truly national in scope about 1906, when ambitious projects to mark local roads were undertaken by the automobile clubs in Illinois, California, Pennsylvania, Ohio, and Minnesota. Among the automobile manufacturers, Thomas B. Jeffery was especially active in the signboard movement; he set aside a $25,000 fund in 1907 to enable Rambler dealers to erect guideposts at intersections and danger points in Wisconsin and Illinois. The touring-information board of the American Automobile Association (AAA) initiated a program in 1909 to erect some 10,000 wooden road signs in those districts of the United States where progress in erecting signboards had been slowest.

There was also evidence that agitation by motorists and farmers had led to some gain in improved-road mileage. Although only 8.66 percent of the roads in the United States were surfaced in 1909, a gain of but 1.52 percent over 1904, in absolute terms 36,950 miles of improved road had been built since 1904, while total road mileage had increased by 48,266 miles. Another definite gain was that gravel was now being displaced by macadam and other more durable types of road surface.[11]

Any gains in the quantity and quality of surfaced roads seem to have been more than offset by the new demands of automobile traffic. It began to become apparent as early as 1902 that the higher speeds of motor vehicles caused undue wear on roads and that adequate automobile roads necessitated increased clearance and width. Engineers estimated that, to build roads capable of standing up under automobile traffic, road improvements costing from $600 to $3,000 per mile would be mandatory.[12] Heavy automobile traffic had already seriously damaged the main highways of Massachusetts by 1907: "The binder is swept from the road, and the stone from ½ to 1½ inch in size has been disturbed, in some cases standing on the surface, and

[11] J. E. Pennybacker, Jr., and Maurice O. Eldridge, *Mileage and Cost of Public Roads in the United States*, Office of Public Roads, Bulletin no. 41 (Washington, D.C.: Government Printing Office, 1912).
[12] "The Wear of Roads by Automobiles," *Scientific American*, 86:137 (March 1, 1902).

in other cases being left in windrows along the roadside."[13] The Massachusetts Highway Commission considered such wear "extraordinary" and was convinced by 1909 that changes in the construction and maintenance of stone roads were necessary. But it was evident that macadamized roads were no solution: "A vehicle weighing from 1,000 to 3,000 pounds, running at speeds of from 20 to 30 miles an hour on pneumatic tires, will break down, and very quickly break down the type of macadamized road of which we are building thousands of miles throughout the country."[14] Brick roads were probably the most satisfactory, but their cost was prohibitive. Concrete, which was eventually to provide the solution, was first used on a county road in 1908 on a mile stretch of highway in Wayne County, Michigan, and proved so successful that the county added twenty-four more miles of concrete highway in 1910.

One must conclude that the development of adequate automobile roads lagged well behind the diffusion of the motor vehicle in the United States and that the automobile was widely adopted here despite a relative scarcity of suitable roads for its use. *Motor Age* accurately assessed in 1899 that "the motor vehicle industry would starve if it should wait for road improvement. To state that motor vehicles require fine roads first of all is tantamount to damning the motor vehicle in the United States." The periodical warned: "Don't preach that motor vehicles depend on roads. They don't. They depend on good suitable construction to negotiate any kind of road surface and on perfectly reliable motors."[15] American automobiles were consequently improved much more rapidly than the streets and highways on which they were driven, and by 1904 motorists were well aware that "the average automobile is better than the average road. . . . The common cause of delays is defective roads, not defective machines."[16]

[13]*Scientific American*, 97:12 (July 6, 1907).
[14]"The Highway and the Automobile," ibid., 100:238 (March 27, 1909).
[15]"The Road Improvement Fallacy," *Motor Age*, 1:82–83 (October 10, 1899).
[16]"Touring Experience," ibid., 6:8 (July 7, 1904).

There is no tangible evidence either that the automobile first diffused more rapidly into those areas in the United States with the best roads or that the automobile led in the short run to better roads in those areas where it was most widely adopted at first. Using Kendall's "tau," correlations were made between the rank order of states in ratio of total automobiles registered to number of persons eighteen years of age and over in 1910 and the rank order of states on two indices of road conditions for 1904, the first year for which reliable data are available, to determine whether any "causal" relationship existed between the innovativeness of states in adopting the automobile by 1910 and the condition of their roads several years earlier. The 1904 indices used were miles of road per square mile of area and percentage of roads improved. Then, to determine the effect of the automobile upon road improvement, the rank order of states on the basis of total automobiles registered to number of persons eighteen years of age and over in 1910 was correlated with the rank order of states on the basis of the percentage of roads improved in 1914.

The resulting correlations show a minimal relationship between the innovativeness of states in adopting the automobile by 1910 and state road improvement both for 1904 and for 1914. The rank order of states on the basis of ratio of total automobiles registered to number of persons eighteen years of age and over in 1910 correlates with the rank order of states on the basis of miles of road per square mile of area in 1904 at +.23 and with the rank order of states on the basis of percentage of roads improved in 1904 at +.30. The correlation with the rank order of states on the basis of the percentage of roads improved in 1914 is even lower, at +.19, bearing out the short-range deleterious effect of automobile traffic on roads that we have previously noted.

Nebraska and North Dakota, which ranked fourth and fifth, respectively, in ratio of total automobiles registered to number of persons eighteen years of age and over in 1910, provide excellent illustrations of how slight the reciprocal relationship between the automobile and good roads appears to have been during the early years of diffusion. Nebraska had only one mile of road per square mile of area in 1904 and ranked twenty-seventh among the states on this criterion. Only 0.02 percent of Nebraska's roads were improved in 1904, and the state ranked forty-seventh in the nation on this criterion. With 0.3 percent of its roads improved by 1914, Nebraska then ranked forty-eighth. North Dakota had only 0.84 miles of road per square mile of area in 1904, and only 0.35 percent of its roads were improved in 1904, so North Dakota ranked thirty-second in miles of road per square mile of area and forty-third in percentage of roads improved among the states for that year. North Dakota tied with Nebraska for forty-eighth place in 1914, with only 0.3 percent of its roads improved.

Thus the relationship between the adoption of the automobile and good roads appears equivocal at best. Although the adoption of the automobile did lead to the building of better roads, there does not seem to have been any significant relationship at the state level between good roads and innovativeness in adoption of the automobile. Cars were designed to negotiate comparatively poor roads rather than vice versa. Progress in road construction continued to lag behind motorists' needs.

Insurance
The inevitable automobile accidents that resulted from unskilled motorists driving at high speeds created a formidable insurance problem. Not only did the accident rate for automobiles seem inordinately high for the number of cars in use; automobile accidents also usually involved more serious bodily injury and higher property damage claims than accidents involving only horse-drawn vehicles, and the motor

vehicle was generally more costly to repair or replace. Insurance brokers furthermore lacked sufficient experience with the motor vehicle to determine risk adequately, so they shied away from writing automobile insurance policies.

Although several firms began to sell automobile fire and liability insurance through extension of the types of policies issued for horse-drawn vehicles by the turn of the century, experience soon indicated that the automobile insurance business was fraught with new difficulties and was unprofitable. *Motor World* reported in 1902: "It is well known that automobilists experience considerable difficulty in placing insurance on their cars, houses, etc. Nearly all insurance companies fight shy of such risks, seemingly being better pleased if the business does not come to them."[17] In New York, the number of insurance companies writing automobile liability policies had dropped from ten to four by 1902, and the companies remaining in the business raised their average premiums from $25, the standard rate for horse-drawn vehicles, to $100. The majority of insurance companies in Cleveland, Ohio, decided in 1902 to insure automobiles for damage "only when they are standing unused in the barn." A member of one of these firms explained that "one experience [with the high cost of repairing a damaged automobile] was enough to convince us that the business was not desirable. Auto insurance is a thing of the past except when the machine is standing."[18]

Both an acceptable floater policy for automobile fire insurance that extended coverage from the owner's storage facilities to the geographic limits of one or several states and an automobile liability policy that provided coverage up to $10,000 per accident had been innovated by 1903, but the problem of insurance for motorists still existed: *Motor World* reported in 1904 that it was "depressing to learn that the pessi-

[17] "Business Not Wanted," *Motor World*, 4:594 (August 21, 1902).
[18] "Insurance Men Are Shy," *Motor Age*, 2:5 (July 24, 1902).

mism felt is both deeper and more general than it was a year or two ago." The failure of one company that had written "hundreds of thousands of dollars" of automobile insurance seemed significant: "Claim after claim was made in rapid succession. . . . So heavy were these drafts that the premiums were soon swept away, leaving a large deficit, with an enormous amount of 'risks' still outstanding." The result was "a general disposition in insurance circles to write less business of this character. Furthermore the business of the future will be more closely scrutinized . . . the application of the motorist with a record of accidents will be turned down without a moment's hesitation."[19]

State laws affecting insurance proved to be another stumbling block. Problems here included lawful premiums and extent of coverage as well as regulations on the storage and operation of motor vehicles. State laws requiring high minimal capitalization for insurance firms necessitated high premiums, and state laws limiting the business of an insurance company to the field of insurance specified in its registration papers made it difficult for any firm legally to guarantee complete coverage to the motorist, whose needs overlapped traditionally distinct fields of insurance. Conflicts among the insurance laws of the different states also made it difficult at first to write floater policies that would protect the touring motorist. A broker explained in a letter to the editor of *Automobile* in 1903: "During the past two years no firm has remained as specialists in this line [of automobile insurance] for a longer period than three or four months, owing to the fact that it is a most peculiar line necessitating unusual facilities and greater knowledge of insurance laws than the average broker possesses. . . . the broker issuing the business finds himself confronted with conditions which tax him to the utmost to write a form which will not be a violation of any state law under which the policy is to cover."[20]

[19] "As Insurance Men View It," *Motor World*, 8:755 (August 18, 1904).
[20] "Insurance on Automobiles," *Automobile*, 8:156 (January 31, 1903).

By European standards, insurance coverage on motor vehicles in the United States remained complicated and costly throughout the period with which we are concerned. Some marine insurance companies, since they were not subject to the jurisdictions of local insurance exchanges and were accustomed to assuming relatively high risks for moderate premiums, were willing and able to write automobile floater policies providing very limited coverage for damage to automobiles at annual premiums of less than 3 percent. These companies were writing the lion's share of automobile insurance by 1905, when other companies, impressed by the growing number of automobiles in the United States, first began to take a more favorable view of insuring motor vehicles at competitive rates. Fox and Pier issued the only policy in the United States in 1906 dealing exclusively with collision risks to automobiles. For a 3 percent annual premium this policy covered damage by collision with any moving or stationary object, liabilities for damage to other vehicles through collision, and legal expenses incurred in connection with collisions. However, so-called universal policies, covering the full range of the motorist's insurance needs, were still not available here, although they were already common in Europe. The combined cost of complete collision, fire and theft, and liability coverage ran about $7\frac{1}{3}$ percent in annual premiums in the United States versus only about $4\frac{1}{4}$ percent in England.

Storage and Repairs

The lack of adequate storage and repair facilities was considered a major stumbling block to the widespread diffusion of motor vehicles in the United States. Most city residences lacked private stables for horse-drawn vehicles, and the public livery stables usually would not allow motorists to use their facilities. *Scientific American* reported that storage and repair facilities for motor vehicles were so unsatisfactory in

1902 that "the manufacturers of motor vehicles are well aware that a great many people are deterred from buying machines because of the lack of repair shops able to do good, responsible work." It was even feared that many commercial users of motor vehicles would go back to horses "unless a system of storage [and repair] stations comes to the rescue," especially since the few automobile garages that did exist were usually not conveniently located "close to the city's business heart." Conditions appeared even worse outside major cities: "The bicycle repair shop, the blacksmith's shop, and the general mechanic's shop are the only places of refuge, and none of them offer adequate assistance in case of accident. They are merely the local mechanical centers, which the wrecked automobilist goes through, not without a lurking suspicion that he will have to do most of the repairing himself or take a botched job."[21]

Bicycle clubs with dwindling memberships took the initiative in a few instances to provide motorists with storage and repair facilities. The prime example was the 1902 decision of the Century Wheelmen of Philadelphia, one of the country's "crack" bicycle organizations, to transform a portion of its large wheelroom into an automobile garage. More often, however, the need for storage and repair facilities became a primary motive for the founding of an automobile club. Whitney Lyon, who with George F. Chamberlain took the initiative to found the Automobile Club of America, explained to *Horseless Age* that "the necessity of a club was forced upon him by the difficulty he encountered in trying to find a livery stable keeper who would store and care for his motor carriage. When the proprietor of a stable learned that the vehicle was horseless he looked upon it as an enemy to his business and not to be harbored at any price." Consequently, a major aim of the new club became "to establish a depot for the proper storage and care of vehicles, and where all forms of automo-

[21]"Automobile Storage and Repair Facilities," *Scientific American*, 86:226 (March 29, 1902).

biles . . . may be properly housed and cared for by competent mechanics, and where supplies of all kinds for the purpose will be kept."[22]

The most impressive early automobile club garage was opened by the Massachusetts Automobile Club (MAC) on January 1, 1902, in its new clubhouse on Boylston Street near Copley Square in Boston. The ground floor served as a storage room for twenty-five vehicles and included inspection pits and facilities for washing cars. The basement served as a reserve storage room, and a gasoline tank was installed underground outdoors. The third floor contained a repair shop equipped with lathe, upright drill, emery wheel, hoist, and a full line of bench tools. An 8×12 foot hydraulic elevator was used to transport cars from the storage floors to the repair shop, and electric motors supplied the power for the machine tools and the air pump for tire inflation. The MAC's facilities were not surpassed by those of any other club until the Automobile Club of America completed its new $500,000 clubhouse in April 1907. This eight-story building on West Fifty-fourth Street between Broadway and Eighth Avenue was both near Central Park and convenient to the elevated and subway lines. Storage accommodations were provided for three hundred automobiles, and the top floor was given over to a fully equipped repair shop and testing room.

However, the establishment of public garages, particularly the provision of garages by automobile manufacturers as adjuncts to sales agencies, was far more important than the construction of a few elaborate garage facilities by automobile clubs. The early close association of the public garage business with the automobile manufacturer is well illustrated by the establishments operating in New York City in 1901. The Winton garage on Fifty-eighth Street near Third Avenue was "in reality an Eastern Branch of the Winton Company." Thirty-three vehicles belonging to customers were housed there, and the business carried out embodied "about the same features of

[22] "Automobile Club Organized," *Horseless Age*, 4:6 (June 14, 1899).

an ordinary storage and repair station conducted for the public at large." Locomobile and the Steam Vehicle Company of America both supported similar garages in the city. Some public garages not associated with any particular manufacturer were also doing business in New York, but these concerns rented either office space to manufacturers' agents or space for demonstration cars. The Manhattan Automobile Company was representative. This firm's business included "only storing, caretaking, repairs and supplying with gasoline, lubricating oils and electric current. Manufacturers store special vehicles there and use them for demonstrating purposes with customers, but the concern as such has nothing to do with the sale or exchange of automobiles; neither does it let office rooms for this or any other line of business connected with automobilism." An alternative policy was association with many manufacturers. Walter Stearns's New York Automobile Exchange at 114 Fifth Avenue was a successful garage with sales agencies for Packard, the International Company, Locomobile, the United Power Vehicle Company, and Adams and McMurtrie. Other New York garages—the Motor Vehicle Storage and Repair Company, Homan and Schultz, and the Automobile Storage and Repair Company—steered a middle course, and each let space to the agencies of two manufacturers.[23]

New York appears to have enjoyed the distinction in these early years of being the only major city in the United States with sufficient garages for the number of motor vehicles in use. *Automobile* pointed out in a 1902 appraisal of metropolitan garage facilities: "In other large cities some of the local agencies and retail branches have limited facilities for storing a few of the vehicles purchased of them, and in some cities there are a few more or less well equipped storage stations. But these are not well distributed through the residence neighborhoods and cannot in size

[23] "Automobile Storage and Repair Stations in New York," ibid., 8:17–18, 28, 74–75, 122–124 (April 3, 10, and 24 and May 8, 1901).

and number meet the rapidly increasing patronage." There were, for instance, only four garages for the six hundred automobiles estimated to have been in use at that time in Chicago.[24]

To fill the obvious need for automobile garages, a few entrepreneurs with foresight established chains of automobile storage and repair stations shortly after the turn of the century. John Wanamaker, whose department stores were among the first retail outlets for motor vehicles in the United States, also pioneered in establishing garages in New York and Philadelphia. The Philadelphia automobile station that Wanamaker opened in 1901 at Twenty-third and Walnut streets occupied a city block and included a driving school as well as facilities for storage and repair. The labor charge for repairs was $1 an hour, and an emergency service was set up to handle breakdowns in any part of the city. The most impressive early chain of garages was the Banker Brothers Company, the eastern distributor for nine automobile manufacturers, which operated large public garages in New York, Pittsburgh, and Philadelphia. Their Philadelphia garage employed thirty-five people and had storage room for one hundred and fifty motor vehicles. It is reputed to have been one of the largest and best equipped garages in the United States in 1903.

The concept of the modern service station was innovated by other early garage chains that attempted to extend facilities to outlying areas. One of these firms, the Hartford Auto Corporation, controlled fourteen service stations within a fifty-mile radius of Boston by late 1901 and was negotiating to extend its "Harvard system" to other cities in New England. Another such chain was that inaugurated in 1901 by the Columbia Lubricants Company of New York on the routes to Philadelphia, Albany, and Boston. This company had been handling gasoline and lubricating oils and greases for several years and made a specialty of supplying automobile manu-

[24] "Metropolitan Storage Stations," *Automobile*, 6:1–2 (June 21, 1902).

facturers. Realizing that it was difficult for the motorist to obtain products of high and uniform quality at the average small-town general store, Columbia Lubricants tried to get the best available dealer or repairman in each town to act as its agent. It also expressed a willingness to cooperate with automobile manufacturers by passing on any special instructions or cautions about specific makes of car to the owners. In addition, accurate information regarding roads, hotels, and state automobile laws were made available in pocket-sized books given out at the company's service stations.

   Both national automobile clubs attempted to secure high-quality service at reasonable rates for automobile tourists by providing lists of approved stations throughout the country. The American Motor League published a list of "Official Stations," whose proprietors were under contract to allow AML members a 10 percent discount on all bills of $1 or more, as well as a list of approved hotels. The American Automobile Association, through its touring-information bureau, gave official endorsement to a "Blue Book" inaugurated by the Class Journal Company, the publisher of *Automobile*, in May 1906. The *Automobile Official Blue Book* was the first comprehensive road guide for the United States and Canada and included a list of AAA-approved hotel and garage accommodations along with its series of maps. Recommended routes and facilities were checked by an official "Blue Book" car. Another important contribution of the automobile clubs was that plans for cross-country tours and races usually included the improvement of service and repair facilities along the routes of travel.

   Although the garage business had grown phenomenally by 1906, especially in major cities, development was not far in advance of the developing market for storage and repair facilities. *Horseless Age* in 1905 noted "a very surprising increase . . . in the number of automobile garages to be found, not only in the large cities but in small towns as well. There is hardly a village of any importance in the thickly peopled parts of the country which does not boast of one or more storage stations, and it appears that in some places the business is in danger of being overdone." But the periodical believed that, "everything considered, the large number of automobile stations which are now doing business, surprising as their increase is, probably do not offer facilities much in excess of the present demand and certainly not in excess of the immediately prospective call for the service which they offer."[25] Denver's dozen garages were about the average number found in the "automobile rows" that had emerged in medium-sized American cities by 1906. New York City led the nation then with over eighty automobile garages.

  The main functions of the automobile garage changed over time and were different in rural than in urban areas. Storage remained the most important function of the big-city garage. Before the introduction of the automobile, there had been little private stabling of horses in big cities. High real estate values and population congestion made it both impractical and undesirable to attach unsightly and unsanitary stables to closely spaced city residences, so city owners of horses had taken to "boarding, baiting and renting stable" at centralized points removed from their living quarters. The public automobile garage thus developed by a natural analogy with the livery stable, and the early urban motorist most often kept his car some distance from his home. Higher insurance rates on property where an automobile was stored, difficulty in securing permission from city officials to store gasoline in one's residence, and the inability of the average city automobile owner to give his car proper care because of his ignorance of practical mechanics and lack of time were other factors that reenforced dependence upon the public garage. Here the city motorist, for $15 or $20 a month, excluding the cost of gasoline and major repairs, could have his vehicle stored, regularly cleaned, and adjusted mechanically. Cars were most often not used

25 "The Growth of the Garage Business," *Horseless Age*, 15:477–478 (April 26, 1905).

during the winter, and the price for winter "dead" storage of an automobile was even more reasonable—from $2 to $5 a month in most places.

Toward the end of the first decade of the twentieth century, however, the private automobile garage in close proximity to city living quarters began to become important. By then it was realized that the main objections to the backyard stable—its filth, odor, and germs—did not apply to the motor vehicle; city ordinances and taxes affecting the storage of motor vehicles had become less prohibitive; and as motoring came to be utilitarian rather than a "sport" pursued on special occasions, automobile owners wanted their cars always at hand for use. By 1908, small portable garages expressly designed for motorcars could be built for as little as $140, and private automobile garages attached to residences were beginning to appear in large- and medium-sized cities.

Outside the larger cities, the garage business never developed well; from the first, storage remained the least important function of the small-town garage. The developing rural market was in response to the farmer's needs for more efficient transportation of his crops to market and easier access to the social life of the city. These needs were incompatible with storing a car in town for use on an occasional outing. Also, knowledge of practical mechanics was much more widely diffused among farmers accustomed to fixing complicated agricultural machinery than among city residents. This reduced the farmer's dependence on the garage for minor adjustments and repairs.

Before the rural market for automobiles began to develop about 1906, the small-town garage depended primarily upon tourist trade. But in many outlying areas this was not sufficient to make the establishment of a garage profitable. The situation reported for the Dakotas in 1907 illustrates rural conditions: "As a rule the cars have the appearance of never having been on a washstand or having made the acquaintance of a polishing rag, no pride whatever being taken in their appearance. Should a replacement of parts be necessary there is nothing to do but lay the car up and wait for new ones. . . . In the majority of the small towns automobile repairs are made by the village 'smithy' who has a very limited knowledge of the working parts of a motorcar. . . . His equipment of tools consists generally of a forge and anvil, ax, heavy hammer and a cold chisel, and the delicacy and accuracy of some of his repairs may well be left to the imagination."[26]

Even in large cities motorists complained constantly about the quality of repair work done at the average garage. *Motor World* summarized this general dissatisfaction in 1904: "The repair departments of most of our factories have not proven to be what they ought to be, from the standpoint of the owner of an automobile. Work coming from them has been found to be badly done, expensive and altogether unsatisfactory. The charges made for parts applied and overhauling are out of all reason, as compared with the cost of the machine."[27] It still seemed in 1909 that dealers "devote practically all of their energies to the sale of cars and conduct a garage business only because it is required by their customers." The inevitable result was that "many car owners regard all garages with distrust."[28]

Fortunately, improvements in the design and construction of motor vehicles progressively made both the shortage of repair facilities in some areas and their poor quality everywhere much less of a burden to the average automobile owner. By 1907 it was apparent that, "As these newer and more reliable vehicles take the place of the older ones the repair business naturally suffers very heavily, and the chief business of this branch of a garage becomes the making of adjustments and minor replacements

[26]"The Automobile in the Dakotas," ibid., 20:324–325 (September 11, 1907).
[27]"Repairs and the Charges Therefor," *Motor World*, 9:183 (October 27, 1904).
[28]"The Present Status of the Garage Business," *Horseless Age*, 23:591 (April 21, 1909).

and a certain amount of tire work. . . . the garage is no longer the automobile 'general hospital' that it once was."[29]

Mechanical Expertise

The general lack of automotive expertise among Americans was another major problem. The neophyte driver constituted a grave menace to the public safety. Commentators agreed that the major cause of automobile accidents was "incompetent driving, which may be due to inexperience or lack of mechanical knowledge of the car," attributable to "the simple reason that new drivers are making their debut every day, and it is generally admitted that most of us will insist on gaining our knowledge through experience—sometimes disastrous."[30] Mechanical breakdowns were also considered to be mainly the fault of improper driving and poor care of the car. *Scientific American* lamented "the lack of men trained to manage and care for the high-powered cars which are being turned out" and pointed out that "manufacturers of popular cars have estimated that three-quarters of the troubles reported to them by automobile owners are the results of inefficient handling rather than of inherent defects in the machine."[31]

Garages capitalized on the ignorance of owners and charged high prices for the shoddy work done by inexperienced so-called mechanics. Early motorists complained: "A job that should take an hour will consume a day, for it takes about eight hours to find out what needs to be done and how to do it. In many cases when one part is duly fixed something else is thrown out of adjustment, and then comes a puzzling search, sometimes taking several days. . . . the owner just sits down and trembles until

[29]"Changes in the Garage Business," ibid., 19:365–366 (March 13, 1907).
[30]C. O. Morris, "The Cause of Automobile Accidents," *Country Life in America*, 15:375 (February 1909).
[31]"An Automobile School," *Scientific American*, 94:435 (May 26, 1906).

the job is finished."[32] Conditions did not get much better. Most garages were obliged to hire young men with a mechanical turn of mind who had no special training. Some city garages during slack periods sent their mechanics to school at the factory represented by the garage, but this was not typical.

Most automobile manufacturers took no action to train drivers and gave negligible instruction to mechanics. The few notable exceptions were to be found among the companies that made relatively high-priced cars, and even their courses of instruction were designed primarily to convert the former coachmen of wealthy owners into chauffeurs in as short a time as possible. Locomobile initiated such a factory school for chauffeurs at its Bridgeport, Connecticut, plant in 1904; the course included on-the-job training in assembling and repairing cars as well as driving lessons. After 1906, Pierce-Arrow conducted similar two-week sessions at a factory school from February through May for chauffeurs and mechanics who had been recommended by Pierce-Arrow dealers; special segregated sessions were initiated for Negroes and the owners themselves in 1909. Packard made the most conspicuous efforts of any manufacturer to provide training for drivers and mechanics. As early as 1903, Packard instituted the first factory school to educate its own employees about motorcar design, construction, and operation with a series of regular classes held at the plant. Soon branching out into providing instruction for new Packard owners and owners' sons and chauffeurs, Packard established a well-rounded month's course at the factory in fundamental automobile mechanics, which included practical experience in making emergency repairs and minor adjustments. Then in 1908 Packard began a local series of weekly lectures and discussions for the owners of Packard cars in the Detroit area.

Working in close association with local automobile clubs, the Young Men's Christian

[32] "Repairs Are Difficult," *Horseless Age*, 8:441 (August 21, 1901).

Association made the most important attempt to provide formal training for motorists and automobile mechanics. The establishment of YMCA automobile schools in several major cities was viewed as "simply a furtherance" of its educational department's standing policy "to furnish such courses of instruction as are of the most practical and direct benefit to members."[33] Automobile clubs had little difficulty in persuading YMCA officials that there was great demand for young men of good character trained as chauffeurs and mechanics because the clubs offered to bear the brunt of the work and the expense involved in setting up the courses under YMCA auspices. A lack of trained, trustworthy chauffeurs and mechanics motivated the automobile clubs to undertake these responsibilities. The Automobile Club of America, for example, began compiling a register of reliable chauffeurs and mechanics in 1902 in response to a growing concern among affluent automobile owners about the "chauffeur evil." But the club had little success in alleviating the shortage of qualified help. The ACA was therefore anxious to attack the problem at a more fundamental level through staffing and equipping an automobile school for the New York City West Side YMCA. Automobile manufacturers generally cooperated with the YMCA schools by providing courtesy cars for demonstration purposes.

The first YMCA school was established in Boston during the winter of 1903/04 with the support of the Massachusetts Automobile Club and representatives of the White, Pope-Waverley, and Crest automobile companies. Other YMCA schools were then founded with the aid of the local automobile clubs in Detroit, Cleveland, and New York in 1904 and in Los Angeles the following year. Curricula in these schools were virtually identical. The courses given at the Boston YMCA may be considered typical. First, there was a basic course intended "for owners, chauffeurs, and prospec-

[33] "School for Cleveland," *Motor Age*, 5:16 (May 12, 1904).

tive purchasers." It consisted of twenty-four illustrated lectures on "the general principles, construction, operation, repair, and care of all styles of cars." A course designed "for those who wish to drive their own carriages, or prepare themselves as professional chauffeurs," which was to be taken in conjunction with these lectures, provided "several weeks' instruction in the engine room." The third course offered a more advanced and thorough exposition, "especially for draughtsmen and machinists who wish to enter the automobile industry."[34] Public response was enthusiastic. By mid-1905 more than 2,000 people were enrolled in the various YMCA schools. The most popular course appeared to be the one that emphasized driving instruction and practical mechanics for budding professional chauffeurs and owner-operators.

Prior to the inauguration of the YMCA program, the Scranton International Correspondence Schools had offered a course by mail in "gas engineering." A few automobile driving schools had also been opened. But *Horseless Age* believed that "to the YMCA branches must be given the credit for the first establishment of resident schools in several of the larger cities." Because of the impetus provided by the successful example of the YMCA schools, by 1908 "each large city could boast of several [automobile schools], and schools also sprang up in many of the smaller cities and towns, in some of which not more than a dozen or so cars were owned."[35]

As one might expect, the quality of the instruction offered varied widely. Not uncommonly, automobile schools were obvious frauds; for high rates of tuition, the practical instruction given consisted of taking a carload of students out for a few hours' ride, and the students spent most of their time "standing in front of the building with no visible means of employment." The result was that "many of the graduates find themselves totally incompetent to render the kind of service for which they are supposed to be prepared," and employers "complain that the graduates do

[34]"Learn Automobiling at School," ibid., 4:11 (August 6, 1903).
[35]"Automobile Schools—Their Purpose and Methods," *Horseless Age*, 21:313 (March 18, 1908).

not come to them with any practical knowledge."[36] Even when honestly conducted, correspondence instruction was considered completely inadequate, and "garage schools" were generally considered inferior to the YMCA courses.

The New York School of Automobile Engineers, founded in 1905, was typical of the better private automobile schools. Professor Charles E. Lucke of the Department of Engineering at Columbia University planned and supervised its program of instruction, which consisted of a six-week course emphasizing practical matters. During the first four weeks, the morning sessions were devoted to lectures "couched in as plain a language as possible" and the afternoons to shopwork, for which the school was adequately equipped with a large supply of tools and demonstration equipment as well as with eight automobiles for instructional purposes. The final two weeks were devoted to "practice driving in the garage and on the road."[37] *Scientific American* reported, after the New York School of Automobile Engineers had been in business a year, that "of the hundred students who have completed the course, none has failed to give satisfaction to his employer."[38]

The contribution of automobile schools to the dissemination of automotive expertise is difficult to assess. Many schools offered instruction of extremely poor quality, and even at the better schools courses were too short and basic to provide students with more than a general smattering of knowledge. On the other hand, it is evident that a large number of men received some training in the fundamentals of automobile mechanics and driving. According to figures available for the two most prominent New York City schools, for example, by late 1908 nearly 2,000 students had taken the courses at the West Side YMCA, and about 1,500 students had been graduated from the New York School of Automobile Engineers.

[36]"Automobile Schools," ibid., 17:625–626 (May 2, 1906).
[37]"A Typical Institution for Training Automobile Drivers," ibid., 23:59 (January 23, 1909).
[38]"An Automobile School," p. 435.

Three things were at least as important as the rise of automobile schools in overcoming the early general lack of automotive expertise. First, most automobile owners were eager to learn all they could about their cars and to communicate this knowledge to others. The large amount of space devoted in trade journals to the mechanisms and mechanical problems of the motorcar and the "experience meetings" that were a common part of the agenda of automobile clubs played an important role in the dissemination of mechanical knowledge among automobile owners. And as the automobile diffused, it became increasingly possible for the novice to obtain adequate informal instruction from his acquaintances.

Second, the problem of mechanical expertise diminished appreciably once the motor vehicle began to be widely adopted in rural areas because the farmer already possessed considerable knowledge of practical mechanics. As *Cassier's Magazine* noted, "Many a motor enthusiast, when stranded by the wayside, has found that the man in the blue jeans and wide-brimmed straw could locate the trouble of his machine and repair it as well as an expert mechanic. Why? Because years of close association with stationary and portable gasoline engines has acquainted him with the simple mechanism of this type of power-producer."[39]

Finally, by 1910 the American motorcar had been vastly improved, and an automobile was easier for the average owner to drive and care for. The simple and rugged Ford Model T was the most conspicuous example of this trend. In 1908, when the Model T first appeared, *Horseless Age* predicted that "the tendency in construction will probably be toward greater simplicity and dependability, so that there will be relatively less need of wide mechanical knowledge and skill on the part of the driver." As the number of such cars in use increased, the periodical expected that "many boys and young men will have opportunity to become familiar with the operation

[39]George E. Walsh, "The Gasoline Motor in Farm Development," *Cassier's Magazine*, 33:527 (March 1908).

of these machines by simple observation without any special instruction, and this distinction between the coachman and the chauffeur will then vanish."[40] Although this was beginning to prove true already by 1910, good mechanics were still scarce, and the neophyte automobilist, if only because his number increased daily, was still about as much a peril on the highway as ever.

[40]"The Status of the Chauffeur," *Horseless Age*, 22:39–40 (July 8, 1908).

8

Developing the
American Motorcar

The rapid displacement of steam and electric cars by the gasoline automobile was not foreseen at the turn of the century. There was uncertainty about which type of motive power, if any, would win out over the others. Steam and electricity appeared initially to offer some distinct advantages over the internal-combustion engine. Consequently, the early production of both steam and electric cars outstripped the manufacture of gasoline-driven automobiles in the United States. Production figures for 1900 listed 1,681 steam, 1,575 electric, and only 936 gasoline cars, with Locomobile steamers alone accounting for about 5,000 of the 22,000 automobiles made in the United States between 1899 and 1902.[1] Early reports from various localities on the relative popularity of the three motive powers also showed that gasoline cars were generally less prevalent than one or the other alternative types. Taking the fifteen makes of automobiles most represented in New York registrations for early 1902, for example, there were 438 Locomobile and Mobile steamers, 320 gasoline cars, and 104 electric cars. It was estimated that about half of the 100 automobiles in Los Angeles at the beginning of 1902 were electrics, the other half being about equally divided between steam and gasoline automobiles.[2]

Despite the initial popularity of steam and electric cars, however, the dominance of the internal-combustion engine was well established by 1905. Its meteoric rise to a position of unchallenged prominence can be seen in the shift in the manufacturers' image of market demand revealed in the trend in relative numbers of models representing the three types of motive power displayed at New York automobile shows from 1901 to 1905. In 1901, 58 steam, 23 electric, and 58 gasoline cars were exhibited, but by 1903 the figures were 34 steam, 51 electric, and 168 gasoline cars. At the 1905 Madison Square Garden show, 9 steam, 20 electric, and 219 gasoline automobiles

[1] J. T. Sullivan, "New England a 1900 Leader," *Motor Age*, 19:2 (March 2, 1911).
[2] "The Fifteen Leaders," *Motor World*, 4:225 (May 22, 1902), and "Roads in Southern California," *Motor Age*, 1:10 (January 4, 1902).

were displayed. Similarly, an analysis of total registrations for ten eastern states for 1905 showed 9,153 American and 597 foreign gasoline automobiles versus 1,407 steamers and 576 electric cars.[3]

The Steam Car

Before the steamer could enjoy even its brief flurry of popularity, a general lack of enthusiasm about its potential that was prevalent in the mid-1890s had to be overcome. An 1896 article in *Engineering Magazine* summed up the objections: "For the purpose of propelling the general run of vehicles, it may be safely said that steam will never be made acceptable. It will furnish all the power required for the purpose, and at a very economical rate, but it is dirty, noisy, more or less dangerous, and requires so much attention that it would be almost impractical for one man to run a steam wagon through the busy streets of a city."[4] A major disadvantage at this time was that it was still necessary to wait to get up steam before the vehicle could be operated.

However, the early steamer did have some decided merits. Compared with the electric car, the steamer was economical to run, had a significantly wider functional range of operation, with the availability of fuel being no problem, and was powerful enough to negotiate steep grades impossible for the electric. The steam engine was a more flexible engine with fewer moving parts than the internal combustion engine and was less critical of exact tolerances for minimal efficiency. The steam engine could not stall, permitted much smoother transmission of power to the wheels, thus simplifying operation by reducing the formidable problems of shifting gears, and was a good deal easier to manufacture.

[3]"Uncle Sam and John Bull," *Motor Age*, 8:8 (August 3, 1905). Estimates of the number of motor vehicles exhibited at the shows vary, but all illustrate the same general trend. The most generous estimates for each year have been used here.
[4]William Baxter, Jr., "Electricity and the Horseless Carriage Problem," *Engineering Magazine*, 11:248 (May 1896).

The American steam car therefore became popular once it had been improved in the closing years of the nineteenth century with the introduction of liquid fuel and the flash boiler, which allowed instantaneous starts provided the pilot light had been left on. Especially in hilly areas where soft water in horse troughs was abundant, several American makes of steamers gained rapid and wide acceptance. New England was one such area; San Francisco was another. The Locomobile steamer was undoubtedly the most popular single make of automobile in the United States in 1900 and 1901.

However, the popularity of the steam car declined as quickly as it had risen. In addition to the water it consumed, the steamer used as much petroleum fuel as the gasoline-powered car. Once the internal-combustion engine had been made more powerful for its weight and more flexible through better basic design and closer precision in the machining of parts, the steam-powered engine could not compete in horsepower generated for weight of engine and fuel supply carried. Boilers were ultimately greatly improved, but in the years immediately after 1901 the development of the steamer reached a technological stalemate that was in sharp contrast with the rapid improvement of the gasoline automobile. At the 1907 Madison Square Garden show, the point had been reached where "the sole representative of the steam machine . . . has as its chief improvement a thermometer gauge on the footboard to show the temperature of the steam."[5]

The implications of technological stalemate in the development of their product were apparently not missed by the manufacturers of steam cars. At the height of the Locomobile steamer's popularity, Locomobile in 1902 switched over entirely to the production of gasoline automobiles. White, Stanley, and five other small companies were the only remaining American manufacturers of steam automobiles

[5] "The Eighth National Automobile Show in Madison Square Garden," *Scientific American*, 97:354 (November 16, 1907).

Plate 29.   Restored 1900 Locomobile "No. 2" steamer, the most popular make of car in the United States at the turn of the century. This car could develop about 10 to 12 horsepower and sold for $750. Courtesy Smithsonian Institution.

by 1907, and two years later White replaced its famous steamer with a gasoline-driven car. Although the Stanleys continued to produce steam cars into the 1920s and ultimately refined their product considerably, they catered to an increasingly diminishing market.

The Electric Car

The electric car was the most conservative form of the automobile in that it bore the closest resemblance to the horse-drawn vehicle in both appearance and performance. Manufacturers of electric vehicles closely copied fashionable carriage forms. The Woods Motor Vehicle Company, a prominent early maker of electric cars, for example, hoped to supply "hundreds of thousands of gentlemen's private stables with fine carriages in all variety of styles rather than the creation of a machine which will transport a man from town to town, or on long country tours."[6]

The electric car was clearly superior to the horse-drawn vehicle as well as the gasoline automobile on three grounds — noise, the emission of objectionable odor, and ease of operation. The silent, odorless electric car came to be especially favored by women, who were concerned foremost with comfort and cleanliness and had a hard time controlling a spirited team or learning to shift gears. The electric was also considered the ideal automobile for city use at the turn of the century. *Scientific American* reported in 1899, for example: "There seems to be a general impression that for passenger transportation in and around our cities the electric automobile is the best. . . . It has the great advantage of being silent, free from odor, simple in construction and gearing, capable of ready control, and having a considerable range [flexibility of performance at different rates] of speed."[7]

[6] "The Woods Electric Vehicles," ibid., 83:308 (November 17, 1900).
[7] "Automobile Motors," ibid., 81:82 (August 5, 1899).

Plate 30. Sales catalog illustration and specifications of a 1906 Woods electric car. Note the retrogressive style and relatively high price. Courtesy Free Library of Philadelphia.

WOODS MOTOR VEHICLE
COMPANY

Surrey

Style 119
Price $1850
Canopy Top
$100 extra

Four passengers; 43-inch seats; battery 40 cells 9 M. V.; 76-inch wheel base; weight 2,800 pounds

These advantages for city use notwithstanding, the electric car stood no chance for widespread adoption as an all-purpose, practical road vehicle. A representative 1900 article in the *Review of Reviews* explained that the many faults of the early electric car were "things having to do with practical efficiency. . . . It is the handsomest automobile, the easiest to drive, the pleasantest to ride in; but it is not adapted for general use — say, in rural districts, nor for touring." The electric car at the turn of the century had a range of only twenty miles before batteries had to be recharged. Recharging took two or three hours, and facilities were not usually available outside big cities. The storage batteries of the day also deteriorated rapidly. The hill-climbing ability of the early electric was so poor that "if your electric carriage brings you to a 20 percent hill (easy for other kinds), you must retrace your steps or make a detour." The range of initial prices for electric cars in 1900 was $1,250 to $3,500, compared with $1,000 to $2,000 for gasoline and $650 to $1,500 for steam automobiles. Regarding operating expenses, "One cent a mile or less will cover the running expenses of the two last named as against two or three cents a mile for an electric carriage."[8]

Well aware that the range of operation of the electric car was severely limited to a short radius around the few available local charging stations, early backers of the electric expressed the vague hope that a network of charging stations would soon emerge and be extended into outlying areas. Mainly due to the efforts of local electric light and power companies, the facilities for charging electric cars did improve markedly after 1900 in the larger cities and on main highways through the more populous areas of the eastern states. By the summer of 1901, the installation of six charging stations in New Jersey towns on the route to Philadelphia made it possible, for example, to drive an electric automobile from New York City to Philadelphia, where four other charging stations had recently been established. Progress was illustrated

[8] Cleveland Moffett, "Automobiles for the Average Man," *Review of Reviews*, 21:707 (June 1900).

well in Boston, where the task of improving charging facilities had been assumed by the Edison Electric Illuminating Company. Hoping to profit from the promotion of a greater use of electric vehicles, the Edison Company installed a large number of charging stations for automobile batteries on its Boston lines in 1903. These stations were accessible twenty-four hours a day every day in the year, and the rate was 10 cents per kilowatt. By July, thirty-two stations were available to motorists in Boston and vicinity, with eight more scheduled to open on August 1. Conditions in other large metropolitan areas were comparable. For example, by 1905 there were forty-one places where electrics could be charged in New York City. However, since charging facilities were still not generally available in rural areas, the electric car remained fairly well confined to city use, and the cross-country tourist and the farmer, two significant purchasers in the developing market for automobiles, consequently turned to the more flexible gasoline automobile.

It remains a moot question whether a well-developed system of charging stations could have altered the demise of the electric car unless the cost of electric power could also have been reduced substantially in the short run to make it competitive with gasoline. Better service facilities were needed as well. For example, an electric car equipped with a charging plug and rheostat was driven from Boston to New York City in October 1903, setting a new long-distance record for an electric automobile. No difficulty was experienced in obtaining the five rechargings necessary during the trip. However, "the cost for recharging was $15, or between four and five times the cost of gasoline for propelling a four passenger gasoline car the same distance."[9] Another frequent complaint, which convinced one commentator that many promoters of the early electric car "were either fools or knaves," was "the lack of knowledge

[9] "The Long Distance Record Run of an American Electric Automobile," *Scientific American*, 89:310 (October 31, 1903).

shown by the garages and agencies everywhere as to the care and proper method of charging. The electric car was looked upon by the dealer as somewhat of a 'side line,' and no proper effort was made to learn its mechanical and electrical makeup."[10]

Although by 1909 the range of the electric car had been increased from 20 to about 50 to 80 miles on a single battery charge at less expense, the general feeling was still that "electrics are expensive to maintain" and that "the electric vehicle does not compete with the gasoline car for touring, but has a large field of its own in city and suburban needs."[11] The weight of storage batteries remained inordinately heavy for the horsepower generated, and they still deteriorated rapidly. For years Thomas A. Edison had been rashly promising that he would soon develop an improved storage battery that would make the electric more practical than the gasoline automobile. At first Edison had been taken seriously, but by 1908 he was being ridiculed for his persistent failure. As *Motor Age* commented in 1908, "Mr. Edison's bunk has come to be somewhat of a joke—a real joke."[12] The growth in automobile touring after 1903 and the shift in the automobile market to middle-income brackets and rural areas after 1906 combined to seal the doom of the electric car. The electric remained in 1910 what it had been in 1900—a "horsey" car for "horsey" people.

The Gasoline Car

The gasoline automobile always had a decided edge over the electric in over-all performance. It was a better "compromise car," and its many practical advantages more than outweighed its few drawbacks. Common stove gasoline could be purchased cheaply at any general store, and even in remote hamlets an individual with some practical knowledge of stationary gasoline engines could very likely be found. An

[10] F. A. Babcock, "The Electric Motor of Yesterday and Today," *Harper's Weekly*, 51:374 (March 16, 1907).
[11] "Automobile Notes and Suggestions," *Scientific American*, 100:60 (January 16, 1909).
[12] "Bunk, Then More Bunk," *Motor Age*, 13:12 (February 13, 1908).

adequate supply of cheap gasoline seemed assured after the price of crude petroleum dropped below five cents a barrel after the discovery of a rich new source in Texas with the bringing in of the gusher "Spindletop" near Beaumont on January 10, 1901. The gasoline automobile was less expensive in both initial cost and maintenance than the electric. In addition, it could negotiate rougher terrain and longer distances without a time-consuming stop to refuel, and its higher ratio of horsepower to weight resulted in fewer mechanical failures and higher average speeds, especially when driven over poor roads. The same 1900 article in the *Review of Reviews* that was quoted on the many faults of the early electric car pointed out that the gasoline automobile "developed more all-round good qualities than any other carriage. In spite of its clumsy and complicated mechanism, it does not get easily out of order. It will climb all ordinary hills; it will run through sand, mud, or snow; it makes good speed over long distances — say, an average of fifteen miles an hour.... It carries gasoline enough for a 70-mile journey, and nearly any country store can replenish the supply."[13]

The manufacturers of gasoline automobiles capitalized upon these early advantages by sustained attention to improvement of their product. The few shortcomings of the gasoline automobile compared with steam or electric cars soon came to be either overlooked or considered merits. In particular, the congruence of the electric car with "horsey" aesthetic standards eventually proved to be a handicap that benefited the gasoline automobile. Gasoline automobiles were by far the most successful in competitions such as reliability runs. Thus the public image of what the car that could be expected to perform well should look like was predominantly shaped by gasoline automobile designs. The departures from adaptations of horse-drawn vehicles that proved to be superior functionally were soon preferred aesthetically as well. By 1905 it was reported that the buyer had been "unconsciously educated away

[13] Moffett, "Automobiles for the Average Man," p. 706.

from shapes that remind one of things not mechanical, toward shapes that are not only mechanical but typical of standard automobile construction." The article went on to explain: "The disdain with which our 'horsey' people regarded the French racing models of four years ago has changed into a very respectable appreciation of approximately the same features in the present American types. The moneyed class of the buying public has finally come to understand why surrey patterns and box seats are out of place in a touring car, and as a general thing they have come to look upon the automobile for what it is — a highway locomotive — and not for what it is not."[14]

The Low-Cost Buggy
Given the comparatively wide distribution of liberal and moderate incomes in the United States and an American manufacturing tradition of volume production for a mass market, it seemed inevitable at the turn of the century that the American automobile manufacturer, unlike his European counterpart, would emphasize the quantity production of low-cost automobiles for the average man. Writers in popular periodicals did not question that this would occur. It was accepted as axiomatic that "American manufacturers have set about to produce machines in quantity, so that the price can be reduced thereby and the public at large can have the benefit of machines which are not extravagant in price, and which can be taken care of by the ordinary individual."[15]

Low-cost cars were in fact available to Americans from the very outset of the diffusion of the automobile in the United States. The original Duryea and Haynes cars had been merely conventional horse buggies equipped with concealed low-horse-

[14] Herman Wade, "Style in Automobiles," *Country Life in America*, 8:449–450 (August 1905).
[15] J. A. Kingman, "Automobile Making in America," *Review of Reviews*, 24:302 (September 1901).

power gasoline engines, and such vehicles could be produced cheaply enough to
sell at about the same price as a decent horse and buggy. This basic design, however,
already primitive in comparison with the best French models by the mid-1890s,
was rapidly abandoned by most American manufacturers of gasoline automobiles
because it appeared synonymous with poor performance. But several companies,
such as the W. H. McIntyre Company of Auburn, Indiana, and the H. K. Holsman
Company of Chicago, continued to build cheap automobiles essentially similar to
the first Duryea and Haynes cars. About 1905, the growing demand for automobiles
among the less affluent in rural areas, especially in the Middle West, gave rise to a
brief revival of these "buggy-type" cars: by 1909 some fifty firms in the United States
were manufacturing them.

Although some slight improvements were progressively made in the buggy-type
car, outdated surrey features were basically retained. A light surrey body equipped
with solid rubber 1½-inch tires on carriage wheels from 36 to 50 inches in diameter
was combined with a one- or two-cylinder, 3½- to 12-horsepower, opposed-hori-
zontal engine mounted under the seat, well above the rear axle. In some of the more
powerful makes, a four-cylinder, opposed-type engine was substituted. The steering
gear invariably utilized a tiller instead of a wheel. A chain or rope drive and a transmission designed to be particularly flexible completed the vehicle, which sold for
between $250 and $600.

The buggy-type automobile for a short while filled a need neglected by most manufacturers. The 1905 automobile of standard design represented a sacrifice of low cost
for better-quality performance over reasonably decent roads and was consequently
both overpriced and ill adapted to the wretched road conditions characteristic of
the developing western market. As *Automobile* commented, "Physical and financial
conditions west of Pennsylvania were and still are so very different from those exist-

Plate 31. Sales catalog illustration and specifications of a 1909 Holsman "buggy-type" car. Courtesy Free Library of Philadelphia.

Model No. 10-K—Runabout
(Code word Tuka)
With Two-Cylinder 12⅕-H.P. Motor. $675.00 without Top

Model No. H-10—Runabout
(Code word Foka)
With Four-Cylinder 26-H.P. All-Ball-and-Roller Bearing Motor.
$900.00 without Top

For description of Motors, see pages 19 and 23.
For Tops and other Accessories, see page 22.

Weight of vehicle without top, 950 pounds; full elliptic springs; wheel-base, 80 inches; any tread from 56 to 62 inches; body, 32 x 84 inches; seat, 19 x 38 inches on top of cushion; space in front of seat, 24 x 31 inches; locker in front of dash, 18½ x 27½ x 13 inches; covered space in rear, 19½ x 31 inches; upholstered with No. 1 machine-buffed leather; patent-leather fenders; roller-bearing axles; brass trimmings; brass hub-caps.

ing in the East as to create a need and persistent demand for a type of machine especially designed and built to meet requirements, and differing radically from the types of cars developed in Europe, which have furnished models for the American manufacturers."[16]

Intended to meet the needs of this developing rural market, buggy-type automobiles were particularly well suited to the poor roads of the rural Middle West. On muddy roads full of ruts and stumps, the high, narrow wheels were a distinct advantage, and if the car did get stuck, it was light enough to be easily pushed out. Moreover, it was low priced and very economical to operate, and the solid rubber tires did away with the most expensive and troublesome aspect of the conventional automobile — the pneumatic tires. Thus if high speed and comfort were not demanded, the buggy-type automobile gave adequate service over rural roads.

The rapid demise of the buggy-type automobile was a foregone conclusion, however, after the introduction of greatly improved, low-priced conventional runabouts in 1906. Technological progress had by then resulted in an all-around automobile that was much more efficient and comfortable for only slightly more money. The Ford Model N, which sold for only $600, was an excellent example of the new 1906 models with which the buggy-type car could not hope to compete for very long. By 1908, the year in which the Ford Model T was introduced at the moderate price of $850, it was feared that "the market will become surcharged with [buggy-type] vehicles which are practically unsalable, and the demand for them will fall as suddenly as it arose." The surrey design also had inherent mechanical weaknesses that had never been eliminated. "The combined influences of the short wheel-base, high wheels and solid tires which are characteristic of the motor buggy, produce a far greater amount of vibration than is encountered in the more ordinary types of automobile. This,

[16] Harry W. Perry, "Development of Buggy Type Western Cars," *Automobile*, 15:143 (August 2, 1906).

coupled with the fact that the lighter bodies used require lighter spring suspension . . . causes even the most trustworthy forms of locking nut to give way at times, and results in a rattling loose of all sorts of fastenings which apparently have no cause to be disturbed."[17]

Design Changes, 1905–1910

The fundamentally unsatisfactory nature of the surrey design became apparent to most American manufacturers shortly after the turn of the century. The single event that served best to underline the basic weakness of this retrogressive style of car was undoubtedly the 1900 Gordon Bennett Cup race from Paris to Lyon, where the sole American entry, a one-cylinder buggy-type Winton, had been hopelessly outclassed by the more powerful, modern-lined Panhards in the race. Carriage styles were rapidly abandoned by American makers of gasoline automobiles during a five-year period of innovation in which contemporary European forms and features of automotive design were widely copied and adapted to the conditions of the American market. Any attempt to depart significantly from basic European features of design was notably absent by at least 1905. As *Scientific American* observed in a review of the 1905 New York automobile show, "Undoubtedly the first impression left by a general survey of the exhibit is that the industry has settled down to the production of a certain number of standard types. In this respect the present show is in marked contrast to those of four or five years ago, when a large proportion of the work done by our manufacturers was experimental, and was prompted by the desire to strike out on original lines, and get away from the designs which had already become standard among the foreign builders."[18]

[17] "Motor Buggies and Their Problems," *Motor World*, 19:143–144 (October 22, 1908).
[18] "The Fifth Annual Automobile Show," *Scientific American*, 92:54 (January 28, 1905).

Plate 32. Restored 1901 Autocar,
one of the first shaft-driven cars
built in the United States. Courtesy
Smithsonian Institution.

The period of experimentation in basic design definitely seemed to have passed by 1907. Competition would henceforth be directed toward producing a better product at a lower price within broad but well-defined limits. By then it was obvious that "years of experience and experiment have brought manufacturers into such uniformity of ideas that their machines may be said to be practically all built on the same general lines; and each year the differences become less and less conspicuous. . . . the 1908 models, as far as they have been shown, are more alike even than the 1907 cars. Generally speaking there are no radical changes embodied in the new models built by the more important factories."[19]

The typical moderately priced 1909 car weighed between 1,500 and 2,000 pounds and had a wheelbase of from 100 to 115 inches. It also had pneumatic tires about 34 inches in diameter with about a 56-inch track and a 4-inch tread; a pressed-steel riveted frame; either semielliptic or elliptic springs; a steering wheel rather than a tiller; and an open, side-entrance body that seated four passengers, with the motor mounted in front of the driver under a hood. The car was powered by a four-cylinder, four-cycle vertical engine of from 20 to 30 horsepower and had magneto ignition with battery ignition in reserve, forced-feed lubrication, water-cooled cylinders, and direct-shaft drive. The H-slot sliding-gear transmission with three speeds forward and one in reverse was standard, as was the leather-covered cone clutch, but two-speed planetary transmissions and multiple-disc clutches were found on many models. There was also considerable variation in lubrication systems and in the details of steering mechanisms.

The typical American gasoline car of the period represented a compromise between European extremes — the heavy, luxurious touring car and the underpowered economy car, frequently a motorized cycle, for the masses. The motorized cycle never

[19] Joseph Tracy, "The 1908 Automobile," *Country Life in America*, 13:65 (November 1907).

became very popular in the United States, perhaps because its operation required comparatively good roads. Despite a brief vogue here for the two-passenger "runabout," cars low powered for their weight were never an important feature of the American industry. By 1908 a trend had clearly developed in the United States toward the dominance of the four-passenger family car. Compared on grounds other than its significantly lower price with the typical European touring car of the period, the American "type car" was light and sat high on its chassis; had an appreciably higher horsepower to weight ratio, a more flexible (though less efficient)* engine, and simpler controls; was poorly designed with respect to safety standards; and showed considerably less attention to finesse in the details of fit, finish, and appointment.

The typical moderately priced American gasoline car by 1909 was a fairly reliable motor vehicle. Observers agreed by about 1908 that "it is very rare, indeed, that an automobile has such a serious breakdown as to require towing to a repair shop, or to necessitate its abandonment by the passengers. Such stoppages as have to be made on the road are usually only for simple adjustments, the cleaning or changing of a spark plug, connecting up of a fresh ignition battery cell or the substitution of a new inner tube for a punctured tube in a tire."[20] Most important, one could now expect this from automobiles that sold for $1,000 or less. As *Scientific American* reported, "Unquestionably, the low-priced car, costing less than $1,000 has come to stay. . . . 'the biggest show for the money,' if we may be allowed the phrase, was presented [at the New York automobile show] by the runabouts costing $800 to $1,000. These machines contain all the essential elements of the elaborate high-powered, high-priced machines."[21]

*Engine efficiency refers in technical terms to "brake mean effective pressure." The best layman's definition is probably the horsepower generated for the amount of fuel used.

[20] Harry W. Perry, "The Dependability of the Automobile," *Harper's Weekly*, 52:24 (February 1, 1908).

[21] "The 1909 Automobile," *Scientific American*, 100:40 (January 16, 1909).

All this definitely had not been true a few years earlier. Although low- and moderately priced automobiles had always been available, few had performed as adequately relative to high-priced models as the famous curved-dash Oldsmobile (1901–1906) and the Ford Model N (1906–1907), which had sold, respectively, for the modest prices of $650 and $600. Until about 1908, automobiles priced under $1,000 had been generally, if not invariably, poorly designed and constructed. No moderately priced car could even begin to be compared with the Locomobile, Thomas, Peerless, Packard, and other expensive makes, and even these automobiles usually left something to be desired in ruggedness and performance.

Table 8.1 lists the most popular American gasoline automobiles in ten eastern states in 1905. The twenty-two most popular makes, which accounted for 7,881 of the 9,067 American gasoline automobiles registered in these states, sold sixty-seven different models of cars in 1905, ranging from a $375, one-cylinder, 4-horsepower Orient Buckboard to a $7,500, four-cylinder, 40- to 45-horsepower Locomobile. No model selling below $1,000 had more than a two-cylinder engine, and none except the Pope-

Table 8.1 Most Popular Makes of American Gasoline Automobiles in Ten Eastern States* in 1905

Make	Total Number Registered
Cadillac	1,131
Oldsmobile	750
Pope (three makes)	701
Rambler	663
Locomobile	581
Autocar	535
Ford	432
Winton	424
Franklin	414
Knox	298
Packard	294
Pierce	239
Thomas	227
Stevens-Duryea	202
Orient	197
Maxwell	170
Columbia	138
Northern	131
Elmore	115
Reo	112
Buick	109
Peerless	108

Source: "Uncle Sam and John Bull," *Motor Age*, 8:8 (August 3,1905). Note: The totals for other American gasoline cars were Wayne, 70; Haynes, 60; Yale, 60; National, 60; Crest, 59; Cameron, 58; Standard, 57; Queen, 54; Acme, 43; Premier, 43; Royal, 42; Jackson, 40; Marion, 36; American, 35; Studebaker, 32; Apperson, 31; Searchmont, 29; Walter, 27; Buckmobile, 26; Mitchell, 21; St. Louis, 19; Stearns, 17; Covert, 17; Matheson, 17; Phelps, 17; S. & M. Simplex, 15; Cleveland, 15; Ranier, 15; Stoddard, 15; Union, 14; Jones-Corbin, 14; Worthington, 13; Buffum, 12; Reliance, 10; Berkshire, 9; Pungs-Finch, 6; Ardsley, 6; Rochester, 5; Upton, 5; and twenty-one other makes, 61.

*Connecticut, District of Columbia, Massachusetts, Maine, New Hampshire, New Jersey, New York, Pennsylvania, Rhode Island, and Vermont.

Plate 33.   Sales catalog illustration
of the 1907 Thomas Flyer, one of
the finest and most expensive early
American cars. Costing $4,000,
the Thomas Flyer had a 118-inch
wheelbase and weighed 3,200
pounds. Its four-cylinder, 60-horse-
power engine gave the car a top
speed of about 64 mph. Courtesy
Free Library of Philadelphia.

THOMAS FLYER, 60 HORSE-POWER—$4,000, f. o. b. Factory

Plate 34.   Sales catalog illustration of the 1910 Packard "Thirty" limousine, a luxury car that sold for $5,450. The Packard "Thirty" had a 123½-inch wheelbase and a four-cylinder, 30-horsepower engine. Courtesy Free Library of Philadelphia.

Tribune (12 horsepower) was rated at more than 10 horsepower. Wheelbases were only 66 to 82 inches. A 1905 automobile comparable to the typical intermediate-price 1909 car in engine specifications and wheelbase alone cost a minimum of $2,000, and the makers of quality 1905 automobiles priced their least expensive models at about $3,000. Of the sixty-seven models offered by the twenty-two most popular makes in 1905, only eighteen models were priced at $1,000 or lower; twenty-six models sold for between $1,100 and $2,000; and twenty-three models commanded from $2,100 to $7,500.

Low Cost versus Quality

Perceptive entrepreneurs became increasingly aware after 1905 that the American automobile industry was reaching a critical turning point. The luxury market for high-priced cars appeared to be nearing the saturation point. Most people in the upper-income brackets already owned cars, and the more expensive 1905 models were quite serviceable automobiles compared with models for previous years. As the product was further improved, the high annual replacement demand from wealthy owners, which had thus far sustained many manufacturers, could not be expected to continue at the same level. Consequently, attention now began to be directed to new classes of purchasers — the middle-class citizen and the newly prosperous middle western farmer. The revival of the buggy-type automobile was, as we have seen, one response to this changing conception of the market. But the more viable alternative was to find some way to sell decent conventional automobiles at significantly lower prices.

Encouragement to exploit these new markets was provided by the growing trade in secondhand cars. New York City, which had become the center for the used-car trade, alone boasted some dozen thriving concerns that dealt exclusively in secondhand cars. These New York dealers sold and shipped used automobiles to all parts of the country. Even unpopular old steamers were being sold for as much as one-fifth of their original price, but the greatest demand was for small gasoline runabouts. Recent models of the better makes in excellent condition could frequently be obtained at bargain prices because "the item of depreciation appears to remain stationary despite the improvement that has been brought about. . . . The car that sold for $2,000 when new will seldom bring much more than half that price when a year old and at the end of its second year this will practically be halved again despite the fact that as a well-built piece of machinery it may have several years of efficient life before it."[22]

In retrospect, the reason why high demand for secondhand cars coincided with low prices for them appears to be that prices were necessarily fixed at the maximal amounts that new, less affluent classes of purchasers could afford to spend for motor vehicles, regardless of how efficient the cars might be. The man of means who had thus far constituted the backbone of the market for automobiles could well afford to purchase the most recent models at relatively high prices and was consequently not particularly interested in buying a used car at what was to him only a slightly lower price than that of a new one.

The Brush Runabout (1907–1912), which enjoyed a brief flurry of popularity, represented one of the more notable attempts to design a low-priced conventional car for the developing new middle-class and rural markets. Frank Briscoe formed the Brush Runabout Company of Detroit in 1907 to produce a small car designed by Alanson P. Brush, who also designed the motor for the first Cadillac and served as chief engineer for Oakland. The Brush car combined the body style, front-mounted engine, and steering wheel of the conventional runabout with the solid rubber tires

[22]"Depreciation of Used Cars," *Motor World*, 14:21 (October 4, 1906); see also "About Second-Hand Cars," ibid., 12:594 (April 12, 1906).

and the chain drive of the buggy-type car. Weighing only 900 pounds, it was powered by a one-cylinder, 7-horsepower engine, had a 74-inch wheelbase, and sold for under $500. Wood was used extensively to reduce construction costs. But by 1910 the Brush Runabout Company was on its last legs because its cheap car had not proved able to compete with better-designed and better-built automobiles such as the Ford Model N and Model T, which cost only a few hundred dollars more to buy. Disgruntled owners complained that the Brush Runabout had a "wooden body, wooden axles, wooden wheels, and wooden run."

   Low initial price at the expense of quality was clearly not the course for an automobile manufacturer to pursue, as Ransom E. Olds was forced to realize. The famous curved-dash Oldsmobile, which should be considered the zenith of surrey-influenced automobile design, was rapidly becoming outmoded by 1903, but Olds had stubbornly insisted that the Olds Motor Works should continue production of this low-priced model. After resigning from the Olds Motor Works under pressure from his partners, Samuel and Frederick Smith, in January 1904, Olds went on to form the REO Motor Car Company in August. The first REO models indicated that Olds had come to accept the very type of automobile design he had previously opposed. Both the new REO touring car and a lighter $650 runabout departed from the curved-dash's surrey style of design, and the heavier touring car was the model emphasized in REO's advertising. The touring car weighed 1,500 pounds, was powered by a two-cylinder, 16-horsepower engine, and was priced at $1,250. Ray M. Owen, Olds's sales manager at REO, had considerable difficulty in getting dealerships established before the design of these models became known. As Owen informed Olds, the trouble was that "throughout the country the general impression is, that you are very much inclined to cut the material down in your cars. They cite . . . several well-known weak points in the [curved-dash] Oldsmobile, as being directly up to you. You will,

Plate 35.   1907 advertisement for
the Brush Runabout, a low-priced
conventional runabout made largely
of wood that was soon outclassed
by the Ford Model T. Courtesy
Free Library of Philadelphia.

Brush $500 Runabout

NOW READY TO DELIVER

This wonderful little car,
the sensation of the season,

is now being produced in quantities.   Several improvements and
refinements delayed us for about 6 weeks but the car is even better
than as originally laid out.

The sales have been phenomenal. Dealers and public have taken
hold way beyond our greatest hopes.

Orders (not inquiries, but orders) have been received from every
conceivable point in the United States, and up to date, from Canada,
Sweden, Holland, Ireland, Russia, Java, Cuba, Mexico, Guatemala,
and New Zealand.

Our first year's product will serve as little more than samples.
We simply suggest to you now that you get in line for next year when
we can give you all you want. We also want to educate people to just
what the car is:—not a sporty plaything but a hard work, long service,
economy, reliability car with limitations as to speed and carrying
capacity.

*Final specifications on opposite page.   Write us again and pardon us if
we may not have given your previous inquiries the attention they deserved.
We are better organized now to handle a big mass of correspondence.*

BRUSH RUNABOUT CO.,   :-:   Detroit, Mich.

Brush $500 Runabout

ENGINE: 6 H. P., single cylinder, vertical, 4 cycle, under hood; valves, connecting rod bearings, piston and spark plug all instantly accessible without disconnecting anything but nuts; almost no vibration; speed range 200 to 2200 R. P. M.; water cooled on thermo-syphon system, no pump; 3 point suspension.

FUEL SYSTEM: Tank lowest member, connections in top only; no pressure but feed is by pulsation pump to floatless fuel cup which maintains level by overflow back to tank; carburetor instantly regulated and completely accessible; absolutely safe in case of leak.

TRANSMISSION: 2 speeds forward and reverse by means of 2 internal and 2 spur gears in mesh all the time; gear action on planetary principle but it has no brake bands, all being contained inside stationary case; no adjustments; absolutely noiseless; runs in oil; has all the advantages and none of the disadvantages of both planetary and sliding gear types and less friction loss than either.

DRIVE: Shaft through bevel gear to countershaft with 2 short side chains.

CONTROL: Lever, selective type with 4 positions for the 3 speeds and brake; also foot brake.

STEER: Wheel, with gear in oil-tight case; irreversible; slow acting at straight ahead but accelerates as it turns; located on left side for convenience in driving as well as getting in and out.

AXLES AND FRAME: Hickory and oak; stronger and more durable than steel.

BEARINGS: Extra liberal throughout; spindles as large as used on cars 400 lbs. heavier.

SPRINGS: Spiral at extreme corners, checked by friction radius rods

OILING: Automatic sight feed on dash supplies engine.

WHEEL BASE: 74 inches. **TREAD:** 56 inches.

WHEELS: Standard are 32 inch artillery, with 2 inch solid rubber tires. With pneumatics 28x3 add $50.00 to price.

Many other features must be seen to be appreciated. We believe this car will stand up for 10 years and is the most economical in the world. It's up to you now.

BRUSH RUNABOUT CO.,   :-:   Detroit, Mich.

Plate 36.   Sales catalog illustration and specifications of the 1901 curved-dash Oldsmobile. Courtesy Free Library of Philadelphia.

Oldsmobile Regular Runabout

SPECIFICATIONS

CAPACITY -- Two passengers.
WHEEL BASE -- 66 inches.
TREAD -- 55 inches.
FRAME -- Angle steel.
SPRINGS -- Oldsmobile side springs.
WHEELS -- 28-inch wood artillery.
TIRES -- 3-inch detachable.
MOTOR -- 5 x 6-inch 7 H. P. horizontal.
TRANSMISSION -- All-spur gear, two speeds forward and reverse.
FINISH -- Black with red trimming.

EQUIPMENT -- Complete set of tools and pair of large brass side lamps.
RADIATOR -- Copper disk.
CARBURETOR -- Oldsmobile.
IGNITION -- Jump spark.
STEERING GEAR -- Tiller.
DIFFERENTIAL -- Bevel-gear type.
BRAKES -- Differential and rear wheel.
WATER CAPACITY -- Five gallons.
CIRCULATION -- Gear pump.
GASOLINE CAPACITY -- Five gallons.

Plate 37.   Sales catalog illustration and specifications of the 1906 REO touring car, illustrating the big change in Ransom E. Olds's concept of automotive design after he formed REO. Courtesy Free Library of Philadelphia.

REO LIGHT TOURING CAR

With Cape Top and Full Lamp Equipment. $1,325 f.o.b. Factory
Searchlight extra

16 horse-power. 1,600 pounds. 90-inch wheel base. Five passengers. Side-door stationary or detachable tonneau. Two speeds and reverse. Speed 35 miles per hour. With cape top, front and rear oil lamps and 2 gas lamps as shown in cut.

therefore, have this prejudice to overcome, and I would not hesitate, if I were in your place, to put in the best material obtainable in these cars, even at a slight additional cost."[23]

The early popularity of the Cadillac car can be attributed to the fact that the Cadillac Automobile Company, organized in Detroit on August 22, 1902, was the first American automobile manufacturer to reconcile advanced design and high-quality construction with moderate price. Cadillac originated from the Detroit Automobile Company, formed by a group of prominent Detroit businessmen who had initially backed Henry Ford. Cadillac agreed to use a motor developed by Leland and Faulconer, a nationally known Detroit manufacturer of high-quality machine tools, bicycle gears, and marine gasoline engines. The Cadillac Motor Car Company resulted from the consolidation of the Cadillac Automobile Company and Leland and Faulconer on December 27, 1904. Henry M. Leland became general manager of the new firm.

Leland and Faulconer had introduced processes that allowed castings to be machined to closer tolerances than their competition found possible to duplicate. The firm commonly worked to tolerances of 1/10,000 of an inch and could undertake production requiring tolerances of 1/100,000 of an inch. Henry M. Leland had been trained at the Brown & Sharpe Manufacturing Company of Providence, Rhode Island, then the leading precision toolmaker in the United States. Leland had been enthusiastic about the possibilities of the gasoline automobile and had first entered the automobile industry as a manufacturer of transmission gears and motors for the 1901 curved-dash Oldsmobile.

Alanson P. Brush, then one of Leland and Faulconer's engineers, set out to improve

[23] See Glenn A. Niemeyer, *The Automotive Career of Ransom E. Olds* (East Lansing: Michigan State University Press, 1963), pp. 72–80. The quotation is from this source (p. 80). Niemeyer cites a letter of September 22, 1904, from R. M. Owen to R. E. Olds as its origin.

the Olds motor. Through closer machining alone, the one-cylinder Olds engine was initially raised from 3 to 3.7 horsepower. The introduction of larger valves and a better timing system resulted in further improvement to 10.25 horsepower. An associate of Leland recalled: "On taking the improved article to the Olds company, we were dismayed by the refusal to use it. Mr. Olds was getting all the business he could handle and I suppose such a radical change in power plant would have necessitated alterations in many directions. The point is significant however as a key to a future of accuracy methods in manufacturing."[24]

The motor rejected by Olds was used in the popular 1903 Cadillac Model A, which also featured superior workmanship, steering by wheel instead of tiller, and room for four passengers. The Cadillac Model B, another one-cylinder car introduced in 1904, featured interchangeability of parts. These two models, each selling for under $1,000, accounted for most of Cadillac's output until after 1905, and ultimately 16,126 cars of both models were produced. A more expensive four-cylinder model of advanced design was introduced by Cadillac in 1905. This car became the famous Cadillac Model Thirty, a four-cylinder, 25-horsepower car that sold for a moderate $1,400 in 1908. Over 67,000 of these excellent cars were produced before the model was discontinued, demonstrating that quantity production did not necessarily entail sacrifice of quality.

Concentrating upon reconciling high standards of workmanship with quantity production, Cadillac won the Dewar Trophy of the Royal Automobile Club of London in 1908 for the greatest advance shown by any motorcar during the year — namely, the achievement of previously unparalleled interchangeability of parts. Three Cadillac cars had been disassembled by officials of the Royal Automobile

[24]Quoted in Arthur Pound, *The Turning Wheel: The Story of General Motors Through Twenty-Five Years* (Garden City, N.Y.: Doubelday, Doran, 1934), p. 103.

Plate 38.   Restored 1903 Cadillac
Model A. The one-cylinder Model
A cost $850 and was considered
a very reliable car in its day. Courtesy Smithsonian Institution.

Club and the parts mixed. In a shed at Brooklands race track in England, Cadillac mechanics then reassembled the cars, which were immediately given a 500-mile test drive. The Cadillacs finished with perfect scores.

Buick also made significant progress under William C. Durant in becoming a leading manufacturer of quality automobiles at moderate prices. When Durant took over its management in late 1904, Buick was in precarious shape. The resources of the automobile company founded in 1902 by David D. Buick, a Detroit manufacturer of plumbers' supplies, had been exhausted in developing its Model F car. The chief asset of the firm in 1904 was its patent on the valve-in-head engine developed by Eugene C. Richard and Walter L. Mar of the Buick staff. Frank and Benjamin Briscoe, manufacturers of sheet metal who had lent Buick considerable money, had to assume financial control and were anxious to sell the company. They found a buyer in James H. Whiting, a Flint, Michigan, carriage manufacturer, and Whiting soon induced William C. Durant, owner of the Durant-Dort Carriage Company and already a millionaire at the age of forty-two, to assume management of the Buick Motor Company.

Durant had built Buick into the leading automobile producer in the United States by 1908. That year the company had a net worth of almost $3.5 million and occupied the largest automobile plant in the world. From an output of only 31 cars in 1904, Buick came to produce 2,295 automobiles in 1906 and 8,487 in 1908. (The second largest American producer in 1908 was Ford with 6,181 motor vehicles, and the third largest was Cadillac with 2,380.) Durant entered boldly into volume production of a reliable car in the intermediate-price range. Large assembly plants were built at Flint and Jackson, Michigan. Considerable attention was given to building up an efficient national system of wholesale and retail distributors. Companies that had supplied Durant's carriage enterprise were shifted to automobile work. Manufacturers of essential components were purchased and moved to Flint. Last, but certainly not

Plate 39.   Sales catalog illustration
and specifications of the 1909 Cadillac "Thirty" touring car, a moderately
priced automobile of exceptional
quality. Courtesy Free Library of
Philadelphia.

CADILLAC "THIRTY" TOURING CAR

Price, $1400.00, F. O. B. Detroit

(Including three oil lamps and horn)

SPECIFICATIONS OF CADILLAC "THIRTY"
IN BRIEF

MOTOR—Four-cylinder, four-cycle; cylinders cast singly. 4-inch bore by 4½-inch stroke. Five-bearing crank shaft.

HORSE POWER—A. L. A. M. rating 25.6. Actual, dynamometer test, 30.

COOLING—Water. Copper jacketed cylinders, gear driven gear pump. Radiator of ample efficiency. Fan attached to motor and running on two-point ball bearings. Center distances of fan pulleys adjustable to take up stretch in belt.

IGNITION—Induction coil and jump spark current with storage battery and dry cells. Optional equipment extra charge, see page 29.

LUBRICATION—Automatic splash system. Oil uniformly distributed. Supply maintained by mechanical force feed lubricator with positive sight feed on dash.

CARBURETOR—Float feed type, our own make.

CLUTCH—Cone type, leather faced with special spring ring in fly wheel.

TRANSMISSION—Sliding gear, selective type, three speeds forward and reverse.

DRIVE—Direct shaft in housing to bevel gears of special cut teeth to afford maximum strength. Universal joint enclosed in housing and running in oil bath.

AXLES—Rear, special alloy steel live axle shafts running on special roller and ball bearings. Front, tubular with drop forged yokes. spring perches, tie rod ends and steering spindles, the latter having ball thrust bearings. Front wheels fitted with two-point ball-bearings.

BRAKES—One internal and one external brake direct on wheels, large drums.

STEERING GEAR—Our own worm and sector type, adjustable, with ball thrust bearings.

FRAME—Dropped, pressed steel, channel section. Width, 30 inches in front, 33 inches in rear.

GEAR RATIO—On Touring Car, 3½ to 1. On Demi-Tonneau 3½ to 1. On Roadster 3 to 1. Options 3 to 1, 3½ to 1 or 4 to 1.

WHEELS—Wood, artillery type, fitted with quick detachable rims. Special large hub flanges and special strength wide spokes.

WHEEL BASE—106 inches.

TIRES—32 x 3½ inches. For options see page 22.

TREAD—56 inches. Option 61 inches.

SPRINGS—Front, semi-elliptical 36 inches long by 2 inches wide. Rear, three-quarter platform; sides, 42 inches long by 2 inches wide; rear 38 inches long by 2 inches wide.

CONTROL—Spark and throttle levers at steering wheel. Steering wheel 16-inches in diameter. Clutch operated by foot pedal. Service brake (external) operated by foot lever. Emergency brake (internal) operated by hand lever. Speed changes by hand lever operating in "H" plate. Throttle accelerator by foot lever.

SPEED—5 to 50 miles per hour on high gear.

GASOLINE CAPACITY—About 13 gallons.

OIL CAPACITY—6 pints.

UPHOLSTERING—Black leather over genuine curled hair and deep coil steel springs.

FINISH—Royal Blue body and chassis striped. For options see page 29.

EQUIPMENT—One pair side oil lamps and tail lamp, one horn and set of tools, including pump and repair kit for tires.

least, the Buick car in just a few years was substantially improved in value for the price asked.

By 1909 Durant had come out with several models in the $1,000-price range that performed as well as the much higher-priced machines of many of his competitors. The 1905 Buick was a very satisfactory two-cylinder, 22-horsepower car that weighed 1,750 pounds and cost $1,200. Characteristically, Durant rapidly diversified his product, and by 1909 he was manufacturing two two-cylinder and four four-cylinder Buick models. The most popular of these was the Buick Model 10, a $1,000, four-cylinder, 22-horsepower runabout introduced in 1908. The Model 10 gained a reputation for reliable performance at a moderate initial price.

Significant as the accomplishments of Buick and Cadillac were, the Ford Motor Company, organized in 1903, emerged as the industry leader in making the high-quality, modestly priced automobile a reality. Following a policy diametrically opposed to the early trend toward diversification of product we have noted at Buick, Ford moved rapidly toward concentrating its resources on the development and production of a single model. During 1904–1905, Ford produced three models—the B, C, and F. And until October 1, 1909, Ford always offered at least two models to the public. After that date only the Model T was manufactured. For several years previous to this, only one of the various models offered for sale each year had really captured the fancy of the buying public. The Model K, a relatively heavy, six-cylinder car designed to appeal to the luxury market at a price of $2,800, had in particular proved almost impossible to sell in 1907.

Henry Ford's great contribution was not that he was the first to produce a cheap car in large quantities; rather, Ford produced the first low-priced automobile that gave as good or better service than the much more expensive cars of the period. Ford was committed equally to precision and to volume production and conclusively demon-

Plate 40.   Sales catalog illustration
of the 1908 Buick Model 10 surrey,
a 22-horsepower, $1,000 car that
rivaled the Ford Model T in popularity. Called the "nifty" Model 10,
some 23,102 were sold between 1908
and 1910. Courtesy Free Library of
Philadelphia.

MODEL 10 SURREY

Plate 41.   Sales catalog illustration and specifications of the 1910 Buick Model 16 Toy Tonneau, another fine, but fairly expensive, car. Courtesy Free Library of Philadelphia.

MODEL 16 TOY TONNEAU

Buick Model 16 Toy Tonneau

SPECIFICATIONS

BODY . . . . . Wood, toy tonneau type. Detachable.

COLOR . . . . Red body and gear, or blue body with ivory white gear.

SEATS. . . . . Five persons.

WHEEL BASE . . 112 inches.

TREAD . . . . 56 inches.

TIRES . . . . . 34 x 4 inches.

BRAKES . . . . Internal expanding hub and external contracting on driving shaft.

SPRINGS . . . . Full elliptic rear, semi-elliptic front.

FRAME . . . . Pressed steel.

STEERING GEAR . Semi-irreversible type.

HORSE POWER . Thirty

CYLINDERS . . . Four vertical. 4½ x 5 inches. Valve-in-the-head construction.

MOTOR SUSPENSION Sub-frame.

COOLING. . . . Water, circulated by pump.

IGNITION. . . . Jump spark.

CURRENT SUPPLY Magneto and reserve set of dry cells.

CARBURETOR . . Schebler.

LUBRICATION . . Self-contained system, oil circulated by pump.

MOTOR CONTROL . Spark and throttle levers on top of steering wheel.

CLUTCH . . . . Cone, our special design.

TRANSMISSION . . Sliding gear, selective type. Three speeds forward, one reverse.

CONTROL . . . Foot pedals for service brake and clutch; side lever for change gear; side lever for emergency brake.

DRIVE . . . . Shaft.

PRICE. . . . . $1,750 f. o. b. factory. This price includes oil lamps, tail lamp, generator, gas headlights, horn and repair outfit.

EXTRAS . . . . Top, glass front, speedometer.

Prest-O-Lite equipment will be furnished instead of gas generator as an extra, if desired.

strated that they were compatible. The Model N had the distinction of being the first conventional four-cylinder automobile costing under $1,000 and available in large numbers. The Model N was also one of the better-designed and better-built cars available at any price in 1906. It was an attractive car that weighed only 1,050 pounds; its four-cylinder, 15-horsepower motor could do 45 miles per hour; and at 20 miles per gallon of gasoline, the Model N was economical to run. Aiming for the newly apparent mass market, Ford initially had hoped to sell the Model N for $500, but to maintain the desired high quality of the car, the price soon had to be raised to $600. Ford justly boasted to reporters early in 1906: "I believe that I have solved the problem of cheap as well as simple automobile construction. . . . the general public is interested only in the knowledge that a serviceable machine can be constructed at a price within the reach of many." He rightly believed that the Model N was "destined to revolutionize automobile construction" and at the time considered it "the crowning achievement of my life."[25]

Despite Ford's own optimism, however, the Ford Motor Company's announcement of its new four-cylinder car did not cause much consternation at first among competing manufacturers. Before the Model N had been exhibited, *Motor Age* reported, "The competing manufacturers might have been expected to say unpleasant things of the company responsible for this low-priced car, but such is not the case to any great extent." It was clear that the industry did not expect the introduction of the Model N substantially to alter competitive conditions. The makers of other low-priced cars were content to believe "that this act will bring into the market the prospective buyer who has waited 4 or 5 years for the price of automobiles to come down." They expected to share this new market with Ford. Similarly, the makers of higher-priced automobiles operated on the false assumption that they were confronted

[25]*Detroit Journal*, January 5, 1906.

Plate 42.   Sales catalog illustration
and specifications of the 1906 Ford
Model N, the first reliable, low-
priced, four-cylinder runabout.
Courtesy Free Library of Philadelphia.

Specifications, Model N

Motor, 4-cylinder, vertical, cylinders 3¾″ bore a 3⅜″ stroke, 17.09 H. P.

Speed, 40 miles an hour down to 3 miles on high gear.

Improved planetary transmission, with improved clutch.

84-inch wheel base.

Pressed steel frame.

Water cooled.

Ignition, two sets of dry cells.

Gasoline Tank, under seat, containing 10 gallons, sufficient for 200 miles.

Water contained in radiator.

Hub brakes—internal expansion, with lever control.

Emergency brake on driving shaft, controlled by foot pedal.

Tops Extra, Prices on application.

Springs, full elliptic in rear, and half elliptic in front.

"Famous Ford" Direct Drive Construction.

Roller bearings on rear axle, with ball-bearing thrust—special design.

Ball Bearings on Front Wheels.

Wheel Steering (Fitted with Ford reduction gears) takes all the strain from steering over the roughest road; an exclusive Ford feature.

Luxurious Body, carrying two passengers.

Weight, 800 pounds.

56-inch tread.

Wheels, artillery, 28-inch.

Tires, 2½ inch, double tube clincher.

Lubricating oil sufficient for 200 miles.

Color, Maroon.

Equipment, two side oil lamps and horn.

Price, $500.00, f. o. b., Detroit.

3″ TIRES, $50.00 EXTRA.

with competition from merely another cheap and unsatisfactory car, so they considered "the Ford company's movement to be a means of feeding the market; that it will make purchasers who will sooner or later desire larger powered and more expensive cars to meet what they believe to be their requirements." *Motor Age* itself felt that if the as yet unseen Model N would "sustain the maker's reputation, the possible effect will be a lowering of prices." But the periodical considered it just as likely that "a car of this grade and price will be the means of producing so many automobilists that there will be little chance to even supply the demand for all grades of machines."[26]

Once the Model N was exhibited at the automobile shows, however, opinions changed rapidly. *Cycle and Automobile Trade Journal* echoed the general sentiment: "This car is distinctly the most important mechanical traction event of 1906. This Ford Model N position of first importance and highest interest is due to the fact that the Model N supplies the very first instance of a low-cost motorcar driven by a gas engine having cylinders enough to give the shaft a turning impulse in each shaft turn which is well built and offered in large numbers."[27] Deluged with orders now, the Ford Motor Company installed improved production equipment and techniques and after July 15, 1906, was able to make daily deliveries of 100 cars.

That the Ford Model N introduced a new competitive standard in the automobile industry is unquestionable. The four-cylinder, low-priced car was soon definitely considered a threat by many manufacturers, especially those committed to the low-volume production of expensive automobiles. For example, a rumor circulating in January 1907 that Buick planned to introduce a sensational new four-cylinder car at a price of $650 brought "no sparing of criticism." *Motor World* reported that "not even Buick's best friends undertake to approve or defend the announcement" and that

[26]"Cheap Car Not a Disturbing Element," *Motor Age*, 8:10 (November 23, 1905).
[27]Hugh Dolnar, "The Ford 4-Cylinder Runabout," *Cycle and Automobile Trade Journal*, 11:108 (August 1, 1906).

"agreement is quite general that a disturbing element has been unnecessarily projected into the industry and one that cannot bring corresponding benefit to even the projectors."[28]

Encouraged by the success of the Model N, Henry Ford was determined to build an even better low-priced car. The outcome was the legendary Model T, first offered for delivery to dealers on October 1, 1908. Designed for utility rather than beauty, the Model T appeared ungainly, with a body that sat high above the roadbed. But this made the Model T particularly well adapted to the worst roads of the period, as did its novel three-point suspension of the motor, improved arc springs, and an enclosed power plant and transmission. Extensive use of new heat-treated vanadium steels helped make the Model T a lighter and tougher car, and new methods of casting parts (especially block casting of the engine) kept the price still within reach of the middle-class purchaser. The Model T had a four-cylinder, 20-horsepower engine, a 100-inch wheelbase, and weighed only 1,200 pounds. Its improved two-speed planetary transmission made shifting gears easier for the average driver and was ideally suited to rocking out of ruts on muddy roads. A steering wheel on the left-hand side, more ample fuel capacity (10 gallons in the touring car and 16 in the runabout), a well-designed magneto ignition instead of dry batteries, and a detachable cylinder head were still other improvements over the Model N.

Ford initially priced the Model T at $825 for the runabout and $850 for the touring car. Although prices in 1909 were briefly raised to $900 and $950, respectively, they were dropped again in 1910 to a low $680 for the runabout and $780 for the touring car. Thus a definitely superior automobile became available at a bargain price. Ford became the undisputed leader of the industry by selling 10,607 Model Ts in the fiscal year 1909/10 and 34,528 in the fiscal year 1910/11. The Ford advertising

[28]"Sensation Out of Season," *Motor World*, 15:177 (January 7, 1907).

Plate 43.   Sales catalog illustration and specifications of the 1908 Ford Model T. Courtesy Free Library of Philadelphia.

Summary

MOTOR: 4 cylinder, 4 cycle, vertical, 20 h. p. 3¾ in. bore, 4 in. stroke, Cylinders cast in one block with water jackets and upper half of crank case integral, water jacketed cylinder head detachable, fine grain gray iron castings.

VALVES: Extra large, all on left side and offset.

SHAFTS: Crank and cam non-welded drop forged heat treated Ford Vanadium steel, bearing surfaces ground, cams integral and ground.

CRANK CASE: Upper half integral with cylinder casting. Lower half pressed steel and extended to form lower housing for magneto and transmission.

COOLING: Gear driven centrifugal pump.

IGNITION: Ford magneto generator, low tension, direct connected to engine drive.

CARBURETOR: New design, float feed automatic with dash adjustment.

TRANSMISSION: New design Ford spur planetary, bathed in oil,—all gears from heat-treated Vanadium steel, silent and easy in action.

LUBRICATION: Combination splash and gravity system—simple and sure. Insures against insufficient or excessive lubrication.

CLUTCH: Multiple steel discs, operating in oil.

CONTROL: All forward speeds by foot pedal. Reverse by hand lever. Spark and throttle under steering wheel.

FINAL DRIVE: By cardon shaft with single universal joint to bevel drive gears in live rear axle. Ford three point system (patented in all countries) with all moving parts enclosed in dust proof casing, running in oil. Vanadium steel throughout.

FRONT AXLE: One piece drop forging in I-beam section, specially treated, Vanadium steel.

STEERING: By Ford reduction gear system; irreversible.

BRAKES: 2 sets. (a) Service band brake on transmission; (b) Internal expanding brakes in rear hub drums.

WHEELS: Artillery wood type. Hubs extra long.

TIRES: Pneumatic; rear 30 x 3½ inches, front 30 x 3 inches.

NUMBER OF PASSENGERS: Normal load touring car, 5 adults.

SPRINGS: Front and rear, semi-elliptic.

FENDERS: Enclosed full length of car.

WHEEL BASE: 100 in., tread 56 in.; 60 in. for Southern roads where ordered.

GASOLINE CAPACITY: 10 gallons. Cylindrical gasoline tank mounted directly on frame.

STANDARD EQUIPMENT: Side oil lamps, tail lamp, tube horn and gas lamp brackets. Touring car ironed for top.

WEIGHT: 1200 lbs.

PRICE: Touring car $850.00. Coupe, $950.00. Cab $950.00. Town Car $1000.00 F. O. B. Detroit.

HIGH PRICED QUALITY IN A LOW PRICED CAR.

boast was essentially correct: "No car under $2,000 offers more, and no car over $2,000 offers more except the trimmings."

Now fully committed to large-volume production of the Model T as a static model at an ever-decreasing unit price, the Ford Motor Company began to introduce mass-production techniques at its new Highland Park plant on a scale heretofore unheard of. Model T prices were reduced to $345 for the runabout and $360 for the touring car on August 1, 1916; and in the fiscal year 1916/17, Ford sold 730,041 cars. Plans were already being developed for further expansion into a gigantic plant at River Rouge that would employ over 100,000 workmen. The American automobile for the masses had indeed arrived with the advent of the Ford Model T.

Automobile Improvements, 1900–1910

Several of the more striking improvements in American motorcar design from 1900 to 1910 should be made more explicit.[29] Changes in body style toward the form of the modern automobile in the United States began in 1900 when the first American cars appeared that had adopted the French practice of placing the engine under a hood in front of the driver. The following year the French tonneau body, which had a rear door and rounded seats that looked like cut-down barrels, was introduced and widely used by American manufacturers. As the engine came to be placed in front of the car and became larger and more powerful, the hood was lengthened and wheel-bases became longer. The replacement of high carriage wheels and narrow solid rubber tires with smaller-diameter wheels and wider pneumatic tires also made for

[29]An indispensable and well-written work on the design and mechanical aspects of the early motorcar is Anthony Bird, *Antique Automobiles* (New York: E. P. Dutton, 1967). Automobile Manufacturers Association, *Automobiles of America* (Detroit: Wayne State University Press, 1962), is also an invaluable compendium of factual information. By far the most useful trade journal for technical information is *Cycle and Automobile Trade Journal*, which emphasized the mechanical features of the cars of the day to the rather complete neglect of other aspects of the automobile movement.

a much lower-slung body. The running board was introduced in the 1903 Northern, the side entrance began to replace the rear door of the tonneau body about 1905, and bumpers became available as extras on some cars in 1906. The introduction of shock absorbers in 1904, gradual improvements in spring suspension, and trends toward longer wheelbases and moving the seats forward in the body made for a much more comfortable ride and reduced strain on the mechanism by 1908.

Automobile riding became more pleasant in inclement weather and possible at night with the general adoption of several other innovations. Canopy tops with glass fronts and side curtains first appeared in 1904, followed by cape and folding tops in 1905 and the "one-man" fabric top in 1909. Although the open car remained fairly universal in the period, as early as 1903 several American closed-car models were available. Special kerosene lamps for automobiles that cast a 200-foot beam were being made by the R. E. Dietz Company by 1900, but the turning point for safe driving after dark was the development of improved acetylene lamps for motor vehicles by Prest-O-Lite in 1904.

Little of the carriage style remained in the conventional American gasoline automobile by 1907, and new aesthetic standards of style in automobile design had by then come to be widely accepted. *Scientific American* reported, for example, that "it is coming to be realized that longer bodies and straight lines produce a car, which is not only . . . more shipshape, but which possesses more of that inherent beauty that belongs to a properly proportioned self-propelled vehicle, whether it be intended for use upon steel rails, or upon a macadam road." Even minor details in design reflected this trend. "Elements which have helped to improve the appearance are the better designed mud guards, which are now frequently brought up to a junction with the frame of the cars, and are designed in long, easy, sweeping lines of decided grace and beauty, and the provision of continuous running boards in place of the earlier and rather crude looking step, which like the curved car bodies, was a relic of the carriage builder's influence." The periodical concluded that, "thanks to the care with which the carriage builders have accommodated the bodies to the necessities of the chassis, the majority of the automobiles shown [at the 1907 ALAM New York automobile show] are marked by no little beauty and distinction."[30]

Controls too were greatly improved, making the operation of a motor vehicle possible for the average man. The steering wheel replaced the tiller on most models as early as 1901, and by 1908 the steering wheel began to be generally placed on the left side, the position best suited to driving on the right-hand side of the road. Eliott's steering knuckle, which enabled the front wheels to turn without the entire front axle turning also, came into general use after 1902. The corrugated steering wheel, designed to keep the driver's hands from slipping, was introduced in 1909.

The development of more flexible engines and better carburetors shortly after the turn of the century allowed the general adoption of the throttle pedal. As Andrew Bird has commented, "The present day driver would be nonplussed to find no throttle pedal with which to control engine and car speed, but before about 1903 many carburetors had no throttle valves and the accelerator pedal found on a few makes, or its equivalent hand lever, was concerned only to over-ride the mechanical governor which normally prevented the engine running too fast. This gave nothing like the sensitivity of control we now take for granted."[31]

Even the crude contracting-band foot brakes, generally operating on some part of the transmission rather than on the wheel drums, used in the early motorcar had been vastly superior to the almost brakeless horse-drawn vehicle. American manufacturers led the way in the adoption of foot brakes that operated on the wheel drums,

---

[30]"The Seventh National Automobile Show at Madison Square Garden," *Scientific American*, 96:22 (January 12, 1907).
[31]Bird, *Antique Automobiles*, p. 72.

and internal expanding brakes replaced contracting brakes about 1906. Larger brakes lined with woven asbestos material instead of leather began to be in common use on American cars about 1907–1908, and several American makers even introduced primitive air brakes on their cars as early as 1905.

Before the introduction of syncromesh in the 1920s, shifting without clashing gears posed a formidable problem for the average driver who had not mastered the fine art of "double declutching." Transmissions, however, had already been greatly improved and made easier to operate by 1910. Packard introduced the H-slot gearshift, which became the standard type, in 1904, and selective transmissions with three speeds forward and one in reverse were the rule on American cars by 1910. The Model T's two-speed planetary transmission, operated by a simple foot pedal, was the height of simplicity in a manual transmission, and its comparative ease of operation undoubtedly helped sell the neophyte driver on the Model T. Although the planetary transmission did not become standard in its day, the development of modern automatic transmissions involved a reversion to some of the basic principles involved in the planetary design. Neither the cone clutch with leather-covered friction facings most commonly used in the period nor the multiple-disc clutch of the day withstood hard use well, but the clutches used by 1910 represented a great improvement over those that had been available at the turn of the century.

Unskilled American drivers from the outset demanded minimal mechanical responsibility while operating a motor vehicle. Pronounced aversion to shifting gears was the most notable example. Compared with Europe, where horsepower taxes and high gasoline prices dictated that the motor be designed to give maximal performance for the amount of fuel used and that horsepower be kept within reasonable limits for the total weight of the car, the seemingly inexhaustible supply of cheap gasoline and lack of any horsepower tax allowed the American manufacturer to sacrifice engine efficiency to obtain maximal engine flexibility. The characteristic large-bore, short-stroke "American engine" that emerged permitted the American driver to reduce shifting to an absolute minimum. A tendency was evident by 1906 "to a steady increase in the cylinder capacity, which is due, no doubt, to the national temperament, which makes the driver prefer, if possible, to run continuously on the high speed, even where sharp hills have to be negotiated."[32]

To many writers some form of automatic transmission seemed ultimately to offer the best solution to the average American driver's distaste for shifting gears. As early as 1906, for example, Winthrop E. Scarritt, the first president of the American Automobile Association, predicted, "The present unsatisfactory system of change-speed gears will be supplanted by a variable-speed device. There are not wanting good judges who believe that the problem will be solved by a system of hydraulic transmission."[33] A primitive automatic transmission had already been introduced in the 1904 Sturtevant, which had a centrifugal clutch with low- and high-speed ranges; then in 1908 another crude form of automatic transmission appeared in the Columbia "gasolect" automobile, which used a gasoline engine to drive a generator that in turn powered separate electric motors attached to the wheels. But neither of these alternatives proved acceptable, and the modern automatic transmission was not developed until several decades more had passed.

The most onerous, and dangerous, part of the procedure of operating a motor vehicle by 1910 was dependence upon a hand crank to start the car. Although Alexander Winton designed a pneumatic self-starter for his six-cylinder model as early as 1907, the first efficient self-starter was the electric starter developed by Charles F. Kettering under the direction of Henry M. Leland, which appeared in the 1912 Cadillac. The

[32] "The Seventh Annual Show of the Automobile Club," *Scientific American*, 95:442(December 15, 1906).
[33] Winthrop E. Scarritt, "The Horse of the Future and the Future of the Horse," *Harper's Weekly*, 51:402 (March 16, 1907).

following year saw the electric self-starter come into general use, when nearly fifty other manufacturers adopted the innovation.

In 1900 and in 1910, the most satisfactory component of the motorcar was the engine, the least satisfactory the pneumatic tire. Both, however, underwent substantial improvement during the decade.

One of the more striking changes in the American motorcar from 1900 to 1910 was the significant increase in the ratio of the horsepower of the engine to the total weight of the automobile. This resulted in a motor vehicle that by European standards was greatly overpowered for its comparatively light weight. The 1901 curved-dash Oldsmobile weighed about 900 pounds and was powered by a 5-horsepower engine versus the 1,200-pound weight of the 20-horsepower 1908 Model T Ford. Americans became convinced by at least 1903 that "nothing is more unsatisfactory than a car too heavy for its horsepower. These were turned out in quantities not long ago, and today they are for sale secondhand for what they will bring."[34]

The increase in horsepower was associated with a trend toward multiple cylinders and water-cooling that began in the 1901 American models. The Franklin was one of the few popular cars that retained for very long the air-cooled engine, which until after World War II remained quite inefficient compared with water-cooling. The four-cylinder, water-cooled, front-mounted engine that had become standard by 1910 was first introduced in an American gasoline car by Locomobile in 1902. Although yearly gains in the number of models featuring six-cylinder engines were evident after 1906, when a brief craze for them developed, engines having more than four cylinders were generally considered too expensive for the advantages they afforded until well after 1910.

The increased horsepower resulted from better design and construction of the engine

[34]Henry Norman, "The Coming of the Automobile," *World's Work*, 5:3305 (April 1903).

as well as from simply adding cylinders and making it larger. Engines became more efficient, giving more horsepower for the size of the engine and the fuel expended, and more flexible, capable of generating sufficient power without stalling at a greater range of rpm. Larger cylinder capacity and closer machining of parts were only two of the many factors involved here. Few specific features related to the engine failed to undergo substantial improvement; even in beginning to enumerate the changes made, one could easily end up with a catalog of details. Perhaps just a few examples will adequately illustrate the general point. The early adoption of float-feed spraying carburetors that could be throttled and choked to adjust the amount of fuel and the fuel-air mixture allowed a flexibility impossible for the primitive stationary gasoline engines used in the first motor vehicles, which had been designed to run only at the speed best suited to fuel economy. The magneto generator began to be adopted in 1901, and by 1910 magnetos and high-tension ignition systems had replaced make-and-break ignition on the majority of American cars. In 1902, porcelain insulation of the spark plug was designed at Autocar by Lewis S. Clarke, the inventor as well of the double-reduction principle in rear axle construction. Three-point suspension of the engine was introduced in the Silent Northern by Jonathan D. Maxwell and Charles B. King. Timing mechanisms began to undergo improvement about this time, too, and were soon enclosed. Valves became larger, allowing better "breathing"; mechanically operated valves, first used in the United States on the 1903 Rambler and Oldsmobile models, were adopted quickly by most other American automobile manufacturers. Forced-feed lubrication by means of an oil pump after 1903 rapidly replaced the crude, early "splash" system of lubrication, which had depended merely upon the connecting rods dipping into and spattering about the oil contained in the crankcase.

The higher speeds resulting from improvements in the engine necessitated that tires also be greatly improved. Pneumatic tires replaced the solid rubber tires initially used, and their cushioning effect both increased riding comfort and reduced strain on the mechanism of the car. But it was generally agreed that the pneumatic tire was the weakest and most unsatisfactory part of the car. Proper pressure was difficult to maintain, and poor treads resulted in skidding. Tires were expensive to replace, easily damaged, and wore out quickly: 2,000 miles was considered extraordinary mileage for a set of tires; 1,000 miles was a more reasonable expectation. Time-consuming delays to repair tires were to be expected on any automobile trip. Finally, although an improvement over solid rubber tires, the pneumatic tires of the day still cushioned the passengers and mechanism inadequately against the shocks of hitting bumps and ruts on poor roads. Some blame was placed on the abuse of tires by the motorist, but tire and automobile manufacturers were considered most at fault, the latter because they often fitted cars with tires too small for the weight and power of the vehicle.

Really satisfactory tires did not become available until low-pressure pneumatic (balloon) tires were developed in the 1920s. By 1906, however, some improvement in tires was evident, and in 1909 it seemed to motorists that "tire trouble is becoming less serious, and the life of the individual tire is greatly prolonged."[35] The greatest advance was undoubtedly in the developments that allowed tires to be changed more easily. Standard quick-demountable rims first came into general use in 1904. The following year the Goodyear Tire and Rubber Company developed universal rims that took either clincher or straight-side tires, and the power tire pump was introduced. Tire chains were another 1905 innovation that made tires more adequate for

[35]"1909 Automobile," p. 40.

Plate 44.   Fashionable lady motorists having tire trouble with a 1909 Ford Model T. Courtesy Smithsonian Institution.

winter driving conditions. Despite these improvements, tires remained the most frequent cause of mechanical failure with which the motorist had to contend.

The manufacture of reliable, durable motor vehicles also depended upon the development of new steel alloys that combined light weight with great resistance to stress. Pressed-steel frame construction, introduced by Peerless in 1903, soon became standard, but the early steels used in automobile construction were not satisfactory. As Henry Ford explained in his 1907 *Harper's Weekly* article on vanadium steels, "The problem was not merely to obtain a steel that would carry a load or withstand the severest single strain or shock to which a car would be subjected in the life of the machine, but a metal of such toughness and tenacity as would successfully resist the ravages of vibration and fatigue. . . . steel which showed great toughness and ductility under static loads was found to fracture like glass in some cases under the influence of shock or of constant vibration, such as that with which we have to reckon in an automobile."[36]

Automobile and steel manufacturers engaged in extensive experiments to determine the qualities and kinds of steels best suited for automobile construction. As early as 1904 it was evident that steel components were becoming more uniform in quality. Improved chrome nickel and high carbon steels began to be generally used in American automobile construction in 1906. Then in 1907 vanadium steels, which had already been used in some of the better European cars, were introduced in the United States.

The Ford Motor Company is generally given credit for introducing vanadium steels in the American automobile industry. There can be no question that sufficient information on vanadium steels had been printed in American automobile trade journals and other technical periodicals, so that few persons in the industry could have been unaware of the potentialities of vanadium for automobile construction very

[36]Henry Ford, "Special Automobile Steel," *Harper's Weekly*, 51:386G (March 16, 1907).

long after 1905, the year in which Ford executives first became interested. It is certain that the ALAM engineers too were experimenting with vanadium steels by early 1907. And Henry Ford himself recognized in his 1907 *Harper's Weekly* article that metallurgists had been well aware of the implications of vanadium steels for some time but that the mineral had not been available in commercial quantities until very recently, when large deposits of vanadium had been discovered in South America. Regardless, it does appear definite that the Ford Motor Company was in this, as in so many other aspects of motorcar construction and design, well ahead of its competition in the effective implementation of an innovation. Ford guaranteed a small steel plant in Canton, Ohio — the United Steel Company — against loss if it would run the first vanadium heats in the United States and set up a metallurgical laboratory under John Wandersee to test and develop vanadium steels. The extensive use of vanadium steels was then immediately incorporated into the basic design and the production engineering of the contemplated Model T.

The introduction of vanadium steels was one of the major innovations in automobile design and construction. Vanadium steels made possible a much lighter car that was also tougher and better able to withstand "dynamic stress." Before the introduction of vanadium, the most promising prospect for a lighter metal car had probably been the cast-aluminum body featured in the 1906 Marmon. But with vanadium, light weight could be obtained without sacrificing superior strength in either the chassis or body; the all-steel body, introduced in the 1912 Oakland and Hupmobile cars, now became possible. It was later demonstrated at Ford that, for many of the purposes for which vanadium steels had been initially used in the Model T, scientifically heat-treated older steels were in fact far superior. However, it was equally evident that the introduction of vanadium steels had increased the maximum possible tensile strength of the steels used in Ford cars from 70,000 to 170,000 pounds.

Standardization of Parts

Relative to the progress that was to be made in the next decade, concrete achievement toward industry-wide standardization of parts and fittings was slight before 1910. Nevertheless, a foundation was laid by then that greatly benefited the purchaser of an automobile. The adoption of standards for bolts and nuts based on United States standards to which carriage bolt sizes and threads conformed meant that a lost or broken bolt could be replaced in any hardware store. Established high standards for automobile steels meant that cars were more durable and safer. Agreement among rim and tire manufacturers on standard forms and dimensions for steel-clincher rims of tires meant that any car could be fitted with almost any leading make of tire. Head-lamp brackets and spark plugs were among the other components that were standardized early, and in 1907 the industry also adopted a standard formula for the determination of horsepower.

Manufacturers who sold similar parts and tires to a number of automobile manufacturers from the very beginning of the industry acted as a check upon diversity in the design of components because it was easier and more economical to furnish one or only a few standardized parts to all customers. Representatives from these related industries were admitted as associate members when the National Association of Automobile Manufacturers was formed in 1900, and within the trade association they continued to push for standardization.

Both the Association of Licensed Automobile Manufacturers (ALAM), through a mechanical branch established in 1905, and the American Motor Car Manufacturers' Association (AMCMA), through a provision in its charter for interchange of technical information, encouraged intercompany standardization of components. However, leadership in the movement was definitely assumed by the ALAM Mechanical Branch between 1905 and 1909. It attempted to establish steel specifications, screw-thread dimensions, and spark plug and rim standards for the companies associated under the Selden patent. But since the ALAM standardization program had been conceived primarily as a legal tactic in the Selden patent litigation against nonmember companies, the program collapsed when the patent was initially upheld by the courts in 1909. The activities of the ALAM Mechanical Branch were then transferred to the Society of Automotive Engineers in 1910. When the Selden patent was voided in 1911, the SAE continued its work in conjunction with the Motor and Accessory Manufacturers' Association, a separately organized trade association of parts and tire makers.

  The Society of Automotive Engineers (initially the Society of Automobile Engineers) began as a small but influential group of automobile trade journalists and automotive engineers who organized in 1905 to improve the state of automotive technology through the publication of articles. Under the leadership of Howard E. Coffin, the vice-president of Hudson who was elected president of the SAE in 1910, the organization blossomed into an important force in the industry. Coker Clarkson, former manager of the ALAM Mechanical Branch, was hired, and the SAE formed a standards committee headed by Henry Southern, a former consulting engineer under Clarkson for the ALAM. The SAE increased its membership from 300 to 900 within a year.

  Most SAE members were small automobile manufacturers, and this interest group dominated the standards committee. A general shake-up due to adjustments to new market conditions had resulted in relatively high rates of failure among both small automobile concerns and their suppliers of components. Also, while large automobile producers could count on their own ability to manufacture needed parts or upon well-established lines of supply, the small automobile makers were often unable by now to obtain the components they needed in sufficient quantity or at reasonable prices. These small producers were therefore eager to inaugurate through the SAE a standards program that would enable them to buy readily available standard components at a lower price than they had been paying for specially designed parts. Howard E. Coffin was in agreement and voiced the opinion that the lack of intercompany standardization was "responsible for nine-tenths of the production troubles and most of the needless expense entailed in the manufacture of motorcars."[37] To remedy this situation, the SAE began in 1910 to carry out a vigorous standards program that resulted in 224 different sets of standards being adopted by 1921.

Ultimately, however, progress toward the standardization and interchangeability of parts was due less to agreement on the formulation of industry-wide standards than to the development of mass-production techniques within individual companies. First pioneered at Cadillac under Henry M. Leland's direction, this characteristic of the American automobile industry was perfected by the Ford Motor Company in its production of the Model T. Of necessity, mass-production techniques leading to increased standardization of product and consequent lower costs could be effectively implemented only by the well-established firm with a car of superior design. As *Scientific American* recognized in January 1909, "In the long run, standardization and interchangeability of parts will have the effect of giving us a higher grade of motorcar at a lower price, but this is dependent in considerable degree upon the production of one model in great numbers and the elimination of extensive annual changes in design that necessitate the making of costly jigs, gauges, and special machinery."[38] The small firm could not hope to amass either the capital or the engineer-

[37] *The Society of Automotive Engineers Transactions* (1910), pp. 125–126, as cited in George V. Thompson, "Intercompany Technical Standardization in the Early Automobile Industry," *Journal of Economic History*, 14:1–20 (Winter 1954). For intercompany standardization, see also Alexander Johnston, "Standardization Turns the Wheels of Progress," *Motor*, 29:84 (November 1917), and J. K. Barnes, "The Men Who Standardized Automobile Parts," *World's Work*, 42:204–208 (June 1921).
[38] "Standardizing the Automobile," *Scientific American*, 100:40 (January 16, 1909).

ing talent necessary to do this. Thus it became inevitable that technological improvements in the design and production of the American motorcar from 1910 on would be due far less to the collective movement for industry-wide standards by the numerous small firms in the American automobile industry than to the actions of the few large producers that had already begun to dominate the manufacture of motor vehicles in the United States.

9
Industrial Organization:
Entrepreneurial
Environment, Strategies,
and Structures

Entrepreneurial Environment

The automobile industry developed under optimal entrepreneurial conditions in the United States. Of primary importance were the higher per capita income and better income distribution relative to European countries, which made possible a much larger domestic market here. That the American manufacturer would cater to a mass market was also inherent in the American manufacturing tradition. The volume production of standardized commodities for a national market had become well established early in our industrial history. In contrast with European conditions, a chronic shortage of labor and an abundance of natural resources in the United States resulted in high wages and low material costs, making possible a mass market for consumer goods. These conditions also encouraged the mechanization of industrial processes, which necessitated the standardization of products and allowed economies in production that could be passed on to the consumer in the form of lower prices. The lack of tariff barriers between the states, in addition, encouraged sales over a wider geographic area. Thus the European pattern of small-scale, individualized production of motor vehicles at necessarily high prices was never expected to become characteristic of the American automobile industry.

From the outset, the demand for automobiles in the United States was consistently much greater than the supply. Operating in a seller's market, early American automobile manufacturers most often had little difficulty in obtaining more orders for cars than they could fill — even before production started and although cars were then sold on a cash-on-delivery basis without warranty. John W. Anderson, one of the original investors in the Ford Motor Company, expressed this point in a letter from Detroit to his father just prior to the Ford incorporation in 1903: "Now the demand for automobiles is a perfect craze. Every factory here ... has its entire output sold and cannot begin to fill orders. Mr. Malcomson has already begun to be deluged with

orders, although not a machine has been put on the market and will not be until
July 1.... And it is all spot cash on delivery, and no guarantee or string attached of
any kind."[1]

Entry into automobile manufacturing was extremely easy in the industry's early
years. One important reason, first pointed out by Lawrence H. Seltzer in 1928, was
that requirements for fixed and working capital could be met mainly by shifting
the burden to parts makers, distributors, and dealers. Since the automobile was a
unique combination of components already standardized and being produced for
other uses — for example, stationary and marine gasoline engines, carriage bodies
and wheels — the automobile manufacturer, once the basic design of his car was established, became merely an assembler of major components and a supplier of finished cars to his distributors and dealers. The latter bore the responsibility for dis-
posing of them directly to the public. By jobbing out the manufacture of component
parts to scores of independent suppliers rather than undertaking it himself, the entre-
preneur minimized his capital requirements for wages, materials, expensive machinery, and a large factory. This capital was instead provided to him indirectly
by the parts makers. The modest assembly plant needed could be rented as easily
as purchased, and the process of assembling was shorter than the thirty- to ninety-
day credit period the parts makers allowed. Operating on this basis, the Ford Motor
Company was able to start in business in 1903 with only $28,000 paid-in capital,
a dozen workmen, and an assembly plant just 250 feet long by 50 feet wide. Moreover, demand for automobiles was so high that manufacturers were able to extract
exorbitant concessions from distributors and dealers in exchange for exclusive ter-
ritorial rights. Advance cash deposits of 20 percent were required on all orders, with
full payment demanded immediately upon delivery through a sight draft attached

[1] The letter is quoted in full in the *Detroit News*, January 14, 1927.

to the bill of lading; and cars had to be accepted according to a prearranged schedule, regardless of current retail sales, thereby allowing the manufacturer to gear shipments to production. Roy D. Chapin, organizer of the Hudson Motor Car Company, informed Seltzer in an interview that as late as 1909, when Hudson was beginning in the industry, "Dealers' deposits often paid half the sum necessary to bring out a full year's production; and if the assembling were efficiently directed, drafts against the finished cars could be cashed as rapidly as the bills from parts makers came in."[2]

   The small amount of capital as well as the managerial expertise and technical ability needed to initiate the manufacture of motor vehicles was most commonly provided through diversion from other, generally closely related, business activities and therefore presented little problem in the early years of the industry. John B. Rae has pointed out that most of the successful early automotive entrepreneurs "were less likely to be individual inventors starting a completely new business than men who added the production of automobiles to an existing operation. Most frequently, they were bicycle or carriage and wagon manufacturers, or operators of machine shops, but there were a variety of odds and ends." Rae has also established that, although the great majority of the more important figures in the early automobile industry had received only practical training as machinists or mechanics, "The number of college-trained engineers in this first generation of automotive entrepreneurs is surprisingly large, considering that engineering degrees were something of a rarity in the United States until the twentieth century."[3]

   Documentation for Rae's assertions is indeed superabundant. The Duryea brothers,

[2] Lawrence H. Seltzer, *A Financial History of the American Automobile Industry* (Boston and New York: Houghton Mifflin, 1928), pp. 19–21. The Chapin quotation was transcribed by Seltzer from notes taken in an interview in Detroit on December 11, 1924.

[3] John B. Rae, *American Automobile Manufacturers* (Philadelphia: Chilton, 1959), pp. 8, 203.

who designed and produced the first American gasoline automobile, were bicycle mechanics. Elwood P. Haynes, their closest rival, was a college-trained engineer. Colonel Albert A. Pope, the most important American automobile manufacturer before the turn of the century, was also the largest manufacturer of bicycles in the United States. Hiram Percy Maxim, who headed Pope's automobile division and also designed his own gasoline car in 1896, had an engineering degree. Alexander Winton, Erwin R. Thomas, George N. Pierce, and Thomas B. Jeffery (Rambler) were other bicycle manufacturers whose firms came to be among the more important early producers of automobiles. The carriage and wagon manufacturers who entered automobile manufacturing included Studebaker, the largest producer of horse-drawn wagons in the world, and the Durant-Dort Carriage Company, which produced about 150,000 horse-drawn vehicles a year at the time William C. Durant, already a millionaire, began an automotive career at Buick that was to culminate in the formation of General Motors and Chevrolet. Owners of successful machine shops who became prominent automobile manufacturers included Henry M. Leland (Cadillac), whose firm had among other things supplied parts to the bicycle industry, and Ransom E. Olds, who had made stationary gasoline engines. Samuel and Frederick Smith, the father and son who together with Olds founded Oldsmobile and then took over the company after he left to form REO, had made a considerable fortune in copper and lumber before entering the automobile business.

Examples of important producers of other commodities that in addition became well-known automobile manufacturers include the Peerless Wringer Company and the White Sewing Machine Company. Windsor T. and Rollin G. White held college degrees in engineering. W. T. Barbour, president of the Detroit Stove Works, which claimed to have the largest stove plant in the world, also founded an important automobile company, the Northern Manufacturing Company. Both the American Locomotive Company and the International Harvester Company undertook the manufacture of motor vehicles. Benjamin Briscoe began as a sheet-metal manufacturer. He went on to back David Buick, a bathtub manufacturer initially, and then founded the Maxwell-Briscoe Motor Company. Briscoe also later organized the ill-fated United States Motor Company. James W. Packard, an engineering graduate, started as a manufacturer of electric cables. Prior to becoming president of Packard in 1901, Henry B. Joy, another college-trained engineer from a wealthy family, was an associate of Charles B. King in the Charles B. King Company, which made pneumatic hammers, railway brake beams, and marine engines. King himself designed a successful automobile in 1896, introduced three-point suspension and an integral engine-transmission assembly in his design of the 1902 Silent Northern, and founded the King Motor Car Company in 1910. Nordyke and Marmon was a successful firm of millwrights when it entered the automobile industry.

Entry into automobile manufacturing apparently presented little difficulty for even the unschooled mechanic without previous experience in operating his own business or funds of his own to invest. Despite these handicaps, Henry Ford was able to obtain adequate support from backers to sustain him through four years of failure to produce a car for the commercial market.

Having successfully experimented with motor vehicles as a hobby for several years, Ford left his job as an engineer with the Edison Illuminating Company to become superintendent and a small stockholder in the Detroit Automobile Company on August 15, 1899, in exchange for his automobile patents, without putting up any money. The firm had been organized on August 5 by some of Detroit's leading citizens with only $15,000 of its $150,000 capitalization paid in. Investors included William H. Murphy, a wealthy lumber merchant; C. A. Black, a well-known local capitalist; and William C. Maybury, the mayor of Detroit. Emphasis was put upon building racing cars, and Ford soon gained a national reputation as a racing driver. His most notable feat was a victory over Alexander Winton at the Grosse Point track on October 11, 1901. On November 20, 1901, the Detroit Automobile Company was reorganized as the Henry Ford Company with a capitalization of $60,000, of which only $30,500 was actually paid in. Ford was given 1,000 shares of stock, representing a $10,000 interest, for his contributions. The new company attempted to turn toward the commercial production of passenger cars; but, largely because of Ford's continued concentration upon building racers, the firm (which became Cadillac in 1902) was not successful until Ford, after a period of dissension, left to form the Ford Motor Company with new backers on June 16, 1903.

Nominally capitalized at $150,000, of which only $28,000 was paid in, the Ford Motor Company issued 1,000 shares of stock, representing $100,000 of its total capitalization. Henry Ford received 255 of these shares, as did his most important backer, Alexander Malcomson, an affluent coal dealer. Malcomson's cousin, Vernon C. Fry; his uncle, John S. Gray, the president of Detroit's German-American Bank; and his clerk and business adviser, James Couzens, were also stockholders. Couzens provided the main managerial expertise for the new company, and Gray became its president because of his banking connections. The other investors were John and Horace Dodge, makers of gasoline engines, Albert Strelow, one of Detroit's largest painting and carpentering contractors; Charles R. Bennett of the Daisy Air Rifle Company; Horace Rackham and John W. Anderson, attorneys; and Charles J. Woodhull.

Henry Ford's experience was atypical only in the high degree of success his company ultimately enjoyed. Demand for automobiles was great and potential profits high, credit from parts makers was readily available, and promoters were having little trouble finding backers to provide the modest capital required to enter the automobile business. Consequently, automobile companies, almost always with well-watered capitalization, were springing up like mushrooms throughout the country. As *Motor World* reported the situation in late 1900, "Since January 1 there have been organized in this country vehicle and power companies with a combined capitalization of $329,-500,000. Not one-tenth of these concerns will ever get any nearer turning out a motor vehicle than the permission to do so, which appears in their incorporation papers. But what a sad commentary the whole thing is upon the credulity of humanity and the never deviating certainty that fools can always be counted upon to rush in where angels, celestial, not financial ones, would hesitate to tread or even fly."[4]

By 1910 considerably heavier capital outlays were required to ensure success than had been necessary earlier, but closure of entry into automobile manufacturing in the United States did not occur until the 1920s.[5] Among the first companies that produced successful automobiles, a number of the better-managed firms soon turned toward a policy of reinvesting their high profits in the expansion of plant facilities both to increase the output of completed cars and to undertake the manufacture of many components formerly jobbed out. Their objectives were further to reduce unit costs of production, improve quality, and ensure supply. The results of this trend were pointed out well in January 1910 by Walter E. Flanders, production manager at Ford from August 1906 until he left in April 1908 to produce the E-M-F car with "Barney" Everitt and William Metzger. He remarked that "to equal in quality cars now selling at $700 to $900, it is not only necessary to build them in tremendous quantities, but to build and equip factories for the economical manufacture of every part." The opening of Ford's elaborately equipped, sixty-acre Highland Park plant on January 1, 1910, gave substance to Flanders's asser-

---

[4] "Fools and Their Folly," *Motor World*, 1:5 (October 4, 1900).
[5] On closure in the American automobile industry, see Harold G. Vatter, "Closure of Entry in the American Automobile Industry," *Oxford Economic Papers*, n.s. 4:213–234 (October 1952).

tion that "henceforth the history of this industry will be the story of a conflict between giants."[6]

Despite the higher capital requirements, however, entry into automobile manufacturing was now more than ever encouraged by the comparative prosperity of the automobile industry during the 1907 recession, the notable financial successes of several firms, and the rapidly expanding middle-class market for motorcars. Detroit had eleven automobile companies at the beginning of 1909, with Ford's $2,000,000 capitalization being the largest. By the end of that year twenty-two new Detroit automobile companies with a total capitalization of $4,310,000 had been organized; to meet the new competition, several of the older companies increased their capitalizations considerably.

Entrances and Exits of Automobile Manufacturers

Numerous small companies, widely dispersed geographically, entered automobile manufacturing during the first decade of the twentieth century. The most conservative estimate of entrances and exits has been given by Ralph C. Epstein, who attempted to list "only such firms as seem actually to have produced and sold cars in a commercial way, firms which sold cars to customers other than merely their few principal stockholders or promoters, and which operated plants for more than merely two or three weeks or a month."[7] Table 9.1 presents Epstein's findings for 1902–1912, which show a total of 93 active automobile manufacturers during the ten-year period, with 57 firms remaining active in 1912.

A more comprehensive list of entrances and exits than Epstein's was compiled by

[6] Walter E. Flanders, "Large Capital Now Needed to Embark in Automobile Business," *Detroit Saturday Night*, January 22, 1910.
[7] Ralph C. Epstein, *The Automobile Industry* (Chicago and New York: A. W. Shaw Co., 1928), p. 164.

Table 9.1 Entrances and Exits of Ninety-three Principal Automobile Manufacturers, 1903–1912

Year	1902	1903	1904	1905	1906	1907	1908	1909	1910	1911	1912	Total
Entrances		13	12	5	6	1	10	18	1	3	12	81
Exits		1	1	2	1	0	2	1	18	2	8	36
Companies remaining active	12	24	35	38	43	44	52	69	52	53	57	

Source: Ralph C. Epstein, *The Automobile Industry* (Chicago and New York: A. W. Shaw Co., 1928). p. 176.

Charles E. Duryea for *Motor* in early 1909. Duryea's list is summarized through the end of 1908 in Table 9.2, excluding companies formed or dissolved through change of name, transfer of ownership, or absorption into another company already engaged in automobile manufacturing. Of the 515 companies engaged in automobile manufacturing between 1900 and 1908, the table shows that 253 remained active at the end of the last year.

Epstein's list may provide a useful index of the entrances and exits of the major manufacturers, but it does appear to be overly restrictive, even on the difficult criteria he established. Certainly, it does not give an accurate accounting of the early automobile industry as a whole. Epstein dealt with only 68 of the 515 companies that Duryea reported to have entered automobile manufacturing before January 1909; and a survey of motor vehicle registrations in ten eastern states alone in August 1905 showed 95 American automobile manufacturers that were represented by five or more cars, although Epstein listed only 42 companies active in the industry up to that date.[8] A comparison of Epstein's findings with Duryea's also reveals some striking differences in patterns of entrances and exits, most notably for the year 1907. Accord-

[8] "Uncle Sam and John Bull," *Motor Age*, 8:8–9 (August 3, 1905).

Table 9.2   Entrances into and Exits from Automobile Manufacturing, 1900–1908

Year	1899	1900	1901	1902	1903	1904	1905	1906	1907	1908	Total
Entrances		46	38	43	53	42	41	48	85	89	485
Exits		15	21	16	29	36	23	21	47	54	262
Companies remaining active	30	61	78	105	129	135	153	180	218	253	

Source: "Motor's Historical Table of the American Motor Car Industry," *Motor*, 11:36–42 (March 1909). These data were gathered by Charles E. Duryea with the assistance of Herman F. Cuntz of the Association of Licensed Automobile Manufacturers.

Note: Entrances include companies that were established in another line of business prior to commencing manufacture of motor vehicles; both entrances and exits exclude companies formed or dissolved through change of name, transfer of ownership or assets, or absorption into another company already engaged in automobile manufacturing.

ing to Epstein, 1907 was quite stable, with only one entrance and no exits, whereas Duryea shows 1907 to have been one of the industry's most unstable years, with 85 entrances and 47 exits. It is pertinent to note that of the 47 firms Duryea found exiting in 1907, 24 (55 percent) had been in the industry for more than one year and were therefore presumably established as automobile manufacturers, even though not successful ones. Furthermore, Epstein's picture of a stable industry in 1907 is not in accord with the qualitative estimates of commentators on the state of the automobile industry at the time.

The more liberal accounting of the number of active automobile manufacturing firms seems to be more useful and meaningful. The presence of a large number of small manufacturers, each producing only a handful of motor vehicles before failing, was one of the most important characteristics of the early American automobile industry. The collective output of these firms was considerable. Their output affected the market for automobiles and created organizational and strategic problems for the more prominent companies. Undoubtedly, only those enterprises that were clearly "fly-by-night" should be eliminated — namely, firms that entered and exited in the same year.

Table 9.3 Proportion of Total Exits from Automobile Manufacturing Accounted for by Companies That Were Active in Only One Year, 1900–1908

Year	1900	1901	1902	1903	1904	1905	1906	1907	1908	Total
Number of companies entering and exiting in same year	11	13	6	6	11	5	6	21	16	95
Companies as percent of total exits that year	73	62	37	21	31	21	29	45	30	

Source: "Motor's Historical Table of the American Motor Car Industry," *Motor*, 11:36–42 (March 1909). These data were gathered by Charles E. Duryea with the assistance of Herman F. Cuntz of the Association of Licensed Automobile Manufacturers.

Table 9.3, which shows the proportion of total exits from automobile manufacturing accounted for by firms active in only one year from 1900 through 1908, establishes that such firms constituted just a small part of the early American automobile industry. Only 95 (18 percent) of the 515 firms active up to 1909 entered and exited in the same year, although the percent of total exits in given years accounted for by such firms ranged from highs of 73 and 62 percent for 1900 and 1901, respectively, to lows of 21 percent for both 1903 and 1905.

The great majority of companies that entered automobile manufacturing did manage to survive their first year. The mortality rate was extremely high after this, however, and prominence was most often fleeting. Over half the firms Duryea listed as having entered the industry from 1900 to 1908 had failed by the latter year, and among the more prominent firms listed by Epstein, 38 percent had failed by 1912. Moreover, between 1900 and 1912 there was a complete turnover in leadership within the American automobile industry, and the geographic center of automobile manufacturing shifted from New England to Detroit.[9]

[9]For the rise of Detroit as the center of automobile manufacturing and histories of its individual manufacturers, see especially "Detroit: The Automobile City," *Cycle and Automobile Trade Journal*, 14:121–161 (December 1, 1909).

Entrepreneurial Problems

The high rate of failure and change in leadership in the early automobile industry were apparently due to three often interrelated factors: overoptimism in the face of technological uncertainties; the lack of any effective industry-wide discipline and control; and poor business judgment regarding organization, product, and market strategy — particularly inability to adjust to changes in market demand.

The most notorious example of misplaced optimism and consequent overcapitalization combined with poor technological judgment was the so-called Lead Cab Trust that resulted from the acquisition of the Electric Vehicle Company by William C. Whitney and P. A. B. Widener interests in 1899. Probably in large part also a stock-jobbing venture, the announced aim of this holding company, formed with an inflated capitalization of $3,000,000, was to place fleets of public cabs on the streets of major American cities. Its manufacturing subsidiary, the Columbia and Electric Vehicle Company of Hartford, Connecticut, then the leading producer of motor vehicles in the United States, produced some 2,000 electric cabs plus a few electric trucks. Heavily overcapitalized, but nevertheless actual, operating companies were formed in New York, Boston, Philadelphia, and Chicago. Ultimate plans went well beyond this, calling for 12,000 vehicles and a capitalization of $200,000,000.

The heavily watered capitalization might not have been such a problem had the Electric Vehicle Company not also made the critical error of backing a poorly designed electric vehicle rather than the gasoline automobile. The failing performance of the company's electric cabs when put into service had an immediate, disastrous consequence on its securities. So did a financial scandal involving a fiscal manipulation that entailed a $2,000,000 loan to an office boy. The operating subsidiaries collapsed, and on June 20, 1900, the Electric Vehicle Company became a manufacturing firm rather than a holding company, which through unwise mergers was again overcapitalized at $20,000,000 by late 1900. The company progressively declined and as a result of the 1907 financial recession went into receivership on December 10, 1907, finally to be reorganized with a more realistic capitalization of $2,000,000 as the Columbia Motor Car Company in 1909. Strangely enough, the chief asset of the firm turned out to be its ownership of the Selden patent on the gasoline automobile, which was ultimately declared worthless by the courts.[10]

Although the high demand for motor vehicles attracted many entrances into automobile manufacturing, it could not ensure the success of inefficient, poorly managed firms that made an inferior car. The problem of inexperienced, and sometimes dishonest, manufacturers who turned out extremely shoddy products in the hope of making a fast dollar from a gullible public eager to purchase motor vehicles was pervasive in the early automobile industry. *Horseless Age*, for example, was concerned in 1902 that "the attitude of the public has, in fact, been so favorable to the new vehicle that promoters and manufacturers have in many cases taken advantage of it to impose upon the public worthless stocks and imperfect vehicles . . . [to] the detriment of the industry as a whole." The periodical concluded: "The worst enemies of the industry are not without. They are within."[11]

Even for the reputable manufacturer, the poor technological choice to back either the steam or the electric vehicle often involved failure as the gasoline automobile rapidly proved superior and gained favor. In sharp contrast with the feverish technological innovation among makers of gasoline automobiles, the manufacturers of both steam and electric vehicles remained either unable or unwilling to overcome defects in their products or to reduce unit prices sufficiently. John B. Rae has noted that "no outstanding automotive engineer appeared in an entrepreneurial role in

[10]For the history of the Lead Cab Trust, see John B. Rae, "The Electric Vehicle Company," *Business History Review*, 29:298–311 (December 1955), and his *American Automobile Manufacturers*, pp. 67–72.
[11]"Who Are the Enemies of the Automobile Industry?" *Horseless Age*, 9:4–5 (January 1, 1902).

connection with either steam or electric automobiles."[12] For the electric car, the result was well expressed in *Harper's Weekly* in 1907 by a writer who did "not think that there ever was a line of goods precipitated on the public that represented so much money value invested that was so utterly worthless practically."[13] Opinion on the steam vehicle was by this time similarly unfavorable.

No one has yet presented a convincing argument that the invariable association of the gasoline automobile with the creative automotive engineer-entrepreneur was due to anything other than the inherently superior technological feasibility of the internal-combustion engine over steam and electric power for the motorcar at the time. Although steam and electric cars each enjoyed some initial advantages over the gasoline-driven automobile, neither was, as we have seen, as susceptible to short-range improvement to obviate its many shortcomings compared with the gasoline-powered car. Charles C. McLaughlin has argued that the demise of the steamer, which he believes (wrongly in my opinion) to have been initially superior to the gasoline automobile, was primarily due to the fact that "White and Stanley, the most prominent makers failed to introduce the innovations in production and selling which would have enabled them to survive in the face of Detroit competition." But McLaughlin himself notes that the early steamer's automatic controls were not good, and "completely satisfactory steam generators were not in use until after the steam car had lost its battle with internal combustion."[14] In the case of the electric car, Thomas A. Edison was unsuccessful in his sustained attempts to improve the storage battery enough to meet even the low minimal performance expectations of the period. At

---

[12]John B. Rae, "The Engineer-Entrepreneur in the American Automobile Industry," *Explorations in Entrepreneurial History*, 8:9–10 (October 1955).
[13]F. A. Babcock, "The Electric Motor of Yesterday and Today," *Harper's Weekly*, 51:382 (March 16, 1907).
[14]Charles C. McLaughlin, "The Stanley Steamer: A Study in Unsuccessful Innovation," *Explorations in Entrepreneurial History*, 7:39, 45 (October 1954).

the present stage of our technological development, the problems involved in designing an electric-powered alternative to the internal-combustion engine still remain formidable for automotive engineers.

The ascendancy of the gasoline automobile also had important implications for regional hegemony in automobile manufacturing. Although the industry was still dispersed geographically in 1910, Michigan, particularly the Detroit area, followed by neighboring Indiana, had emerged as its geographic center. Several reasons for this seem apparent. From the outset, the eastern firms had tended to produce mainly electric and steam vehicles, while manufacturers in the Middle West had concentrated upon the gasoline-powered car. The overwhelming choice of the internal-combustion engine over other motive powers by middle western companies was influenced by the region's comparatively poor roads, which were near impossible for electrics to negotiate, and by the universal availability of gasoline for fuel in the sparsely settled rural areas lacking electricity, which composed a large part of the potential middle western market. What had appeared to be initial drawbacks for the western manufacturer turned out to be advantages: as the demand for steam and electric cars quickly declined and rural markets replaced urban ones, the New England producer, if he were now to switch to the gasoline-powered car, faced immediate, unfamiliar problems of both design and production engineering. Furthermore, while it would be erroneous to say that most of the important western manufacturers were committed to producing for predominantly middle-class and rural markets, more manufacturers in the Middle West than elsewhere appear to have been concerned early with the production of moderately priced cars for a mass market. Perhaps this was true because the local markets that were expected to provide the mainstay of a small firm's business in the Middle West rarely afforded the amount of upper-class clientele one could count on in a large eastern city. In addition, Michigan and Indiana had been the center of the carriage and wagon trade because of their excellent hardwood forests. Finally, these states were also important for the production of stationary gasoline engines, widely used on farms, as well as for the production of marine engines in the Detroit area. Thus southern Michigan provided an ideal environment for the manufacture of gasoline automobiles, affording close proximity to suppliers of the two major components, bodies and motors.

Among the manufacturers of gasoline automobiles in Detroit and throughout the United States, competition was sharp: failure to keep abreast of the most recent technological improvements in design or bringing out an inferior new model might well spell ruin for the established company that had risked plowing most of its profits back into improved plant and equipment as well as for the new firm operating on slender resources. Benjamin Briscoe recalled that, despite the success of Maxwell-Briscoe by 1908, "there was always the thought that if we should ever experience a 'silly season,' should ever drop so far behind competition as to make it difficult for us to sell our product 'off the fire,' we . . . would find ourselves in a very unfortunate position." Briscoe found conditions in the spring of 1908 "somewhat ominous, especially for such concerns as had large fixed investments in plants, machinery, tools, etc." The main problem was that a large number of companies were outright "manufacturing gamblers," and all firms "plunged" to some extent by risking unduly large amounts of capital in light of the existing technological uncertainties. The policies of several of the bolder companies forced "even the sanest among the manufacturers . . . into business risks which they would not have entered had they not been fearful that some other concern would gain a few points on them." Briscoe had also been worried about the "menace to the industry" posed by "concerns which did not have a worthy car or any manufacturing ability, but with large stock issues to sell, and by ingenious exploitation would succeed in stirring up the trade and the public, creating the impression that . . . they, through some newly discovered combination of geniuses, were enabled to sell gold dollars for fifty cents in automobiles." His final source of anxiety was that many parts makers, "by extending accommodations and taking long chances with small automobile manufacturers, threatened a demoralization by encouraging into the business undercapitalized concerns and inexperienced makers, and although such companies were generally short-lived . . . and even though their scope was limited to their own localities, the business which they did in the aggregate was very considerable."

The answer to these problems of uncontrolled competition in the face of technological uncertainty appeared to Briscoe and others, most importantly to William C. Durant, to be an industrial combination strong enough to order the industry effectively through control of the leading automobile manufacturers. Briscoe remembered that "in this year of 1908, many of us thought that the industry was beset with difficulties and so came the desire to some of us to form a combination of the principal concerns in the industry, not with the desire to sell all of the automobiles that were to be sold, but rather for the purpose of having one big concern of such dominating influence in the automobile industry, as for instance, the United States Steel Corporation exercises in the steel industry, so that its very influence would prevent many of the abuses that we believed existed."[15]

Discipline Through Combination

Benjamin Briscoe and William C. Durant became the key figures in several unsuccessful attempts to discipline the early automobile industry through industrial combina-

---

[15] Benjamin Briscoe, "The Inside Story of General Motors," *Detroit Saturday Night*, January 15, 22, and 29 and February 5, 1921.

tion.[16] They first cooperated in a plan to merge Maxwell-Briscoe and Buick, their own companies, with several other leading producers of gasoline automobiles, most importantly with Ford and REO. Such a combination might have accomplished the end intended, as about one-third of the output of American gasoline automobiles would have been controlled. But the plan did not materialize, allegedly because first Ford, then Olds each demanded $3,000,000 in cash, rather than securities, to sell out. Undaunted, Briscoe and Durant tried another consolidation scheme by securing a New Jersey charter for an International Motors Company, to be built around the nucleus of Buick and Maxwell-Briscoe. J. P. Morgan & Co., from whom Briscoe had previously obtained financial aid for his automotive ventures, was to underwrite the stock issue. However, Morgan withdrew support because it appeared that Durant, intending to profit personally by enlarging his stockholdings, had neglected to inform the other Buick stockholders of the plan. Briscoe and Durant parted company.

Working alone now, Durant moved quickly to form the General Motors Company as a New Jersey holding company with a nominal capitalization of only $2,000 on September 16, 1908. The holding company structure allowed Durant to finance his combination with minimal cash, since companies could be purchased mainly through exchange of stock. Consequently, although Durant was short of both cash and bank credit, the capitalization of General Motors reached an astonishing $60,000,-000 within a year. Cadillac, purchased for a premium $4,400,000, was the most notable of the few companies for which cash had to be paid. General Motors soon acquired control of thirteen motor vehicle and ten parts and accessories manufacturers that varied considerably in strength, prominence, and potential.

[16]For the material on industrial combinations in this section, see especially Rae, *American Automobile Manufacturers*, pp. 86–97; Arthur Pound, *The Turning Wheel: The Story of General Motors Through Twenty-Five Years* (Garden City, N.Y.: Doubleday, Doran, 1934), pp. 111–130; and Alfred D. Chandler, Jr., *Giant Enterprise: Ford, General Motors, and the Automobile Industry* (New York: Harcourt, Brace & World, 1964).

Far from serving as a force for order in the automobile industry, General Motors proved in the short run to be an example of the worst contemporary business practices. As a result, the combination floundered so badly within two years that it had to be reorganized under banker control. Any role General Motors might have played as a stabilizing force within the industry was seriously handicapped from the outset by Durant's inability to gain control of a sufficient number of the industry's leading producers. Ford, the most conspicuous example, now more confident due to the initial success of the Model T, had upped his asking price to an impossible $8,000,000 in cash. Only four of thirteen motor vehicle manufacturers in the General Motors combination—Cadillac, Buick, Oldsmobile, and Oakland—had national sales networks, and just two producers, Cadillac and Buick, were making money. As Durant dispersed his energies, Buick too began to decline, threatening to leave Cadillac alone among the automobile manufacturing units to support the heavily overcapitalized holding company. Although the parts and accessories units included important firms such as the Northway Motor Manufacturing Company and the Champion Ignition Company, here too there were costly liabilities.

Durant's propensity to speculate recklessly was unfortunately combined with poor technological and poor business judgment. With the four-cylinder, four-cycle engine well-nigh universal and the horsepower-weight ratio increasing each year, Durant nevertheless bought the Elmore Manufacturing Company for $600,000 on the slim chance that its outdated two-cylinder, two-cycle engine might prove the most popular in the future. Although the H-slot sliding-gear transmission was well established and the planetary transmission also widely used, $140,000 was paid for the Carter Car Company to obtain its patent on a poorly designed friction drive. The most spectacular error was the purchase of the Heany Lamp Company for $7,000,000 in General Motors stock to obtain a patent on an incandescent lamp that turned out to be fraudulent. Compounding these blunders, Durant was so optimistic about demand that he failed to build up cash reserves, relied on cash from sales to pay his operating expenses, and made no attempt to achieve economies through coordinating and integrating the constituent units of General Motors. He further lacked adequate information about the combination's financial condition.

When sales unexpectedly dropped as the result of a slight business recession in 1910, Durant was unable to meet his payroll and bills from suppliers. The First National Bank of Boston, to whom Buick was indebted for $7,000,000, called in a banking syndicate composed of Lee, Higginson & Co. of Boston and J. & W. Seligman and the Central Trust Co. of New York. The syndicate agreed to intervene to save the General Motors combination only after receiving assurances of feasibility and support from Henry M. Leland of Cadillac and extracting stiff concessions, which on the basis of the holding company's extremely poor condition appeared necessary to the bankers to justify the risk involved. They received over $6,000,000 in General Motors stock plus $15,000,000 in 6 percent notes for a $12,500,000 cash loan. Durant was to remain officially president of Buick as well as vice-president and a member of the board of directors of General Motors, but he was forced to retire from active management, and the banking syndicate gained control of the combination through a five-year voting-trust agreement. To the leadership of General Motors, the bankers appointed James J. Storrow, a senior partner in Lee, Higginson, who served first as the temporary president and then directed operations as chairman of the finance committee. Charles W. Nash, a Durant-Dort production engineer who had succeeded Durant as head of Buick in 1910, was moved to the presidency of General Motors in 1912 to replace Thomas Neal, a Detroit businessman who held the office briefly after Storrow. Walter P. Chrysler, manager of the American Locomotive Company, was then brought in to take over Nash's position at Buick.

The Storrow-Nash regime followed a sound, conservative policy of retrenchment during their five-year period of control. Organizational efficiency and product were both improved. The weak units in the combination were quickly liquidated, and only five companies were allowed to continue to manufacture motor vehicles — Buick, Cadillac, General Motors Truck, Oakland, and Oldsmobile. A centralized research and testing program, which became the General Motors research department, was initiated. Storrow also attempted to attract top-flight administrative talent, and internal administration was greatly improved.

Perhaps the greatest error the Storrow-Nash administration made was to withhold common stock dividends. This increased the propensity of General Motors stockholders to sell their shares to Durant, who had gone on to build up Chevrolet as he earlier had Buick and, with the aid of the du Ponts, was secretly purchasing General Motors stock in an attempt to regain control of the combination. Succeeding in this in 1915, Durant once again inaugurated a period of speculative expansion that within five years resulted in another severe financial crisis for General Motors and culminated in his final dismissal from its management.

Benjamin Briscoe's independent attempt to form a combination of companies revealed the same basic flaws that characterized General Motors under Durant and proved even less successful. The International Motors Company was revived by Briscoe as the United States Motor Company in January 1910. Briscoe received his principal backing for this venture from Anthony N. Brady, a traction magnate who had been associated with William C. Whitney in the Electric Vehicle Company's "Lead Cab Trust." Brady had also been an early advocate of consolidation in the automobile industry, but he had been deterred from acting on his initial impulse through fear, needless as it turned out, that the 1907 financial crisis would have dire consequences for the automobile business.

The United States Motor Company came to involve, at least tangentially, some 130 affiliated companies and a capitalization of $42,500,000 in its short existence. The nucleus of the combination's automobile manufacturing firms was Maxwell-Briscoe. The Briscoe Manufacturing Company and the Providence Engineering Works were its most important parts and accessories units. Another seemingly important acquisition at the time was the Columbia Motor Car Company, which as successor to the Electric Vehicle Company owned the Selden patent on the gasoline automobile. Thus Briscoe, president of the American Motor Car Manufacturers' Association, the trade association organized to oppose the Association of Licensed Automobile Manufacturers' attempt to monopolize the production of gasoline automobiles under the Selden patent, now paradoxically gained control of his adversary's chief asset. Three other automobile producers in Briscoe's combination were important enough to deserve mention also: the Alden Sampson Manufacturing Company, which made gasoline-powered trucks; the Brush Runabout Company, producer, as we have already noted, of a one-cylinder $500 car made largely of wood that was designed to become the automobile for the masses; and the Dayton Motor Car Company, whose Stoddard-Dayton automobile was an innovator in the adoption of the Silent Knight sleeve-valve engine.

For essentially the same reasons that General Motors had failed in 1910, United States Motor went into receivership in September 1912 with liabilities of $12,250,000 versus realizable assets of $9,250,000. Here again, major problems were the inability to include a sufficient number of prominent companies, combined with heavy investment in too many weak firms producing unpopular automobiles. Maxwell-Briscoe was the only manufacturing unit in the combination that made money. The Brush Runabout was completely outmoded by new low-priced, four-cylinder cars that appeared after 1908, particularly by the Ford Model T, and soon proved impossible to sell. Neither the Stoddard-Dayton nor the Columbia had ever been very popular, and the Knight engine, now used in both makes, did nothing to attract buyers. After Henry Ford's ultimate victory in the Selden patent suit in 1911, Columbia's ownership of the patent on the gasoline automobile also came to mean nothing. Like Durant, Briscoe had made poor technological choices and had expanded his empire well beyond reasonable limits for its earnings. Another analogous error was that the component companies in Briscoe's combination were too far dispersed geographically; despite some attempt to integrate and consolidate operations, United States Motor remained loose organizationally. Finally, Briscoe too was so optimistic about sales that he failed to maintain adequate cash reserves to pay operating expenses. Consequently, when sales did not materialize, catastrophic failure became inevitable.

Under the reorganization of the United States Motor Company by the banking firm of Eugene Meyer, Jr. & Co., Walter E. Flanders was induced to assume leadership of the combination for the phenomenal price of purchasing his weak Flanders Motor Company, an additional $1,000,000 in cash, and $2,750,000 in stock of the reorganized combination. Flanders followed a policy of organizational consolidation and liquidation of weak units much more severe than that which occurred under banker control at General Motors: only the Maxwell Motor Company ultimately emerged as a going concern from the reorganization of the Briscoe combination. Flanders entirely abandoned the idea of an industrial combination offering several different makes of cars to the public for the more common strategy of building up a single firm to a position of strength within the industry. Benjamin Briscoe remained in the automobile industry to found several more companies, but he never regained his earlier position of prominence as a manufacturer.

Walter E. Flanders's severe solution to the problems of the Briscoe combination was very likely conditioned by his previous involvement as a key figure in still another combination attempt, Studebaker-E-M-F. After leaving his position at Ford in 1908 for one at the Wayne Automobile Company, Flanders joined forces with "Barney" Everitt, the general manager at Wayne, and William E. Metzger, an organizer of the Northern Motor Car Company who had begun his automotive career at Cadillac, to form the Everitt-Metzger-Flanders Company (E-M-F) from Wayne, Northern, and three Detroit parts and accessories firms. In sharp contrast with the practice of both General Motors under Durant and Briscoe's United States Motor Company, E-M-F's operations were integrated organizationally and centralized geographically. The Wayne and Northern cars were discontinued for two new models, the E-M-F and the smaller Flanders. Then Studebaker, on the basis of great gains in the sales of its own automobiles during the 1907 recession, purchased a third of the E-M-F stock for $800,000 and arranged to market the E-M-F output as an expedient way for the manufacturing firm to expand its automobile sales.

   The relationship between Studebaker and E-M-F disintegrated almost immediately. After legal action failed to halt an E-M-F attempt to set up its own sales organization, Studebaker bought complete control of E-M-F for $5,000,000. J. P. Morgan & Co. financed the purchase. Now primarily committed to the manufacture of gasoline automobiles rather than horse-drawn vehicles and electric cars, Studebaker reorganized as the Studebaker Corporation and dropped the use of the E-M-F name on its products. Flanders remained with Studebaker as general manager until 1912, when he rejoined Everitt and Metzger to organize the ephemeral Flanders Motor Company. Thus the pattern of development at Studebaker-E-M-F was simply one of merger to strengthen a single company's competitive position rather than a strategy of combination. Flanders quite naturally continued this policy of consolidation when given the opportunity in the reorganization of United States Motor.

   The basic problem with a strategy of combination was that no combination could hope to control a sufficient proportion of the total output to exert much influence over the industry, or even to succeed as a business enterprise, unless it included many of the leading producers. But the firms currently on top of the heap, for example, Ford and REO in 1908, were apt to be those most confident of their ability to go it alone. Consequently, the likely candidates for combination were the weaker companies, whose assets consisted primarily of uncertain patents and radical innovations that might or might not prove profitable. The difficulty of determining which firms among these had real potential led to costly errors in judgment and indiscriminate expansion. The resulting combination then faced the formidable task of improving the product and operations of a number of floundering firms, which tended to absorb the profits from its few strong units. Thus the problems faced in building up a single company were greatly compounded without gaining the main objective of combination — control over a sufficient proportion of the total output to achieve security within the industry. Given these circumstances, the sounder course of action at the time was Henry Ford's strategy of an individual company attempting to capture the lion's share of the market through effective competition, that is, producing a better car at a lower price.

The Selden Patent Controversy
The Selden patent controversy provided the most important confrontation in the early automobile industry between the philosophy of unregulated competition and the forces for industry-wide concentration and control.[17] George Selden sold the rights to his patent to the Electric Vehicle Company of New Jersey on November 4,

[17]William Greenleaf, *Monopoly on Wheels: Henry Ford and the Selden Patent Suit* (Detroit: Wayne State University Press, 1961), is the most complete and scholarly study of the Selden patent controversy. For a short treatment that is less critical of George Selden and the ALAM, see Rae, *American Automobile Manufacturers*, pp. 75–81.

1899, for $10,000 and one-fifth of any royalties gained from the patent. Probably the main motive underlying purchase of the patent by a company strongly committed to the electric car was to hedge against the possibility that the gasoline automobile might prove superior. The Electric Vehicle Company had no plans to switch to the production of gasoline-powered cars, but it had begun experimental work with the gasoline automobile and had been advised by Herman F. Cuntz, the Pope Manufacturing Company's expert on patents, that Selden's claim appeared valid and might cause trouble. With the patent, the Whitney syndicate would in any event be able to profit from any success the gasoline automobile might have by extracting tribute from its producers.

In an attempt to enforce the Selden patent, the Electric Vehicle Company chose in 1900 to begin litigation against the Winton Motor Carriage Company, then the country's leading manufacturer of gasoline automobiles. On March 20, 1903, a decree was finally entered that the Selden patent was valid and that Winton had infringed. But before the case was determined, Winton came to terms with the Whitney interests rather than continue what appeared to him a hopeless legal battle.

Following Winton's agreement with the Electric Vehicle Company to recognize the Selden patent, several other prominent manufacturers of gasoline automobiles who had initally viewed the patent as a threat began to realize that it might provide a means to regulate competition and prevent disruptive practices in the industry. The leaders among these manufacturers were Henry B. Joy of Packard and Frederick L. Smith of the Olds Motor Works. Negotiations with the Electric Vehicle Company were concluded on March 6, 1903, at the Manhattan Hotel in New York City to form a trade association under the Selden patent—the Association of Licensed Automobile Manufacturers. Nineteen companies were granted licenses entitling them to manufacture gasoline automobiles; within a year the ALAM included in its ranks some thirty leading producers of motor vehicles. Firms allowed to join the ALAM paid an initiation fee of $2,500, plus $1,000 to cover in full the royalties on their previous production, and agreed henceforth to pay quarterly as royalties to the association 1¼ percent of the retail price on every gasoline automobile they produced. The ALAM retained two-fifths of these royalties to defray the expenses of litigation to enforce the Selden patent and for other services rendered to the industry. Another two-fifths went to the Electric Vehicle Company, and one-fifth was received by George Selden. The affairs of the ALAM were administered by a five-man executive committee and a board of managers composed of representatives from each member company.

The ALAM was initially well received in many quarters. *Motor Age* believed, for example, that "the association will be beneficial to the trade for the reason that it will prevent the incursion of piratical hordes who desire to take advantage of the good work done by the pioneers to flood the market with trashy machines, made only to sell and not intended to go — at least for any great length of time."[18] *Motor World* felt that "for the industry of motor vehicle making, for the dealer in automobiles, and for the persons who purchase them the perfection of this association is quite the most important event that has occurred in this relation in this country." The periodical assured its readers that the ALAM "does not propose to exercise any cramping suzerainty over the trade, but instead to promote the industry and conserve the interests of the public. This it has a peculiar power to do."[19] Unfortunately, these optimistic expectations proved unfounded.

William Greenleaf has argued that the ALAM threatened to monopolize automobile manufacturing in the United States. Despite the fact that member companies

[18]"Selden Patent Ownership," *Motor Age*, 3:7 (April 16, 1903).
[19]"Nine Years Agreement on Selden Patent," *Motor World*, 6:17 (April 2, 1903).

were not prohibited from competing with one another, it is clear that the ALAM did try to exercise arbitrary power over entrances into the industry by establishing a criterion of prior experience in the automobile business, which theoretically froze the admission of new firms. Attempts were also made to preserve the status quo in the industry by setting production quotas. One might not wish to call this monopoly, but certainly the Licensed Association's intention was to restrict competition severely.

However, as Greenleaf recognizes, the ALAM was never able to carry out this intention. The threat of litigation proved to be an ineffective deterrent to new entrances, and the Selden patent was widely disregarded. There were, for example, only 32 licensed makers among the 218 American automobile manufacturers active in 1907, the vast majority of whom produced gasoline-powered cars. Even though the ALAM companies, as a select group of established firms, accounted for the bulk of total output — about 80 percent in 1907 — the association evidently lacked sufficient power to stabilize the automobile industry. For had the ALAM accomplished much toward this goal, the circumstances that motivated Briscoe and Durant to form stabilizing combinations in 1908 would not have existed.

The failure of the ALAM to achieve its intended goals stemmed mainly from several internal weaknesses. First, members remained organizationally discrete units in competition with one another, and the Licensed Association lacked sufficient sanctions to discipline them. Second, there is no evidence that the licensed manufacturers were more dedicated either to sound, progressive policies within the industry or to the interests of the consumer than were responsible so-called independents such as Henry Ford, Ransom E. Olds, and Benjamin Briscoe. The contrary, in fact, appears often to have been the case. The comparatively much larger percentage of fly-by-night operations among the nonlicensed makers indicates little beyond the

Licensed Association's inability to keep irresponsible or incompetent firms out of the industry by its policy of legalistic exclusiveness. With market demand high, technology uncertain, and the financial conditions for entrance relatively easy, the threat of litigation over the violation of a questionable patent due to expire in the foreseeable future was a risk one might well be inclined to take.

From its inception, the ALAM also had to contend with deeply entrenched attitudes in the industry favoring free competition and weak organizational loyalties beyond the level of the individual company. Patterns of cooperation among early automobile manufacturers were typically tenuous and superficial. The first trade association formed in the industry, the National Association of Automobile Manufacturers, exhibited this general lack of industry-wide cooperation on important problems. The NAAM was organized on November 10, 1900, "to advance and protect the interests of the trade, procure lower freight rates, more equitable legislation . . . hold shows and exhibitions and give attention to such other matters as required attention." Membership policy was liberal and the cost ridiculously low: active membership (limited to automobile manufacturers) involved payment of a $25 initiation fee and $10 annual dues, while associate members (makers of parts and accessories, sales agents, and trade journals) paid $15 for initiation and only $5 for annual dues. At the end of its first year, the NAAM had a balance in its treasury of $350, forty active members (claimed to include all except three manufacturers of recognized standing), and fifty associate members.[20]

Up to the end of 1903, the NAAM had accomplished little more for the industry than establish a meaningless standard warranty, sponsor several successful automo-

---

[20] For the early history of the NAAM, see especially "Origin and Rise of the N.A.A.M.," *Automobile*, 16:217–218 (January 31, 1907); "N.A.A.M. Constitution," *Motor Age*, 5:17 (May 12, 1904); and "Turbulent Annual Meeting," ibid., 5:8–9 (January 28, 1904).

bile shows and runs, and make a feeble attempt to influence motor vehicle legislation. The 1904 annual meeting was characterized by petty bickering among the thirty-four active members who attended (out of 135 manufacturers then active in the American automobile industry) about show space, endurance run awards, and the procedure for electing directors. The financial records for the preceding year showed total receipts of $36,261, of which $31,439 represented profits from the New York and Chicago automobile shows, versus disbursements of $31,000, the largest items here being $5,095 for an endurance run and $6,030 for influencing legislation. The best effort the NAAM was able to put forth to curb what seemed undesirable practices in the industry was to urge members, through its "moral influence" over them, to make better cars and to avoid overinflating the market by voluntarily limiting their production. After 1904, even the NAAM's role as sponsor of national automobile shows was taken over by the ALAM and its newly formed rival trade association, the American Motor Car Manufacturers' Association.

Formed at the 1905 Chicago automobile show with twenty charter members, the AMCMA had as its primary objective the protection of the so-called independent manufacturers who refused to recognize the Selden patent. It ultimately came to have forty-eight members, among the more important of which were Ford, REO, Maxwell-Briscoe, Nordyke and Marmon, Mitchell, and National. James Couzens, Henry Ford's right-hand man who became the organization's first chairman, explained: "This Electric Vehicle Company can't force us to pay royalties. . . . We can fight their suit of infringement on the ground that no infringement exists. We manufacturers on an independent basis have simply decided to take the bull by the horns and cooperate for mutual benefit."[21] Like the ALAM, the AMCMA had as secondary motives the pro-

[21]"Independent Makers Meet in Detroit," *Automobile*, 12:349 (March 4, 1905). For the Ford Motor Company's initial response to the ALAM, see also James Couzens, "Ford on the Selden Association," *Cycle and Automobile Trade Journal*, 8:17 ff (October 1, 1903).

motion of automobile shows; technical improvement of product and standardization of parts; and securing better freight and insurance rates, improved roads, and favorable motor vehicle legislation.

But regarding its major objective, the AMCMA proved to be a strikingly apathetic and ineffective organization. *Automobile* reported in late 1906: "No fight is made against the [Selden] patent by the association, although the members, along with some forty other makers, do not believe in it. The Ford Motor Company, one of the leading members of the AMCMA, is fighting the idea single handed, in an effort to disprove the claims made."[22]

Several other important manufacturers were also involved in infringement suits, but Henry Ford indeed bore the brunt of the battle against the ALAM, which had initially denied him a license on the basis that he had not demonstrated his competence as a manufacturer of gasoline automobiles. Assured of the support of John Wanamaker, his eastern agent, Ford nevertheless determined to continue to make and sell cars and to contest to the limit of his resources the legal action begun against him by the ALAM in 1903. Ford commented: "I am opposed to the Selden patent first, last, and all the time, and I will fight it to the bitter end."[23] In an attempt to discourage sales of unlicensed makes of automobiles, the ALAM advertised extensively. It warned prospective purchasers, who were also subject to legal action: "Don't buy a lawsuit with your car." Ford effectively countered this threat by an offer to bond his customers against any suit for damages the ALAM might bring against them. Furthermore, in a clever propaganda campaign, Ford gained public sympathy by contrasting his humble middle western origins and status as a pioneer automotive inventor and small businessman with the image of the ALAM as a group of powerful eastern

[22] "American Motor Car Manufacturers' Association," *Automobile*, 15:704 (November 29, 1906).
[23] "Independent Makers Meet in Detroit," p. 349.

monopolists who had contributed little if anything to the advance of automotive technology.

The ALAM won a fleeting victory when the United States Circuit Court of the Southern District of New York upheld the suit against Ford in 1909. The AMCMA immediately disintegrated. Most of its members sought and obtained licenses from the ALAM, whose active membership swelled to eighty-three. Alfred Reeves, general manager of the AMCMA, even became manager of the ALAM with Ford's blessings. The royalty terms offered by the ALAM had by now been substantially reduced to 0.8 per cent, and the independent makers who joined were allowed to pay this reduced rate on their production since 1903 for their licenses. This liberality was due both to the recent bankruptcy of the Electric Vehicle Company and to the ALAM's anticipation of the expiration of the Selden patent in 1912: restrictive policies on membership were abandoned in a final attempt to gain as much additional revenue as possible. Ford too was now invited to become a licensed manufacturer, but he rejected membership because the ALAM refused to reimburse him for his legal expenses in the suit against him. Ford decided to continue the fight by appealing the decision in the higher courts.

The United States Circuit Court of Appeals for the Second Circuit handed down a written decision on January 11, 1911, which, while sustaining the validity of the Selden patent, declared that Ford had not infringed upon Selden's claims. The basis of the court's decision was that the Selden patent covered only motor vehicles that used the Brayton two-cycle engine. Since Ford and almost all other manufacturers powered their cars with Otto four-cycle engines, the decision, in effect, made the Selden patent worthless. Ford's victory therefore resulted in the complete collapse of the ALAM. However, since in any event the period of exclusive rights under the Selden patent was to expire the following year, this late legal decision merely formalized and hastened a bit the imminent breakup of the Licensed Association.

Plate 45. 1903 ALAM advertisement warning against infringement of the Selden patent. Courtesy Free Library of Philadelphia.

CYCLE AND AUTOMOBILE TRADE JOURNAL.

NOTICE

TO MANUFACTURERS, DEALERS, IMPORTERS, AGENTS, AND USERS OF

Gasoline Automobiles

United States Letters Patent, No. 549,160, granted to George B. Selden, Nov. 5, 1895, controls broadly all gasoline automobiles which are accepted as commercially practical. Licences under this patent have been secured from the owners by the following-named manufacturers and importers :—

Electric Vehicle Co.
The Winton Motor Carriage Co.
Packard Motor Car Co.
Olds Motor Works.
Knox Automobile Co.
The Haynes-Apperson Co.
The Autocar Co.
The George N. Pierce Co.
Apperson Bros. Automobile Co.
Searchmont Automobile Co.
Locomobile Co. of America.
The Peerless Motor Car Co.
U. S. Long Distance Auto Co.
Waltham Mfg. Co.
Pope Motor Car Co.
The J. Stevens Arms & Tool Co.
H. H. Franklin Mfg. Co.
Charron, Girardot & Voigt Co. of America (Smith & Mabley)
The Commercial Motor Co.
Berg Automobile Co.
Cadillac Automobile Co.
Northern Mfg. Co.
Pope-Robinson Co.
The Kirk Mfg. Co.
Elmore Mfg. Co.
E. R. Thomas Motor Co.
Buffalo Gasolene Motor Co.
The F. B. Stearns Co.

These manufacturers are poineers in this industry, and have commercialized the gasoline vehicle by many years of development and at great cost. They are the owners of upward of four hundred United States Patents, covering many of the most important improvements and details of manufacture. Both the basic Selden patent and all other patents owned as aforesaid will be enforced against all infringers.

No other manufacturers or importers are authorized to make or sell gasoline automobiles, and any person making, selling, or using such machines made or sold by any unlicensed manufacturers or importers, will be liable to prosecution for infringement.

Association of Licensed Automobile Mfrs.

7 EAST 42d STREET, NEW YORK

Plate 46. Ford rejoinder to the ALAM warning, which appeared on the opposite page. Courtesy Free Library of Philadelphia.

NOTICE

To Dealers, Importers, Agents, and Users of our Gasoline Automobiles

WE will protect you against any prosecution for alleged infringements of patents. Regarding alleged infringement of the Selden patent, we beg to quote the well-known Patent Attorneys, Messrs. Parker & Burton: "The Selden patent is not a broad one, and if it was, it is anticipated. It does not cover a practicable machine, no practicable machine can be made from it, and never was, so far as we can ascertain. It relates to that form of carriage called a FORE CARRIAGE. None of that type have ever been in use; all have been failures." "No court in the United States has ever decided in favor of the patent on the merits of the case; all it has ever done was to record a prior agreement between the parties."

We are the pioneers of the GASOLINE AUTOMOBILE. Our Mr. Ford made the first Gasoline Automobile in Detroit, and the third in the United States. His machine, built in 1893, two years prior to the issue of the Selden patents Nov. 5, 1895, is still in use. Our Mr. Ford also built the famous "999" Gasoline Automobile, which was driven by Barney Oldfield in New York on July 25th, 1903, a mile in 55 4-5 seconds, on a circular track, which is the world's record.

Mr. Ford, driving his own machine, beat Mr. Winton at Grosse Pointe track in 1901. We have always been winners.

Ford Motor Company

688-692 Mack Ave., Detroit, Mich.

Write for Catalogue

The secondary functions that the ALAM and AMCMA had filled as trade associations were now assumed by the Society of Automotive Engineers and by the Automobile Board of Trade, which became the National Automobile Chamber of Commerce in 1914 and the Automobile Manufacturers Association in 1932. All too aware of the inevitable costs of another patent controversy, the NACC, under the leadership of Alfred Reeves, instituted a cross-licensing agreement among its members in 1914. Characteristically, the Ford Motor Company, which then dominated the industry, remained aloof from these trade associations. While Ford continued to take out patents for legal protection, the use of Ford patents was liberally allowed to competitors free of royalty fees.

Adjusting to the Mass Market

The comparative strength of the ALAM companies within the industry began to decline appreciably about 1907. The ascendancy of the independents after this date is indicated by the sharp drop in percentage of total output accounted for by the licensed manufacturers from about 70 to 80 percent in the 1903–1906 period to 45 or 50 percent in 1908. The subsequent rise in the ALAM share of the market to approximately 85 percent in 1910 and 70 percent in 1911 is misleading because it merely reflects the swelling of the licensed makers' ranks by the capitulation of many independents following the ephemeral 1909 ALAM victory over Ford in the Selden patent suit.

This decline of ALAM strength in the market can be attributed to what was perhaps the trade association's greatest shortcoming—its unwillingness to adjust to the needs of a mass market for automobiles. William Greenleaf has pointed out that the members of the ALAM were primarily concerned with filling the replacement demands of a narrow, upper-class market; that they consequently followed a policy of procuring high unit profits from the production of a severely limited number of cars; and that they did not seriously attempt to cater to a broad middle-class market until forced to do so by the more responsible independents. William C. Durant, the outstanding exception to these criticisms among the licensed manufacturers, was considered a maverick within the ALAM fold. The licensed makers in general emphasized the mechanical perfection of the product and gave little consideration to volume production and lower unit prices. Greenleaf has noted: "In any given year between 1903 and 1911, the ALAM never had more than four makes selling for less than $1,000. . . . In contrast, it was generally agreed that the majority of independent makers produced low-priced cars. Their ranks could . . . cite an average price that was $1,500 below the ALAM average. In 1909 the independents offered twenty-six models costing $1,000 or less."[24]

  From its inception, the ALAM had in fact pushed for higher rather than lower unit prices for automobiles. During the early Selden patent litigation, for example, it came to public attention that prices in the first two years of the Licensed Association's existence had been sharply raised: the average selling price of cars produced by ALAM members went from $1,170 in 1903 to an exorbitant $1,784 in 1905.[25] The manufacturers justified skyrocketing prices as being necessitated by the costs of product improvement. The press rationalized: "The current models are cheaper than ever before. . . . Better value is obtained for the same amount of money."[26] What was generally ignored was that each improvement of product also increased market demand, which in turn tended to discourage the production of lower-priced cars at low unit profits. *Outlook* explained, for example: "One firm . . . whose first reputation was

[24]Greenleaf, *Monopoly on Wheels*, pp. 174–175.
[25]"Some Automobile Statistics," *Scientific American*, 94:304 (April 14, 1906).
[26]Arthur N. Jervis, "The Automobile Shows," *Country Life in America*, 7:518 (March 1905).

made on a low-priced car of unusual excellence, now makes that style only on order and does not exhibit or generally advertise it. It is now turning out higher-priced cars, of which, as a representative said 'we can sell all that we make.' "[27]

Such shortsightedness proved disastrous to many firms once the upper-class market for new cars began to be saturated and competitors became able to produce more moderately priced automobiles that met minimal expectations of performance. By at least 1908, automotive design and production techniques had advanced to the point where decent cars could be sold at reasonable prices, and several progressive firms, most notably the Ford Motor Company, aggressively began to demonstrate that quality and relatively low price were not incompatible. This rapidly opened up a broad middle-class market for cars. Production in 1908 alone accounted for about 25 percent of the total of some 230,000 motor vehicles made in the United States up to that date; then a spectacular increase of about 100 percent over 1908 in motor vehicle production occurred in 1909. Furthermore, the upper-class market for automobiles was by then saturated. The demand for high-priced cars began to stabilize in the 1907–1910 period. A trend toward the dominance of the market by automobiles selling for under $1,375 was established in 1908. Cars selling at or below $1,375 comprised about a third of the market in 1907; by 1916 they would account for about 90 percent of the total sales of new automobiles in the United States.

The result was a large-scale reorganization of the American automobile industry during the 1908–1912 period. Well-established firms were forced to either accommodate to these new market conditions or suspend operation, and new companies rose to take advantage of the opportunities that had been created. Epstein's data on the entrances and exits of significant automobile manufacturers gives some indication of the extent of this shake-up. They show 18 entrances and 1 exit for 1909 and 1

[27] "A Notable Automobile Show," *Outlook*, 85:241 (February 2, 1907).

entrance and 18 exits for 1910. Seven of the 1910 exits were accounted for by companies that had been engaged in passenger car production for four years or longer, and 3 of these 7 for as long as eight years.

By 1912 more than half of the total American output of motor vehicles was being produced by seven organizations: Ford, the constituent units of General Motors, Studebaker, Willys-Overland, Hudson, REO, and Packard. With the exception of Hudson, newly formed in 1909, all of these organizations had been engaged in automobile manufacturing before 1908 or were built up from companies active in the industry before that date. But neither Studebaker nor Willys-Overland had been leaders in the industry; and General Motors, as we have seen, underwent extensive internal reorganization in 1910. Packard was the outstanding example of a manufacturer who could produce a high-priced car of exceptional quality and still find a secure place in the industry. However, the surest way to succeed now clearly involved the ability to produce good cars in large volume at prices the average man could afford.

Following this formula, the Ford Motor Company consolidated and extended its already secure position into one of undisputed leadership after 1910. This position was held until the late 1920s, when Henry Ford himself proved inept at adjusting both to later basic changes in the market for automobiles and to the emergence of modern management techniques at General Motors under the leadership of Alfred P. Sloan. During the intervening period of Ford dominance, the automobile and the automobile industry became the most significant force for change in American civilization. Our attention has been focused upon the development of attitudes and an institutional context that made this inevitable by 1910. The important story of the "Fordization" of American life, which began with the initiation of the mass production of the Model T at Highland Park, deserves another volume.

Bibliography

Books

Anderson, Rudolph E. *The Story of the American Automobile*. Washington, D.C.: Public Affairs Press, 1950.

Arnold, Horace L., and Fay L. Faurote. *Ford Methods and the Ford Shops*. New York: Engineering Magazine Co., 1915.

Bird, Anthony. *Antique Automobiles*. New York: E. P. Dutton, 1967.

Chandler, Alfred D., Jr. *Giant Enterprise: Ford, General Motors, and the Automobile Industry*. New York: Harcourt, Brace & World, 1964.

Cleveland, Reginald M., and S. T. Williamson. *The Road Is Yours*. New York: Greystone Press, 1951.

Cochran, Thomas C. *The American Business System*. Cambridge, Mass.: Harvard University Press, 1957.

Cohn, David L. *Combustion on Wheels*. Boston: Houghton Mifflin, 1944.

Cole, Arthur C. *Business Enterprise in Its Social Setting*. Cambridge, Mass.: Harvard University Press, 1959.

Doolittle, James R., et al. *The Romance of the Automobile Industry*. New York: Klebold Press, 1916.

Epstein, Ralph C. *The Automobile Industry*. Chicago and New York: A. W. Shaw Co., 1928.

Ford, Henry, in collaboration with Samuel Crowther. *My Life and Work*. Garden City, N. Y.: Doubleday, 1922.

Glasscock, Carl B. *The Gasoline Age*. Indianapolis: Bobbs-Merrill, 1937.

Greenleaf, William. *Monopoly on Wheels: Henry Ford and the Selden Patent Suit*. Detroit: Wayne State University Press, 1961.

Kennedy, Edward D. *The Automobile Industry*. New York: Reynal & Hitchcock, 1941.

Longstreet, Stephen. *A Century on Wheels: The Story of Studebaker*. New York: Holt, 1952.

Lynd, Robert S., and Helen M. Lynd. *Middletown: A Study in Modern American Culture*. New York: Harcourt, Brace & World, 1929.

MacManus, Theodore F., and Norman Beasley. *Men, Money and Motors*. New York: Harper, 1929.

Mason, Philip P. "The League of American Wheelmen and the Good-Roads Movement." Ph.D. dissertation, University of Michigan, 1957.

Maxim, Hiram Percy. *Horseless Carriage Days*. New York: Harper, 1936.

Mott, Frank A. *A History of American Magazines*, vol. IV, *1885–1905*. Cambridge, Mass.: Harvard University Press, Belknap Press, 1957.

Musselman, Morris M. *Get a Horse!* Philadelphia: J. B. Lippincott, 1950.

Nevins, Allan, with the collaboration of Frank Ernest Hill. *Ford: The Times, The Man, The Company, 1865–1915; Ford: Expansion and Challenge, 1915–1933;* and *Ford: Decline and Rebirth, 1933–1962.* New York: Charles Scribner's Sons, 1954, 1957, 1963.

Niemeyer, Glenn A. *The Automotive Career of Ransom E. Olds*. East Lansing: Michigan State University Press, 1963.

Oliver, Smith Hempstone, and Donald H. Berkebile. *The Smithsonian Collection of Automobiles and Motorcycles*. Washington, D.C.: Smithsonian Institution Press, 1968.

Partridge, Bellamy. *Fill 'er Up: The Story of Fifty Years of Motoring*. New York: McGraw-Hill, 1952.

Pound, Arthur. *The Turning Wheel: The Story of General Motors Through Twenty-Five Years, 1908–1933*. Garden City, N.Y.: Doubleday, Doran, 1934.

Rae, John B. *The American Automobile: A Brief History*. Chicago: University of Chicago Press, 1965.

——. *American Automobile Manufacturers: The First Forty Years*. Philadelphia: Chilton, 1959.

Rogers, Everett M. *Diffusion of Innovations*. New York: Free Press, 1962.

Seltzer, Lawrence H. *A Financial History of the American Automobile Industry*. Boston and New York: Houghton Mifflin, 1928.

Singer, Charles, et al. *A History of Technology*, vol. V, *The Late Nineteenth Century*. New York and London: Oxford University Press, 1958.

Smith, Frederick L. *Motoring Down a Quarter of a Century*. Detroit: Detroit Saturday Night Co., 1928.

Automobile Trade Journals and Industry Publications

Automobile, vol. 1, September 1899.

Automobile Club of America Annual Yearbook (annual editions, 1902–1910).

Automobile Manufacturers Association, Inc. *Automobiles of America*. Detroit: Wayne State University Press, 1962.

Cycle and Automobile Trade Journal, vol. 1, May 1897.

Horseless Age, vol. 1, November 1895.

Motor, vol. 1, October 1903.

Motor Age, vol. 1, September 12, 1899.

Motor World, vol. 1, October 4, 1900.

National Automobile Chamber of Commerce. *Facts and Figures of the Automobile Industry* (various annual editions).

Popular Periodicals

American Agriculturalist

American Monthly Review of Reviews

Cassier's Magazine

Country Life in America

Engineering Magazine

Farm Journal

Harper's Weekly

Independent (New York)

Life

Munsey's Magazine

Outing Magazine

Outlook

Overland Monthly

Scientific American

Scientific American Supplement

World Today

World's Work

Individual Articles

Briscoe, Benjamin. "The Inside Story of General Motors." *Detroit Saturday Night*, January 15, 22, and 29 and February 5, 1921.

Burnham, John C. "The Gasoline Tax and the Automobile Revolution." *Mississippi Valley Historical Review*, 48:435–439 (December 1961).

Cuntz, Herman F. "Hartford: The Birthplace of the Automobile Industry." *Hartford Times*, September 16–18, 1947.

Flanders, Walter E. "Large Capital Now Needed to Embark in Automobile Business." *Detroit Saturday Night*, January 22, 1910.

Lee, Everett S. "The Turner Thesis Reexamined." *American Quarterly*, 13:77–83 (Spring 1961).

Martin, James W. "The Motor Vehicle Registration License." *Bulletin of the National Tax Association* (Lancaster, Pa.), 12:193–208 (April 1927).

McLaughlin, Charles C. "The Stanley Steamer: A Study in Unsuccessful Innovation." *Explorations in Entrepreneurial History*, 7:37–47 (October 1954).

Pierson, George W. "The M-Factor in American History." *American Quarterly*, 14:275–289 (Summer 1962).

Rae, John B. "The Engineer-Entrepreneur in the American Automobile Industry." *Explorations in Entrepreneurial History*, 8:1–11 (October 1955).

——. "The Electric Vehicle Company." *Business History Review*, 29:298–311 (December 1955).

Thompson, George V. "Intercompany Technical Standardization in the Early Automobile Industry." *Journal of Economic History*, 14:1–20 (Winter 1954).

Vatter, Harold G. "Closure of Entry in the American Automobile Industry." *Oxford Economic Papers*, n.s. 4:213–234 (October 1952).

United States Government Publications

Eldridge, Maurice O. *Public Road Mileage, Revenues, and Expenditures in the United States in 1904*. U.S. Department of Agriculture, Office of Public Roads, Bulletin no. 32. Washington, D.C.: Government Printing Office, 1907.

Pennybacker, J. E., Jr., and Maurice O. Eldridge. *Mileage and Cost of Public Roads in the United States*. Office of Public Roads, Bulletin no. 41. Washington, D.C.: Government Printing Office, 1912.

Proceedings of the National Good Roads Convention, St. Louis, Mo., 1903. U.S. Department of Agriculture, Office of Public Road Inquiries, Bulletin no. 26. Washington, D.C.: Government Printing Office, 1903.

U.S. Bureau of the Census. *Historical Statistics of the United States: Colonial Times to 1957*. Washington, D.C.: Government Printing Office, 1960.

U.S. Bureau of Foreign and Domestic Commerce. *Statistical Abstract of the United States*. Washington, D.C.: Government Printing Office, various annual editions.

U.S. Department of Commerce. *Highway Statistics, Summary to 1955*. Washington, D.C.: Government Printing Office, 1957.

Index

SUBJECTS